Youth Employment in Tourism and Hospitality

A Critical Review

Andreas Walmsley

(G) Goodfellow Publishers Ltd

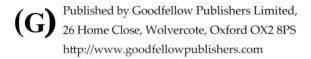 Published by Goodfellow Publishers Limited,
26 Home Close, Wolvercote, Oxford OX2 8PS
http://www.goodfellowpublishers.com

British Library Cataloguing in Publication Data: a catalogue record for this title is available from the British Library.

Library of Congress Catalog Card Number: on file.

ISBN: 978-1-910158-37-1

 Design and typesetting by P.K. McBride, www.macbride.org.uk

Cover design by Cylinder

Printed by Marston Book Services, www.marston.co.uk

Contents

Acknowledgements

I would like to thank former colleagues at Leeds Beckett University where my interest in the area of tourism employment was fostered and where the foundations for this text were laid. In particular I would like to acknowledge Rhodri Thomas and Stephanie Jameson in this regard. I would also like to acknowledge colleagues at the Association for Tourism in Higher Education who provided an open, welcoming forum for discussions and who give up so much of their time to promote the academic study of tourism.

1 Introduction

Overview of content

The tourism and hospitality sector counts among the world's largest in terms of business volume and employment. The United Nations World Tourism Organization suggests one in 11 jobs globally are to be found in tourism (UNWTO, 2013:78). Although precise employment figures in tourism are difficult to establish, as a heavily customer-facing, service-orientated sector it is in many of its operations highly labour intensive. Despite advances in technology, the possibilities of substituting labour by technology in tourism remain limited. For this reason tourism is frequently regarded favourably by policy makers, both in the developed and the developing world, in their attempts to drive down unemployment, particularly youth unemployment which in many countries is at crisis levels. According to the International Labour Organization (ILO), for example, young people are three times more likely to be unemployed than adults.

The general consensus suggests tourism is in fact characterised by high levels of youth employment. However, it is also frequently described as a low-wage sector that provides many low skilled, part-time and/or temporary jobs, where working conditions are poor, where employers are unwilling to provide formal training and where labour turnover is notoriously high. There appear then to be two sides, at least, to youth employment in tourism. On the one hand tourism provides young people with jobs, on the other we may question the extent to which these jobs are desirable and ultimately beneficial to young people's long-term career development. Admittedly, the finer detail of tourism employment is often lost when making such broad brush claims. This book therefore attempts to investigate the scope, nature and determinants of youth employment in tourism. It addresses a gap in the literature on tourism employment, where first there has been little explicit focus on youth (as opposed to say migrant or female employment in the sector), but second where other books on employment in tourism have traditionally adopted a human resource management perspective, i.e. focussing primarily on the needs of organisations. This aligns with what Ladkin (2011:1150) in a review of the study of labour in tourism has hinted at: "Some may argue that tourism labor research has been dominated for too long by management themes, and the real value lies in what it tells us about wider societal issues". This is not to say that no society- or policy-orientated texts on tourism employment exist. Baum (2006) and Riley, Ladkin and Szivas (2002) provide two useful examples of such texts.

It is perhaps surprising, given its policy relevance, that at the time of publication the only substantial work in the area of youth employment explicitly in tourism and hospitality was undertaken by the ILO as part of a series of publications that sought to better understand tourism employment (the other publications focused on gender and migration, see Baum 2012, 2013). This text seeks to provide a more detailed look at youth employment than was initially outlined in the ILO working paper that, given its purpose, had a more scene-setting function. This text therefore aims to make available in a critical and yet accessible format key thinking in the area of youth employment in tourism. While the text is therefore sector-specific, the analysis has implications for other sectors, especially those belonging to the service industries.

In addition to problems of definition, research and writing in the area of tourism and hospitality is hampered, but also made more interesting, by the inextricable nature of the forces that shape it. Lee-Ross and Pryce (2010) point specifically to the complexities in tourism labour markets and provide the example of seasonality, which is often related to low pay and poor working conditions. Another example to stress the point is the relationship between labour turnover and training, where employers frequently suggest they do not train because of high levels of labour turnover in the sector, and employees argue that high levels of labour turnover are the result of poor career development opportunities, which include the lack of training.

Arguably therefore, this text could have been structured in a number of ways and the reader will note some cross-referencing throughout. Nonetheless, as a whole the book endeavours to take a comprehensive review of the many and varied facets of youth employment in the sector and the interrelationships between them, it is structured as follows:

Chapter 1 describes the blight of youth unemployment and its effect on the individual and society. Some of the causes of high levels of youth unemployment relating to the structural changes to labour markets are also discussed.

With the scene thus set, Chapter 2 presents youth employment as a concept, from the perspective of the social meaning of youth and also exploring statistical attempts at defining and operationalising youth employment within the tourism and hospitality sector. Informal employment and its relationship to youth employment is also discussed. Finally, Chapter 2 attempts to assess levels of youth employment in tourism and hospitality drawing on official statistics as well as academic sources and the so-called 'grey literature'.

Chapter 3 discusses the nature of youth employment. Working conditions in tourism are often regarded as poor and yet for some young people tourism is a sector of choice. This chapter therefore tackles the issue of working conditions and the experience of employment in tourism. It also explores the role of trade unions in improving working conditions for youth, by drawing attention to employment malpractices and providing a platform for social dialogue. The chapter then looks at the nature of youth employment in developing countries before turning to the relationship between responsible tourism and youth employment.

Chapter 4 explores reasons for the high rates of youth unemployment generally and considers these as they apply and do not apply to tourism and hospitality. It addresses the question of youth employment from both the supply and the demand side perspectives. The supply side reviews youth perceptions of tourism employment while the demand side discusses the business perspective, whereby emphasis is placed on skills shortages as well as on attitudes towards employing youth. The chapter concludes by describing a range of initiatives that seek to promote youth employment in the sector.

Chapter 5 scrutinises the nature of the relationship between education, particularly higher education, and youth employment. It reviews the development of tourism and hospitality higher education, with a particular focus on perceptions of the purpose of education from the policy makers' standpoint. The relationship between education and economic growth is reviewed, before turning to the notion of employability, whereby a critical look at the ongoing skills debate and the role employers, universities and policy makers play in the provision of a skilled tourism workforce is provided. In continuing with the employability theme the chapter closes with a review of the potential advantages of hiring young people.

Chapter 6 focuses on the education to work transition, as this is regarded as a key 'sticking point' in policy circles when it comes to providing meaningful employment to young people. It begins by outlining current thinking in the area of career decision-making and uses this to review studies in tourism that have sought to explain difficulties in the transition from education to work. It discusses attitudes towards work in the youth population along with the role of placements/internships in easing the transition into employment. The chapter concludes by looking at the role of small and medium-sized enterprises (SMEs) and venture creation as potential sources of youth (self) employment in tourism. The final chapter pulls together key themes that have emerged, summarising dilemmas and issues that may provide avenues for further research and debate in the area of youth employment as well as ultimately providing guidance to policy makers.

The blight of youth unemployment

Youth unemployment presents one of the key challenges of our times. The effects of the 2007/08 global financial crisis are still keenly felt and have exacerbated what has become an ongoing concern. It would however be wrong to assume that high levels of youth unemployment are solely related to the most recent economic troubles. In the UK, for example, a rise in the number of unemployed young people pre-dates 2008 (Keep, 2012). Because of high birth rates and a demographic skewed towards youth in many developing countries, youth unemployment can be regarded as a developing country problem. That this is palpably not the case is demonstrated by European Commission statistics where for some countries youth unemployment has hit crisis levels (in March 2015 both Spain and Greece had youth unemployment rates of 50.1%, 45.5% in Croatia and 43.1% in Italy (Eurostat, 2015)). In the European Union youth unemployment reached a minimum value of 15.1% in the first quarter of 2008, it has since shot up and remains high although it peaked at 23.6% in the first quarter of 2013 in the EU-28 countries (Eurostat, 2014). Youth unemployment in Europe was lower in March 2015 than at the same time the previous year, however, at 20.9% in the EU-28 and 22.7 % in the euro zone rates are still unacceptably high[1] (Eurostat, 2015). What is true for Europe also holds for OECD countries, reports *The Economist* (2011) referring to this generation of youth as the 'scarred generation' or 'those left behind' because of the high and persistent levels of youth unemployment.

The World Economic Forum's (2014) global outlook for 2015 lists the top ten trends facing the world in 2015. Income inequality comes first and jobless

---

1   Youth unemployment ratios are usually lower than youth unemployment rates because they draw on the entire population rather than on those solely in work or looking for work which is the denominator used in unemployment rate calculations.

growth second. Both affect youth (un)employment in developed and developing nations alike. According to this WEF report in the United States the top 1% of the population receives a quarter of the income. Over the last 25 years, the average income of the top 0.1% has grown 20 times compared to that of the average citizen. The effect of inequality on youth is readily spelled out in the report:

> The inherent dangers of neglecting inequality are obvious. People, especially young people, excluded from the mainstream end up feeling disenfranchised and become easy fodder of conflict. This, in turn, reduces the sustainability of economic growth, weakens social cohesion and security, encourages inequitable access to and use of global commons, undermines our democracies, and cripples our hopes for sustainable development and peaceful societies. (World Economic Forum, 2014:9)

It is possible to speak of youth as a new social class. The negative impacts of the financial crisis on young people cut across class boundaries. For Roberts (2012) lower- and middle-class young people in Europe are being pulled into a jilted generation. This began for working class youths at the end of the last millennium but has now spread to young people more generally leading Roberts to speak of a new generation to succeed the baby boomers, the latter being 'the first in a series of birth cohorts who lived better (and knew that they were living better) than their predecessors in terms of levels of income and consumption' (Roberts, 2012:479). Roberts (2012) also refers to the book *The €1,000 Generation* written by Antonio Incorvaia and Alessandro Rimassa which inspired a film describing the lives of 20- and 30-year olds in Italy who continue to live as students, surviving on hand-outs from 'the bank of mum and dad', shopping in discount stores and using low cost airlines for very rare breaks. The salient thing about these young adults was that many of them were university-educated, and had work experience albeit in temporary or part-time, low-skilled jobs with no discernible prospects for progression. Youth unemployment is most certainly not a concern only for the uneducated although education may be the best insurance against unemployment.

In modern societies work has taken up a central, for some the central role in life. Gottfredson (1985) discusses the role of the self-concept in vocational theory and explains how social roles are means for individuals of engaging with society. She continues by arguing how occupational roles are some of the most important roles individuals assume, setting boundaries around individuals' identities and the lifestyles they are able to sustain. The centrality of work

to our lives has been augmented by a growing adherence to a discourse of economic rationality. Individuals are commonly judged based on what they do for
a living, on how much they contribute to the economic goals of society, of how
productive they are. Unsurprisingly therefore, the inability to find work can
lead to long-term negative impacts, both material and psychological. People
do not just work for monetary gain, despite the reduction in classical economic
theory of the employment relationship into an exchange of labour for wages.
The reality of work for most people extends beyond this narrow perspective.
Being employed can provide a sense of worth, esteem and purpose. This is true
at all occupational levels. Bourdieu (1979 cited in Grint, 1991:14) describing
street traders in Algeria of the 1960s notes:

> Those who find themselves in a position where it is impossible to
> get real work endeavour to fill the abyss between their unrealizable
> aspirations and the effective possibilities by performing work whose
> function is doubly symbolic in that it gives a fictitious satisfaction to
> the man who performs it while at the same time providing him with
> a justification in the eyes of others.

The effects of unemployment on young people can be disastrous therefore,
both at the level of the individual and of society. While often viewed through
an economic lens in terms of increased social spending and a loss of productivity, paid employment fulfils a number of functions for young people (many of
which are addressed below, e.g. Chapter 6 on the education to work transition)
including identity formation and the promotion of social inclusion. Jahoda
(1982) determined five latent consequences of employment which serve as a
further reminder that work is about a lot more than just generating income:
employment gives the day structure; it provides contact with people outside
the family; it involves people in a common goal; it provides the individual with
status and identity; and it enforces activity.

For young people, work is particularly important for the transition into
adulthood (Pavis *et al.*, 2002). The recognition that youth is a time when career
identities are formed has long been established (Super, 1957; Erickson, 1956).
Donovan and Oddy (1982) argue that for a young person, losing a job has
greater implications for identity formation than for older individuals because
young people are still in the early stages of identity formation, a view shared
by Hammer (1993). The psychological consequences of unemployment for
young people may therefore be greater than for older individuals. This is not
to downplay the negative consequences of unemployment in the latter stages
of a person's working life which may result in withdrawal from the labour

market and subsequent reductions in pension entitlements. However, early unemployment may be regarded as an accumulation of disadvantage across the life course (Wadsworth *et al.*, 1999). Young people who have experienced unemployment may be more likely to settle for any job, be that low paid or with unusual working hours, i.e. those usually associated with employment in much of the tourism sector, and this may have long term impacts in terms of career development and earnings. So-called wage scarring persists into later working life (*The Economist*, 2011).

A further more contentious issue, because more difficult to establish, is the relationship between youth unemployment and youth crime levels. If the said relationship were to hold true, the already difficult employment circumstances become almost impossible for the young person with a criminal record. Moreover, the long-term negative impacts on health of early unemployment have been demonstrated in numerous studies. Examples include Hammarström and Janlert (2002) who in a Swedish-based study on adult health problems (smoking, excess alcohol, somatic symptoms and psychological symptoms) demonstrated that with only one exception those with early periods of unemployment (those between the ages of 16 and 21) had the highest position in unfavourable habits. Moreover, controlling for possible confounders, including the initial health position, early unemployment was significantly associated with unfavourable health behaviour and symptoms at age 30 (a finding also corroborated by Hammer, 1993). Another longitudinal study (Ferguson, 2011) based on a cohort in New Zealand indicated that unemployment was linked to higher rates of psychological disorders. The authors remind the reader of confounding effects and reverse causality, i.e. that unemployment is also more prevalent within groups who demonstrate some mental illness but as the aforementioned studies demonstrated, even taking initial health positions into account, the impact of early unemployment on negative health outcomes is significant. Expanding on health issues to also focus on the impacts of unemployment on socio-economic position, Wadsworth *et al.* (1999) explored the impact on unemployment on a large cohort of British males. Their analysis demonstrated that early unemployment, particularly that lasting more than a year, had a negative impact on socio-economic and health capital at age 33. This was also the case when controlling for pre-labour market health and socio-economic conditions. What all these studies demonstrate are the negative implications of youth unemployment, particularly persistent unemployment, on health and life chances (notably employment) in later life. While youth is temporary, the impacts of youth unemployment are persistent and negative.

Structural changes in the labour market

There is wide-ranging consensus in policy making and scholarly circles that young people today face quite a different and in many ways more challenging labour market compared to previous generations. As Tomaszewski and Cebulla (2014:1031) explain with reference to the UK, young people 'have seen vocational routes into full-time and long-term employment become scarce and an exception rather than the rule'. In the UK until the mid-1970s over 70% of the population left school before 16 (Bynner, 2001). Joining the labour market at age 16 was the norm as the quotation by Schaffer and Hargreaves (1978:92) demonstrates: 'Most adolescents join the labour market at the age of 16. It is the normal life experience of the adolescent'. However, rapid structural changes in developed economies in the form of a move from manufacturing to services, as well as technological developments, resulted in profound changes in occupational aspirations, outcomes and indeed the transition into work. As Symonds *et al.* (2011:11) ,with reference to the United States, offer in relation to the transition from youth to adulthood '(it) is far more daunting. It takes much longer, and the roadway is filled with far more potholes, one-way streets and dead ends'.

Goos and Manning (2003) also looked at data on employment in Britain, specifically data from the Labour Force Survey and New Earnings Survey between 1979 and 1999. The title of their paper 'Lousy and lovely jobs: the rising polarization of work in Britain' does a good job in summarising the key hypothesis of the paper which is ultimately concerned with the impact skill-biased technical change (SBTC) is having on the structure of the labour market. The 'standard' view of the SBTC hypothesis is that it leads to rising wage inequality as relative demand for skilled workers increases. What is ignored is the fact that SBTC may also lead to an increase in demand for non-routine, least skilled jobs. SBTC can replace labour in the 'middling' jobs that may require high levels of manual and/or cognitive skills, but that are nonetheless fairly routine. This then, so Goos and Manning (2003) contend, has led to a polarization of work. Not only is relative demand for skilled jobs rising, but also for low-paid least skilled jobs. This contrasts with the popular view that low-skilled jobs are in decline. Goos and Manning (2003) also make direct reference to the increase in low-skilled service sector work and one is inclined here to think of tourism employment. Warhurst *et al.* (2000:3) allude quite scathingly to the emphasis in policy circles on high skilled, technical jobs in the service sector directly as follows:

> there is insufficient sensitivity to the heterogeneity of work and employment within the service sector – not just between the high

skill, high wage knowledge 'iMac Jobs' eulogised by policy-makers such as Robert Reich and Gordon Brown on the one hand and the low skill, low wage 'McJobs' …on the other.

There are links between the notion of polarization in the labour market, youth employment, and its precarity. Youth employment in tourism is a case in point in this regard, assuming a prototypical status for changes in modern economies and as such underlines the importance of its study. The remainder of this book explores these and associated issues in detail.

Keep (2012) discusses the contraction of the youth labour market in the UK, suggesting that the proportion of employers who recruit young people leaving education (at any level) has fallen. Furthermore, more than three quarters of 18 year olds were in work in 1976 whereas in 2009 this had fallen to 40%. Keep (2012) is quick to acknowledge that this is partly explained by the increase in the uptake of further and higher education, however, he also argues that young people may be seeking further and higher education in greater numbers due to the lack of employment opportunities. A UK Commission for Education and Skills (UKCES) report (2011) also claims that those who leave school rather than go on to further or higher education are particularly affected as only 6% of employers take on school leavers (the figure for all leavers of education is 25% – UKCES, 2011:14).

However, despite many similarities, differences in policies that effect youth, notably in vocational education, exist. Bynner (2001) discusses how, in contrast to the UK, countries such as Germany and Sweden conceive of youth as a fairly long period of preparation for adult employment. Bynner (2001) describes how in Germany all interested parties, the so-called *social partners,* are responsible for providing training to ensure a successful transition from school to work (Bynner excludes those going into higher education). It appears that in the UK, businesses expect government and educational institutions (or rather via educational institutions) to assume the sole responsibility for preparing young people for employment. Despite similarities, there are evidently also differences in labour market policies and their underpinning assumptions, even across economies in the same trading block and at similar stages of economic development.

One term it is impossible to exclude from discussions around structural changes in labour markets and youth employment is NEETs: those neither in employment, education nor training. As discussed above, it is quite normal today for many young people not to be in employment, but to be preparing for full time employment. Comparing youth employment ratios with overall employment ratios can be misleading precisely for this reason. In many countries however, late modernity has brought about a gulf between those young people in society who manage to find work or are otherwise in education and/or training and those who have slipped through the system and are in neither. The causes of this are manifold. It is not just a case of poor education or training systems. Attitudes to work and education are key too and these are culturally determined, at least to an extent. Whatever the cause, tourism, as a purported low-skills sector may offer that all-important first step into employment.

The foregoing discussion has presented a compelling case that the implications of youth unemployment are grim. Nonetheless, the impact of structural changes in the labour market may be interpreted in a variety of ways. Devadason (2007), for example, has tried to understand how individuals cope with the multiple work transitions that, it is suggested, are becoming the norm for youth in employment. He challenges Sennett's (1998) notion that under insecure conditions of employment individuals find it difficult to create a sense of coherence in their lives. Devadason interviewed 48 individuals divided into three occupational groups: professional and managerial high income earners; intermediate, typically public sector and middle-income earners; and routine service and manual low-income workers. He then identified five different types of causality used by these individuals to make sense of their employment transitions:

1   Climbing the career ladder;

2   Personal development;

3   Avoiding monotony and boredom;

4   At square one;

5   Setback stories.

Devadason (2007) explains that, as expected, the career ladder causality is most readily identifiable with the professional and managerial high income earners and yet he provides examples of low-income workers who also describe strategic thinking in their transitions. In fact, he makes reference to an individual working in hospitality who, starting from the bottom in what many people would describe as a low-skilled, menial job, had worked his way up to manager of a cappuccino bar and who now seeks to advance further. Square one causality is used by those whose work transitions have not demonstrated any form of progression or which do not feature as part of a larger career plan. This comprises both individuals who have remained in low-skilled work for some time as well as workers who were simply looking to earn some income before going on to further study. The final category of Setback stories relates to those who find themselves in a square one situation for an extended period of time and who then try to explain an absence of progress with reference to 'lack of encouragement, confidence or the right networks to fulfil their aspirations' (Devadason, 2007:712). The key point Devadason makes is that for some young adults, transitions into and out of employment, unemployment and education are woven into a narrative that is not necessarily negative. Indeed, it could be argued that we are entering an era where a lengthy period of time with one employer calls for an explanation in a tacit acknowledgement that this is no longer the norm. The extent to which young people will adapt to these labour market changes is yet to be fully understood, although it is likely tourism and hospitality employment will continue to feature in many young people's early work experience.

References

Baum, T. (2006) *Human Resource Management for Tourism, Hospitality and Leisure: An International Perspective*, Thomson Learning.

Baum, T. (2012). Migrant workers in the international hotel industry, *International Migration Papers.* Geneva: International Labour Office.

Baum, T. (2013). International perspectives on women and work in hotels, catering and tourism, *International Migration Papers.* Geneva: International Labour Office.

Bynner, J. (2001) British youth transitions in comparative perspective. *Journal of Youth Studies,* **4** (1), 5-23.

Devadason, R. (2007) Contructing coherence? Young adults' pursuit of meaning through multiple transitions between work, education and unemployment . *Journal of Youth Studies,* **10** (2), 203-221.

Donovan, A. & Oddy, M. (1982) Psychological aspect of unemployment: an investigation into the emotional and social adjustment of school leavers. *Journal of Adolescence,* **5** (1), 15-30.

Erickson, E. H. (1956) The problem of ego identity. *Journal of American Psychoanalytic Association,* **4** 56-221.

Eurostat (2014) *Unemployment Statistics.* Available: http://epp.eurostat. ec.europa.eu/statistics_explained/index.php/Unemployment_statistics [Accessed 28.09.14].

Eurostat (2015) *Unemployment Statistics.* Available: http://ec.europa.eu/eurostat/statistics-explained/index.php/Unemployment_statistics [Accessed 14.04.15].

Ferguson, L. (2011) Promoting gender equality and empowering women? Tourism and the third Millennium Development Goal. *Current Issues in Tourism*, **14** (3), 235-249.

Goos, M. & Manning, A. (2003). Lousy and lovely jobs: the rising polarization of work in Britain. Working paper. Centre for Economic Performance, London School of Economics and Political Science

Gottfredson, L. S. (1985) Role of self-concept in vocational theory. *Journal of Counseling Psychology*, **32** (1), 159-162.

Grint, K. (1991) *The Sociology of Work. An Introduction*, Cambridge: Polity Press.

Hammarström, A. & Janlert, U. (2002) Early unemployment can contribute to adult health problems: results from a longitudinal study of school leavers. *Journal of Epidemoiology and Community Health*, **56** (8), 624-630.

Hammer, T. (1993) Unemployment and mental health among young people: a longitudinal study. *Journal of Adolescence*, **16** (4), 407-420.

Jahoda, M. S. (1982) *Employment and Unemployment. A Social-psychological Analysis.*, Cambridge: Cambridge University Press.

Keep, E. (2012). Youth Transitions, the Labour Market and Entry into Employment: Some Reflections and Questions. SKOPE Research Paper No 108. Cardiff: SKOPE.

Ladkin, A. (2011) Exploring tourism labour. *Annals of Tourism Research*, **38** (3), 1135-1155.

Lee-Ross, D. & Pryce, J. (2010) *Human Resources and Tourism: Skills, Culture and Industry*, Oxford: Channel View Publications.

Pavis, S., Platt, S. & Hubbard, G. (2002) Youth employment, psychological health and the importance of person/environment fit: a case study of two Scottish rural towns. *Advances in Mental Health*, **1** (3), 1-14.

Riley, M., Ladkin, A. and Szivas, E. (2002) *Tourism Employment. Analysis and Planning.* Clevedon: Channel View Publications.

Roberts, K. (2012) The end of the long baby-boomer generations. *Journal of Youth Studies*, **15** (4), 479-497.

Schaffer, H. T. & Hargreaves, D. (1978) Young people in society: a research initiative by the SSRC. *Bulletin of the British Psychological Society*, **31** (91-94).

Sennett, R. (1998) *The Corrosion of Character. The personal consequences of work in the new capitalism,* London: W.W. Norton & Company.

Super, D. (1957) *The Psychology of Careers,* New York: Harper.

Symonds, W., Schwartz, R. & Ferguson, R. (2011). Pathways to prosperity: Meeting the challenge of preparing young Americans for the 21st century. Cambridge, MA: Harvard University Graduate School of Education.

The Economist (2011). The jobless young: Left behind. Available at http://www.economist.com/node/21528614.

Tomaszewski, W. & Cebulla, A. (2014) Jumping off the track: comparing the experiences of first jobs of young people living in disadvantaged and non-disadvantaged neighbourhoods in Britain. *Journal of Youth Studies,* **17** (8), 1029-1045.

UKCES (2011). *The Youth Inquiry. Employers' perspectives on tackling youth unemployment.* UK Commission for Employment and Skills.

UNWTO (2013). *UNWTO Tourism Highlights.* 2013 Edition. Madrid: UN World Tourism Organization.

Wadsworth, M. E. J., Montgomery, S. M. & Bartley, M. J. (1999) The persisting effect of unemployment on health and social well-being in men early in working life . *Social Science & Medicine,* **48** (10), 1491-1499.

Warhurst, C., Nickson, D., Witz, A. & Cullen, A. M. (2000) Aesthetic labour in interactive service work: some case study evidence from the 'New Glasgow'. *Service Industries Journal,* **20** (3), 1-18.

World Economic Forum (2014). *Outlook on the Global Agenda 2015.* Geneva: World Economic Forum.

2 Determining Levels of Youth Employment

Aims of the chapter

The purpose of this chapter is to provide a baseline understanding of the scope of youth employment in tourism and hospitality. The chapter begins by defining youth employment in tourism and hospitality. Following the provision of the commonly accepted statistical definition of youth as it applies to labour markets, attention turns to the concept of youth employment whereby it will become apparent that what counts as youth employment will depend on societal context. The chapter then returns to the measurement of tourism employment and some of the difficulties associated with this, which have implications for understanding youth employment in the sector. Key statistics relating to youth employment in tourism and hospitality are then presented and discussed, drawing on governmental and non-governmental data.

Youth and employment as social constructs

Although frequently encountered in the media, the concept of youth employment, as opposed to the term 'youth employment', is in all likelihood rarely given much attention. Because this is a book on youth employment in tourism and hospitality, but also because reflection on the concept itself reveals a number of intriguing perspectives, a review of the meanings inherent in what might appear to be a relatively innocuous term is both necessary and revealing.

In a statistical sense, defining youth employment is simply about operation-alising the term, setting boundaries around the concepts of youth and employ-ment to arrive at some meaningful way of its measurement. Commonly, youth in studies of labour markets and international statistics are thereby defined as anyone between the ages of 15-24 (see for example ILO, 2012). The boundaries of youth may be somewhat arbitrarily set, and yet they are necessarily clear even though most readers might balk at the upper age limit, expecting it to be lower, and possibly consider the lower age limit too high (this could simply reflect the author's prejudices of course). Possibly the age bracket is drawn too broad; the experiences and outlook of a fifteen year old are likely to differ considerably to that of a twenty-four year old (Heggli, 2001). It is unlikely there will ever be unanimous agreement on where youth begins and where it ends.

The boundaries delimiting employment, or work, from non-work are not as straightforward as establishing age. To begin with, not all societies even accept the concept of work. As Godelier (1980:831) reminds us '…the notion of work is by no means common to all cultures or ages'. Freyssenet (1999) reviews the role and development of the construct of work in modern society. His analysis also underscores just how complex work as a concept is; a concept constantly undergoing change:

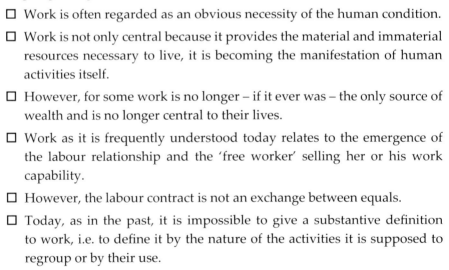

☐ Work is often regarded as an obvious necessity of the human condition.

☐ Work is not only central because it provides the material and immaterial resources necessary to live, it is becoming the manifestation of human activities itself.

☐ However, for some work is no longer – if it ever was – the only source of wealth and is no longer central to their lives.

☐ Work as it is frequently understood today relates to the emergence of the labour relationship and the 'free worker' selling her or his work capability.

☐ However, the labour contract is not an exchange between equals.

☐ Today, as in the past, it is impossible to give a substantive definition to work, i.e. to define it by the nature of the activities it is supposed to regroup or by their use.

Even in advanced economies, where work frequently assumes a dominant role in a person's life, delimiting work from non-work can be problematic. A common area of contention, for example, is domestic labour. As Grint (1991) has argued, virtually all of the chores undertaken at home can also take on the form of paid employment. This reiterates Freyssenet's (1999) view in that an activity itself is not sufficient to determine whether it is work or not. Guiding a group of friends on an ascent of a mountain is, in terms of the physical activity itself, the same as guiding a group of tourists up the same mountain; a perceived difference may lie in the monetary remuneration of the latter activity. The distinction between work and non-work, based on monetary remuneration alone may also be found wanting however. For Grint (1991) the fact that work is frequently regarded as paid employment says as much about the centrality of paid employment in modern societies as it does about the intrinsic nature of work.

The debate is not purely academic. If we exclude unremunerated activities from an analysis of tourism employment, we would be casting aside swathes of workers and work in the sector. Drawing on unpaid family support is widespread practice in many tourism and hospitality firms. Young people in particular can often be found *helping out* in the family business. In many developing countries the reliance on unpaid family support is the norm. This kind of informal work is crucial to the survival of many tourism businesses (see also next section).

The relative clarity pertaining to statistical definitions of youth, in contrast to definitions of work or employment, may detract attention from what is also arguably a complex social construct. Foster (2013) reveals the importance of generation as discourse and by the same token it is possible to talk of a youth discourse. According to Purvis and Hunt (1993:485) discourses shape social relations, they provide 'a vehicle for thought', although they 'channel' more than they 'control'. Just as the concept of generation provides such a vehicle for thought, channelling the way people not only think but consequently act, so does a youth discourse connote certain thoughts and feelings, prejudices and understandings that permit a socially constructed notion of youth. Foster's (2013) investigation of generation as discourse among a cross-section of 52 Canadian citizens (all over 25 years of age) revealed the notion of *generation as an axis of difference*: participants of all ages understood generation to imply differences in attitudes towards work. Whereas the older generation lived to work, the younger generation worked to live. There was also agreement among participants that the younger generation had 'an overblown sense of entitlement' (Foster, 2013:200). These attitudes may prejudice employers when it comes to hiring young people as well as the way young people are treated in the workplace. The consideration of youth as a social construct is far more than just a mental exercise therefore. The discourse particularly around youth has very real practical consequences in both individual and societal terms.

Van Gennep (1960 [1909]) proposed that the lives of individuals can best be understood as the crossing of a series of ritual thresholds from one social state to another, with transitions being assisted by ceremonies, or rites of passage, such as betrothal, marriage, transition to a higher social class and funerals. Rites of passage such as these (also: initiation rites) exist in all cultures. They may be institutionalised such as those mentioned above, but initiation rites are not always immediately recognised as such (Alvez, 1993). It is understood that there may be numerous discourses around youth, possibly within a given society, but certainly between different cultures and societies. In some cultures the transition from childhood to adulthood may be regarded as almost immediate whereas in others the transition from childhood to adulthood may be marked by a series of initiation rites that can extend for a number of years. In this latter case youth may be understood as a liminal period, as a period of transition between the two more defined states of childhood and adulthood, between immaturity and maturation. Career development theory, as discussed later (Chapter 6), is also premised upon life phases, with young people facing particular career development tasks according to their physical age. The successful completion of these tasks may then also be regarded as rites of passage. If, as may be argued, the transition from youth to adulthood includes leaving one's parental home (Pavis *et al.*, 2002) then a case can be made for an extension of youth in many western societies where, largely because of economic circumstances, adults return home to live with their parents (the so-called 'Boomerang Generation') as they are unable to find work and thereby acquire the means by which to support themselves. The UK Office for National Statistics (ONS), for example, estimates that there has been a 25% increase in the number of 20-34 year-olds living with their parents between 1996 and 2013 (ONS, 2014).

Studies on labour issues in tourism commonly revert to what might more fittingly be described as hospitality. Riley *et al.* (2002), for example, refer the reader to standard industrial classifications where tourism is often equated to accommodation, restaurants and cafés. Arguably, in Version 4 of the International Standard Industrial Classification (United Nations Statistics Division, 2008) the tourism sub-sectors '5510: Short term accommodation activities', and '791: travel agency and tour operator activities' might most unequivocally be categorised as belonging to tourism. Frequently when defining tourism, sub-sectors are listed. So, thinking specifically about employment, Australia's Travel Industry Career's Association (2015) suggests:

> The Travel & Tourism Industry has a variety of sectors that include Retail Travel, Wholesale Travel, Visitor Information, Tour Operators, Cruising, Transportation, Events and Services.

The Canadian Tourism Human Resources Council (Discover Tourism, 2015) speaks of tourism as a sector suggesting it comprises five 'industry groups': Accommodation, Food and Beverage Services, Recreation and Entertainment, Transportation, and Travel Services. The UK sector skills charity People 1st, whose *State of the Nation 2013* report is referred to in a number of places in this text, identifies the following as belonging to the tourism and hospitality sector (People 1st, 2013:11):

> Events, food and service management, gambling, hospitality services, hotels, pubs, bars and nightclubs, restaurants, self-catering accommodation, holiday parks and hostels and tourism services.

Rather than focussing on sub-sectors of tourism, what counts as falling within tourism employment may be related to job roles. Here the Canadian Tourism Human Resources Council draws attention to over 400 job roles in tourism (Discover Tourism, 2015):

> Tourism is Canada's (and the world's) fastest growing industry with a choice of over 400 job roles that require varying levels of skill, experience and education. From sales and marketing to guest services, accounting, maintenance, management, fitness, housekeeping, catering, entertainment or grounds management, the list of opportunities goes on!

A further flavour of the wide range of jobs available in tourism and demonstrating that these are not all low-skilled is provided on the UK graduate careers website 'Prospects' (2014). It lists fifteen examples of graduate jobs in hospitality, sports and tourism as follows:

- ☐ Accommodation manager
- ☐ Catering Manager
- ☐ Event organiser
- ☐ Hotel manager
- ☐ Public house manager
- ☐ Restaurant manager
- ☐ Fitness centre manager
- ☐ Outdoor pursuits manager
- ☐ Sport and exercise psychologist
- ☐ Sports coach
- ☐ Sports development office
- ☐ Theme park manager

☐ Tour manager

☐ Tourism officer

☐ Travel agency manager

Finally, it should be noted then that on the basis of an absence of a universal approach this book adopts a pragmatic stance when seeking to define tourism and hospitality. While appreciating the debates around what constitutes tourism we are in the main happy to accept other studies' definitions, i.e. if a study says its focus is on tourism or hospitality, this is taken as given. Indeed, many studies have grappled with this issue and we are not going to attempt to add to these debates – see, for example, Lee-Ross and Pryce's, (2010) useful introduction to the issue of employment in tourism in the aptly named chapter, *The Nature of the Beast*. The reader unfamiliar with these debates is simply reminded that as an economic activity, tourism is a broad church, itself part of the service industries and arguably, many of the points discussed in this book will apply to other sectors within the service industries. The reader is reminded though to bear the generalisation issues mentioned above in mind (indeed, one of the aims of this text to shed light on some of the detail lurking behind blanket statements frequently made about the nature of tourism employment). Unless otherwise stated, henceforth when tourism is mentioned it is taken to comprise tourism and hospitality.

Measurement of tourism and hospitality employment

Tourism and hospitality are dynamic sectors that as we have seen comprise a range of diverse economic activities. Together with an increasingly complex, global business environment, business models are changing. The rise of coffee chains demonstrates how quickly products can become mainstream, while others fall out of fashion (see the fate of the public house sector and licenced bars in the UK). In some cases, products that were deemed outdated and in decline have seen a recent resurgence in interest as the resurrection of the package holiday market has shown (ABTA, 2015).The growth of a travel-savvy, wealthy middle class in emerging economies such as those in India and China is changing the structure of international travel. Leisure travel, to all intents and purposes once the preserve of citizens of the 'developed' world is spreading as economies rapidly develop (UNWTO, 2015). Developments in the area of technology have considerable repercussions for tourism and hospitality, from the way consumers book holidays, to the way social media is transforming destination/attraction/hotel image. The rise of the sharing economy, including the rise of home-exchange networks may still be considered a niche activity (Forno and Garibaldi, 2015) and yet its growth is rapid and justifiably concerns traditional tour operators.

Shorter lead times for bookings means that it is now even more difficult to deal with fluctuations in demand. In the UK this has resulted in an increasing number of employees being on so-called zero hour contracts, i.e. having no guarantee how many hours they will work, and being able to be called upon to work at short notice. The implications for this in terms of regarding tourism employment as desirable is outlined amply in People 1st's *State of the Nation Report*, 2013. The use of labour as a commodity, to be turned on an off in the same manner as water and electricity, has long been an element of criticism of the workings of employment practice in capitalist societies (Vosco, 2000).

Despite these often-touted claims of rapid change, in many respects employment in the sector has changed very little. The sector continues to be very labour intensive, suffering low levels of productivity. Boella and Goss-Turner (2013:4) quote People 1st statistics that suggest hospitality employees only generate between £42 and £81 per hour for their employers, whereas employees in the gambling sector generate on average £120 (£1 = US$1.55 at the time of writing) although it should be noted that productivity calculations are notoriously difficult in service sectors that rely heavily on a customer-facing element such as tourism (McLaughlin and Coffey, 1990).

Difficulties in defining tourism extend into the deceptively simple task of establishing how many people work in the sector. This does not curtail the common practice of promoting tourism development on the basis of its employment-creation potential. To date, despite the common belief that tourism draws heavily on youth employment, statistics as to the proportion of young people employed in tourism vary widely. The first step in trying to establish levels of youth employment is to focus on measuring tourism employment more generally. This in itself is not without problems. Measuring employment in tourism can generally take three forms:

1 Count of persons employed in tourism industries in any of their jobs
2 Count of persons employed in tourism industries in their main job
3 Count of jobs in tourism industries.

While in an ideal world tourism employment may be measured through the aggregation of individuals' output purchased by a tourist (directly or indirectly), this understanding of tourism employment is not observable directly but can only be estimated. For example, some of an individual's output may be purchased by tourists as well as by non-tourists (e.g. a bus driver who transports both locals and tourists), or an individual may have more than one job working part-time in tourism but also in another sector. Here then a need arises to distinguish main job from ancillary employment, insofar as this is possible. Frequently tourism employment is simply equated with employment in tourism industries, although even here which industries belong to tourism is not unequivocal either.

Rather than focus on the number of people employed in tourism, it is also possible to take stock of tourism employment according to the number of jobs in tourism. Typically, the number of tourism jobs available will exceed the number of economically active individuals in tourism because of the existence of part-time work. Despite these data difficulties, relying on job count is generally regarded as an acceptable method where comparisons are to be made between tourism and other sectors or between tourism and employment in an economy more generally. Obviously, the more prone to part-time employment an industry is, such as is the case in tourism, the more its economic contribution with regard to employment is likely to be overestimated if relying on job count to measure employment.

Levels of young people working part time in the tourism sector are generally quite high. Numerous studies have focused specifically on student employment in the sector which appears to be increasing in many countries. Barron (2007) conducted a survey of 486 undergraduate tourism and/or hospitality students in Australia. Of these, 372 (77%) had some form of part-time employment. Barron furthermore cites Australian Government statistics that claim 65% of all students working part-time were working in either the hospitality or retail sectors. Lashley (2005) conducted a survey on student employment in Nottingham, UK, which showed that approximately 40% of students are working; and that bars and restaurants, and retail outlets were the most popular locations for student employment. Student employment will be discussed in greater depth later in Chapter 6.

A further measurement difficulty relates to the seasonal nature of much tourism employment, meaning that tourism employment at an aggregate level usually fluctuates considerably, depending on when it is measured. People 1st (2013) data indicate that 9% of staff in tourism in the UK are temporary, compared to 6% for the economy as a whole, as well as specifying that this is largely down to seasonality, highlighting further that the figures of visitor attractions (39%) and self-catering accommodation, holiday parks and hostels (18%) are indeed much higher. As long as there is some regularity in the rise and fall in tourism demand it is nonetheless possible to estimate tourism employment by making seasonal adjustments.

Another major, arguably even greater, stumbling block in trying to ascertain the extent of tourism employment is the issue of informal employment. Informal activity has been defined as 'work outside the regulative ambit of the state' (Harris-White, 2010:170), and, according to Williams and Nadin (2012:896), "some 45 different nouns and 10 adjectives have been used to denote it such as 'cash-in-hand', 'shadow', 'informal', 'black' and 'underground'". Informal employment is characteristic of much employment in tourism in both developed and developing countries, although it is often associated with developing countries in particular. Schneider and Enste (2002) argue that informal activity accounts for as much as 60% of employment in emerging economies, but it is not as though informal activity plays an unimportant role in developed economies. Here Schneider and Enste (2002) have posited that informal employment accounts for between 10-20% of GDP in mature economies. Informal employment is often the preserve of youth and as such is likely to hamper attempts at measuring youth employment. O'Higgins *et al.* (2001), for example, examined long-term youth unemployment in Bulgaria estimating that at least one fifth of the young registered unemployed were actively engaged in informal income earning.

What do all these measurement issues mean for an assessment of the extent of tourism employment more generally and youth employment specifically? At best they should lead to caution when presented with data on tourism employment, especially when, as frequently occurs, these figures are presented as factual by policy makers in their attempts to justify spending public monies on tourism development, or by the industry itself when it seeks funding or approval for new tourism development on the grounds of tourism's employment-creation potential. At the very worst, one might argue that any measurement of tourism employment is so fundamentally fraught with loose assumptions that any data pertaining to tourism employment, let alone youth employment, are nigh on meaningless. Notwithstanding these caveats, we would argue that it makes sense to at least estimate tourism employment, in particular relative to other sectors. There is surely more room for a greater degree of transparency when publishing employment data related to tourism, to enable policy makers to make sounder decisions, and for evaluations of the spending of public funds to be more accurately assessed.

Levels of youth employment in tourism and hospitality

On the basis of the foregoing discussion it will not come as a surprise that determining a precise level of youth employment in the sector is virtually impossible, although it is generally regarded as high. Nonetheless, despite simply repeating this truism, this section of the book will consider a range of statistics on the levels of youth employment in the sector. It begins with a narrow focus comparing levels of youth employment internationally for tourism overall before moving to a more detailed focus on youth employment by sub-sector and occupation, at least as far as existing data permit.

One would perhaps imagine that locating data on employment disaggregated by age and sector (or industrial classification) is a straightforward affair. For developed economies this holds true but for developing economies, alas, it does not. Focussing therefore initially on developed economies, there is much evidence that levels of youth employment in the sector are indeed elevated, but crucially, levels vary quite considerably between countries. What is meant by 'high' varies even when looking at countries in a relatively close-knit economic zone.

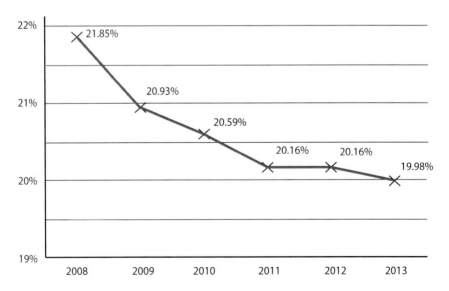

Figure 2.1: Youth employed in accommodation and food services – Europe (28) 2008-2013 (%). Source: Author's figures calculated from Eurostat LFS data.

Table 2.1: Youth employment in accommodation and food services – Europe 2013.
Source: Author's figures calculated from Eurostat LFS data

	Youth as percentage of tourism workforce	Unemployment rate (annual average) %[1]
Spain	9.8	26.1
Portugal	12.3	16.4
Italy	12.4	12.2
Macedonia	12.5	28.7
Czech Republic	12.8	7.0
Cyprus	13.8	15.9
Romania	13.9	7.3
Croatia	14.1	17.3
Luxembourg	14.3	5.9
Belgium	14.5	8.4
Slovakia	15.0	14.2
Slovenia	15.8	10.1
Bulgaria	16.4	13
Hungary	16.6	10.2
Germany	17.7	5.3
Switzerland	18.1	3.2
Latvia	18.5	11.9
France	19.8	10.3
Poland	20.3	10.3
Austria	20.4	4.9
Turkey	22.7	9.0
Ireland	22.9	13.1
Estonia	26.1	8.6
Malta	26.7	6.4
Lithuania	27.3	11.8
Finland	27.9	8.2
United Kingdom	34.6	7.5
Norway	34.8	3.5
Sweden	35.1	8.0
Denmark	46.0	7.0
Netherlands	47.0	6.7
Iceland	50.0	5.4

1   Unemployment data for Macedonia: www.tradingeconomics.com/macedonia/
unemployment-rate, accessed 21.05.15. Unemployment data for Switzerland: www.
statista.com/statistics/263707/unemployment-rate-in-switzerland, accessed 21.05.15

We start with comparisons in Europe, using data from Eurostat, the statistical office of the European Union, and these are derived from individual countries' Labour Force Surveys. Sampling rates in each country vary between 0.2% and 3.3% (Eurostat, 2013). Given the nature of classification of industries in Eurostat's dataset, tourism is equated here to mean 'accommodation and food services'. Figure 2.1 suggests that the proportion of youth employed in tourism in Europe hovers around the 20% mark but has been in decline since 2008 (prior to this a different industrial classification was used).

The proportion of young people employed in tourism varies between countries in Europe, ranging from 9.8% in Spain to 50% in Iceland (see Table 2.1). There appears to be a general tendency that the proportion of young people employed in tourism is higher in northern European countries, which could suggest that the proportion of youth employed decreases with overall levels of unemployment, which tend to be lower in northern than in southern Europe. This was tested using Pearson's Correlation Coefficient (r), with unemployment the independent variable and the proportion of youth employed in tourism the dependent variable. The data in Table 2.1 suggest that there is a weak negative relationship between these two variables ($r = -0.51$), in other words, the higher the unemployment rate, the lower the proportion of young people employed in tourism.

At this stage it is only possible to speculate as to why this may be the case. It could be that as employment opportunities in the labour market decrease, those who ordinarily might not have sought or even considered tourism employment, i.e. older workers with skills and experience, vie for the limited number of available jobs in the labour market. A further argument is that those countries currently not fairing as well economically are also those countries heavily reliant on tourism (tourism is a notoriously fickle industry, [Frechtling, 2001]). Where the contribution of tourism to a country's economy is high, it might be regarded as more mainstream rather than as a contingent form of employment, and consequently mature adults are less inclined to seek employment outside of tourism than in those countries where the economy is more diversified.

It is acknowledged that these are just speculative explanations at present, and empirically they still require support (although Szivas and Riley, 1999 do provide support for tourism's role as a contingent form of employment in their analysis of Hungary's labour market at a time of economic transition with the fall of the Iron Curtain). One important insight nonetheless stands out from a comparison of youth employment in tourism across European nations: levels of youth employment do vary quite considerably on a country-by-country basis. The claim that youth employment is high in tourism will mean different things in different countries and contexts.

A number of further sources from high income countries indicate high levels of youth employment in tourism:

☐ People 1st's (2013) *State of the Nation Report* in the UK suggests that 31% of employees in tourism and hospitality are between 16 and 24 years of age.

☐ According to Sweet *et al.* (2010:9) with reference to US data, approximately 40% of employees in accommodation and food services are under 25 years of age.

☐ Yunis (2009) presents data from Australia's labour force survey that suggests that 35.6% of employees in the accommodation, cafes and restaurant sector are between 15 and 24 years of age.

☐ The Canadian Tourism Human Resources Council (2006) suggests youth (15-24 years of age) constitute a third (32.8%) of the tourism workforce.

☐ Queensland Tourism Industry Council (2012:10): 45.7% of those employed in tourism in Australia were between 15-24 years old.

☐ Data from New Zealand's Ministry of Business, Innovation and Employment (2011) indicated that 'accommodation, cafes and restaurants' was the leading industry sector in terms of youth employment, with 39% of all its workers aged 15-24 years (in 2010).

☐ Further data, based on the author's calculations, suggest that the proportion of youth employed in accommodation and food services in Singapore is 16.4% (the figure relates only to Singaporean residents). Saudi Arabia and Kuwait have far lower proportions of youth employed in the sector (hotels and restaurants) at 6.5% and 6.6% respectively.

Sector data from low or middle income countries broken down by age are more difficult to find. A few publications reveal some insights, e.g. Majcher-Teleon and Ben Slimène (2009) propose that youth employment in the sector in Jordan stands at approximately 10%. In Pakistan, the percentage of youth employed in 'wholesale and retail trade, restaurants and hotels' in 2006 to 2007 is 14.5% (Ministry of Labour, 2008) whereas the percentage or youth employed in 'trade, restaurants and hotels' in 2004 in Zimbabwe was 3.5% (Luebker, 2008). Clearly, these figures need to be taken with a pinch of salt, demonstrating some of the difficulties alluded to above with regard to measuring or even estimating the proportion of youth employment in tourism. It is very likely that the proportion of youth employed in tourism in developing countries is much higher than government statistics might suggest therefore. Non-governmental data from advanced economies suggest that the proportion of youth employed in tourism is approximately one third.

The variation in youth employment rates in tourism across countries raises the question of how tourism employment data might otherwise be segmented, thereby revealing further distinctions in levels of youth employment. As tourism comprises a range of economic activities, it is instructive to understand the extent to which youth employment features in equal measure across tourism's sub-sectors. Unfortunately, tourism employment data already disaggregated by age are then rarely disaggregated further into tourism sub-sectors. A number of sector specific studies, as opposed to published government statistics, do exist however that provide some further disaggregation of tourism employment data.

According to a study conducted by the Canadian Tourism Human Resources Council (2006) food and beverage services nearly drew half their workforce from those 15-24 years old, whereas in travel services the proportion of young people employed is a mere 12%. Overall, nearly one third (32.8%) of tourism employees were young people compared to an all-industry average of just 15%. Yunis (2009) cites Australian Labour Force Survey data which looks at the median age of the workforce. Here the median age of employees in the 'cafes and restaurants' and 'pubs, taverns and bars' sectors stood at only 27 years of age, while the median age in the accommodation sector stood at 40 years.

Understandably given the structure of occupations in terms of hierarchies of skills, educational requirements and levels of seniority, youth employment tends to focus on specific occupations or occupational groupings within tourism. The previously-cited Canadian study (Canadian Tourism Human Resource Council, 2006) also provides data on youth employment at different occupational levels. Specifically those occupations have been highlighted where young people represent over half of employees. Arguably, apart from 'program leaders and instructors in recreation and sport' these are all relatively low skilled occupations, which serves to underpin the notion of tourism being a form of employment for young people looking for temporary or part-time employment, or simply those looking for a first step into the world of work.

Here again it is apparent that levels of youth employment in the sector vary at different occupational levels, and not just between senior and junior positions. The average age of waiting staff (26), bar staff (27) and theme and leisure park attendants (29) in the UK (People 1st, 2013) also demonstrates that youth employment is particularly pronounced in certain tourism sub-sectors. A further report (European Agency for Safety and Health at Work, 2008) also suggests that young workers are mostly concentrated in restaurants and bars. Canteens, camping sites and short stay accommodation tend to have higher proportions of workers in older age categories (45 to 64 years).

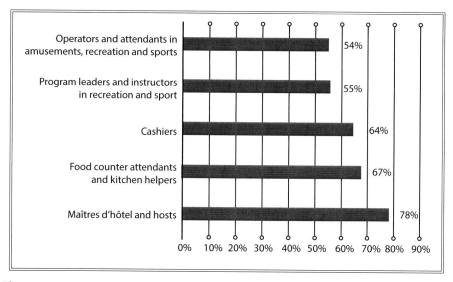

Figure 2.2: Percentage of youth employment in selected tourism sub-sectors, Canada.   Source: CHRC, 2006

References

Abta (2015). ABTA Travel Trends Report 2015. London: Association of British Travel Agents.

Alvez, J. (1993) Transgressions and transformations: Initiation rites among urban Portuguese boys. *American Anthropologist,* **95** (4), 894-928.

Barron, P. (2007) Hospitality and Tourism students' part-time employment: Patterns, benefits and recognition. *Journal of Hospitality, Leisure, Sport and Tourism Education,* **6** (2), 40-54.

Boella, M. & Goss-Turner, S. (2013) *Human Resource Management in the Hospitality Industry. A Guide to Best Practice,* London: Routledge.

Canadian Tourism Human Resources Council (2006). Youth (aged 15 to 24 Years) employed in tourism. Available: http://www.otec.org/Files/pdf/ resources/Demopro_LabourPro_Youth.aspx

Discover Tourism. (2015) Careers. Available: http://discovertourism.ca/en/
careers [Accessed 11.01.15.]

European Agency for Safety and Health at Work (2008). Protecting workers in
hotels, restaurants and catering. Luxembourg: European Agency for Safety
and Health at Work.

Eurostat. (2013) Employment and Unemployment (LFS). Introduction.
European Commission. Available: http://epp.eurostat.ec.europa.eu/portal/
page/portal/employment_unemployment_lfs/introduction [Accessed
30.06.13.]

Forno, F. & Garibaldi, R. (2015) Sharing economy in travel and tourism: The
case of home-swapping in Italy. *Journal of Quality Assurance in Hospitality &
Tourism,* **16 (**2), 202-220.

Foster, K. (2013) Generation and discourse in working life stories. *British
Journal of Sociology,* **64 (**2), 195-215.

Frechtling, D. (2001) *Forecasting Tourism Demand. Methods and Strategies,*
Oxford: Butterworth-Heinemann.

Freyssenet, M. (1999) The emergency, centrality and end of work. *Current
Sociology,* **47 (**2), 5-20.

Godelier, M. (1980) Aide-memoire for a survey of work and its
representations. *Current Anthropology,* **21 (**6), 831-835.

Grint, K. (1991) *The Sociology of Work. An Introduction,* Cambridge: Polity Press.

Harris-White, B. (2010) Work and wellbeing in informal economies: The
regulative roles of institutions of identity and the state. *World Development,*
38 (2), 170-183.

Heggli, G. (2001) Becoming and being a teenager: From childhood to youth
through vernacular writing. In: Heggli, G. & Hauan, M. (eds.) *Younger
Than Yesterday, Older Than Tomorrow. Cultural Perspectives on Contemporary
Childhood and Youth.* Turku, FInland: Nordic Network of Folklore.

ILO (2012). *Decent Work Indicators. Concepts and Definitions.* Geneva:
International Labour Organization.

Lashley, C. (2005). *Student Employment Patterns in Nottingham's Tourism Sector:
A Research Report for East Midlands Tourism.* Nottingham: Nottingham Trent
University Centre for Leisure Retailing.

Lee-Ross, D. & Pryce, J. (2010) *Human Resources and Tourism: Skills, Culture and
Industry,* Oxford: Channel View Publications.

Luebker, M. (2008). *Employment, Unemployment and Informality in Zimbabwe: Concepts and Data for Coherent Policy-Making.* Issues Paper No 32. Harare: ILO Sub-Regional Office for Southern Africa

Majcher-Teleon, A. & Ben Slimène, O. (2009). *Women and Work in Jordan. Case study of tourism and ICT sectors.* Working paper: European Training Foundation.

Mclaughlin, C. & Coffey, S. (1990) Measuring productivity in services. *International Journal of Service Industry Management,* **1 (**1), 46-64.

Ministry of Business, Innovation and Employment . (2011) *Likely Areas of Growth in Employment Opportunities.* Available: http://www.dol.govt. nz/publications/research/growth-employment-opportunities-jun2010/ growth-employment-opportunities_05.asp [Accessed 12.09.13]. Ministry of Business, Innovation & Employment, New Zealand.

Ministry of Labour (2008). *Employment Trends 2008. Youth.* Islamabad: Labour Market Information and Analysis Unit, Ministry of Labour, Manpower and Overseas Pakistanis, Government of Pakistan.

O'Higgins, N., Pastore, F., Beleva, I. & Ivanov, A. (2001) Targeting youth employment policy in Bulgaria. *Economic and Business Review,* **3** (2), 113-135.

ONS (2014). *Young Adults Living with Parents, 2013.* London: Office for National Statistics.

Pavis, S., Platt, S. & Hubbard, G. (2002) Youth employment, psychological health and the importance of person/environment fit: A case study of two Scottish rural towns. *Advances in Mental Health,* **1 (**3), 1-14.

People 1st (2013). *State of the Nation Report 2013. An analysis of labour market trends, skills, education and training within the UK hospitality and tourism industries.* Uxbridge: People 1st.

Prospects (2014) www.prospects.ac.uk. [Accessed 20.04.14].

Purvis, T. & Hunt, A. (1993) Discourse, Ideology, Discourse, Ideology, Discourse, Ideology…'. *The British Journal of Sociology,* **44** (3), 473-499.

Queensland Tourism Industry Council (2012). *Tourism and Hospitality Workforce Development Plan.* Brisbane: Queensland Tourism Industry Council.

Riley, M., Ladkin, A. & Szivas, E. (2002) *Tourism Employment. Analysis and Planning,* Clevedon: Channel View Publications.

Schneider, F. & Enste, D. H. (2002) *The Shadow Economy: An International Survey,* New York: Cambridge University Press.

Sweet, S., Pitt-Catsophes, M., Besen, E., Hovhannixyan, S. & Pasha, F. (2010). *Talent Pressures and the Aging Workforce: Responsive Action Steps for the Accommodation and Food Services Sector.* The Soan Center on Aging and Work.

Szivas, E. & Riley, M. (1999) Tourism employment during economic transition. *Annals of Tourism Research,* **26** (4), 747-771.

Travel Industry Career's Association (2015) travelindustrycareers.org. Available: http://www.travelindustrycareers.org/career-paths-in-the-travel-industry [Accessed 11.01.15.]

United Nations Statistics Division (2008) *ISIC Rev.4.* Available: http://unstats.un.org/unsd/cr/registry/regcst.asp?Cl=27 [Accessed 11.09.14].

UNWTO (2015). *Tourism Highlights 2015 Edition.* Madrid: United Nations World Tourism Organisation.

Van Gennep, A. (1960 [1909]) *The Rites of Passage,* Chicago: Chicago University Press.

Vosco, L. F. (2000) *Temporary Work. The Gendered Rise of a Precarious Employment Relationship,* Toronto University Press: Toronto.

Williams, C. & Nadin, S. (2012) Tackling the hidden enterprise culture: Government policies to support the formalization of informal entrepreneurship. *Entrepreneurship and Regional Development,* **24** (9-10), 895-915.

Yunis, E. (2009). Tourism and Employment: An overview by UNWTO. Tourism: An engine for employment creation. *The Fifth UNWTO International Conference on Tourism Statistics.* Bali, Indonesia: UNWTO.

3 The Nature of Youth Employment

Aims of the chapter

Roan and Diamond (2003) claim that labour market policy in Australia has focussed on the provision of employment and the preparation of young people for employment but entirely neglected quality of working life issues. The same may be said for other developed economies' labour market policies. In the anguish to get young people into work, which is understandable given the youth unemployment crisis, the nature of work itself has, until recently at least, rarely been questioned. In the run up to the May 2015 UK general election, rival parties were at loggerheads over the nature of jobs being created in the economy, with the ruling coalition parties pointing to the fall in unemployment and the opposition arguing that many of these jobs were barely paying the minimum wage and that furthermore many of the jobs now being offered were on zero-hour contracts and also on casual contracts, which are ones where the employer can hire staff without the guarantee of work. Suddenly the nature of work reappeared on policy makers' agendas and this, coupled with tourism's admittedly poor reputation as an employer, suggests the need for a closer look at the nature of youth employment in the sector. Consequently, this chapter presents and discusses different characteristics of youth employment in tourism and hospitality. It aims to provide an insight into the experience of youth employment as well as reviewing the role of trade unions in improving working conditions for young people. The chapter also addresses separately the nature of youth employment in developing countries, and concludes with a review of the relationship between responsible tourism and youth employment.

Working conditions for young people

Working conditions in tourism do not usually get a good press. The common portrayal of tourism employment is one where remuneration is low, formal training is scarce, working hours are long and unpredictable, and union representation is weak. In sum, the picture is not rosy. This characterisation is undoubtedly often justified, but on closer inspection tourism employment presents a more varied picture which is often ignored. The intention here is not to review in length the more traditional claims around working conditions, as these have been discussed at length elsewhere (Wood, 1997, Riley *et al.*, 2002, Baum, 2007). What this chapter will do is provide a nuanced review of youth employment in tourism, discussing challenges but also reviewing the attraction of tourism as a sector. As will be discussed, young people face particular challenges in employment settings and as such a youth-specific focus on aspects of the experience of work is timely.

Labour turnover

Labour turnover is a perennial issue in studies and descriptions of tourism employment. It is also an issue that HR managers continue to engage with, demonstrating its significance compared with other industrial sectors (Boella and Goss-Turner, 2013). Drawing on People 1st (2013) data, labour turn-over figures will vary depending on industry sub-sector, ranging from 31% for 'pubs, bars and nightclubs' to 9% for 'food and service management'. Widespread agreement exists that labour turnover is characteristic of tourism employment, and yet there is no agreement with regard to actual turnover rates, with a range of studies highlighting various statistics. At the higher end of estimates, Graver and Harrison (2002) suggest labour turnover can exceed 120% and Battersby (1990) in an older text claims that in some sub-sectors staff turnover rates are as high as 300%.

Getting to grips with turnover is made more difficult by the various measures that exist and the nature of turnover in the sector. There are various ways of measuring staff turnover but usually recourse is made to the so-called separation rate or 'crude turnover rate' (Johnson, 1981) which measures how many staff have left in relation to average number of staff employed in a specified period of time. Although widely used, what this measure fails to capture is who is leaving, i.e. whether there are certain sub-groups who are more affected by high labour turnover rates. Because of the separation rate's weakness in explaining structural characteristics of the tourism workforce, Tyson and York (2001) advocate using the stability index, which provides insights into the extent to which the experienced workforce is being retained. In practice though this measure is rarely used.

Thus, Johnson (1981) splits the tourism workforce into 'transients', 'opportunists' and 'hard core' each with varying degrees of organisational tenure, a categorisation later picked up by Walmsley (2004) in an analysis of the tourism labour market in the British seaside resort of Torbay. Others have also focussed on the segmentation of the tourism workforce according to tenure. Wood (1997) and Krakover (2000) distinguish between core and peripheral workers, arguing that this distinction is sharper in tourism than in other industries. Lee-Ross and Pryce (2010) take the discussion back to Piore and Sabel's (1984) work on the primary and secondary labour markets, where the primary consists of core workers, and the secondary of part-time staff who are hired and fired as needed.

The causes and consequences of high labour turnover in the industry have likewise received much comment. The prevailing discourse holds that turnover is detrimental to businesses as it incurs administrative costs associated with staff leaving and the recruitment of new staff; staff with organisation-specific knowledge and skills take their skills with them when they leave, and it may be detrimental to staff morale, e.g. where staff have to cover periods of absence. There is also a case to be made for some labour turnover from a business perspective as it leads to the introduction of new talent, the 'fresh blood' argument and crucially it is a means of dealing with seasonal demand fluctuations. It is also often held up as a measure of poor employment practices in the industry and a justification, or excuse, depending on whose point of view one takes, for the low levels of training in the industry. Rowley and Purcell (2001) take issue with what Iverson and Deery (1997:71) describe as a turnover culture in the hospitality industry that is 'the acceptance of turnover as part of the work-group norm'. They argue, based on interviews with 21 managers, that much can be done to reduce labour turnover in the industry, notably improving working conditions and providing training and development opportunities.

Data on staff turnover levels (or its counterpart, tenure) by age, are scant, but what we know about patterns of youth employment in the sector certainly points to elevated levels of staff turnover for young people. First, tourism employment draws to a large extent on individuals who are flexible with regard to employment tenure. This is particularly the case in resorts that are characterised by high levels of seasonality. This kind of work appeals to a range of young people, from students looking for work outside of term time, to those who are desperate to accept any job regardless of tenure or conditions because of labour market circumstances, thereby gaining that all-important 'first step on the ladder', but also young people who work for lifestyle reasons such as those looking at resort employment. What may be a blessing for some young people can represent a blight for others. For those who are looking for permanent employment, for employment that will give them economic security, which will in turn allow them to transition into adulthood by engaging in activities associated with adulthood, seasonal employment provides a mixed blessing.

Working hours

Much, though certainly not all, tourism and hospitality employment is characterised by irregular working hours. Although these are usually regarded as one of the detrimental characteristics of employment in the sector it is clear that irregular and flexible working hours can represent both a downside and an upside for employees. For young people who are still in education, flexible working hours can provide them with an income and experience that would otherwise have been unavailable had only jobs with regular working hours existed. Flexible and irregular working hours can present a draw for young people, who may face fewer family commitments (European Agency for Safety and Health at Work, 2008) and are therefore more readily available for work in a 24/7 hour economy. It has been noted that bar and restaurant employment especially attracts large numbers of students seeking to work around lectures, particularly evenings and weekends (Lashley, 2005). Lee-Ross and Pryce (2010) report high levels of job satisfaction, which they argue conflicts with the ongoing representation of tourism employment as poor due to high levels of temporary and part-time work. Boon's (2006) work, which discusses resort employment within the context of a ski resort in New Zealand, suggests a trade-off between management and youth employees with regard to pay and working hours. Employees may not be paid much and are only able to work during the season but this kind of chalet work provides them with the opportunity to engage in leisure pursuits, i.e. skiing. Again, the extent to which this suits everyone, however, will depend on the precise nature of the work (working hours) and individual preferences as these contrasting views from two resort employees demonstrate (Boon, 2006:601):

> Ashley[1]: 'The hours suit me. I enjoy working nights. It gives me the days off to do things I want to do – to go snowboarding'.

> Carl: 'Yeah, I'm out of here. I'm not really enjoying it...Just the hours because having come here for the snow and then ...doing breakfast

---

1   Not original names

so like you start at 5:30 in the morning and you don't get out until 2
pm and so your day is destroyed if you want to go up the mountain'.

Roan and Diamond (2003) in an Australian study point to the fact that young
employees in hospitality, while not put off by irregular working hours, regard
these as potentially problematic later on in their lives when family commitments
arise. This, so Roan and Diamond demonstrate that hospitality employment is
often regarded as a transitory career opportunity by young people. Roan and
Diamond also provide examples of young hospitality employees who complain that the irregular working hours have curtailed their social life, in that
during times where employees' friends tend to go out and enjoy themselves,
i.e. evenings and weekends, they are having to work. Again, the message that
comes through is that the working hour arrangement is something that suits
some but not others.

Wages

Establishing a wage level for tourism employment is not only challenging
but virtually meaningless without further considerations as to the nature of
a general wage level. Firstly, as has been emphasised in Chapter 2, measuring what belongs within the diverse sphere of economic activity classified as
tourism is contested. Although the straightforward option of counting those
employed in a tourism business presents the most practical solution, arguably,
if an employee gains the majority of his or her remuneration from tourism,
irrespective of whether the actual business is classified as a tourism business,
a case can be made that this is then tourism employment. This is by no means
a trivial argument. For example, aircraft technicians are not considered as falling within the ILO's hotel, catering and tourism sector employment, although
where their job is to maintain passenger aircraft making the case that they are
not employed in tourism becomes difficult.

The view that tourism is a low wage sector is the result of a focus on wages
at the lower end of the occupational spectrum. This is reasonable insofar as
many of the jobs in tourism are not high paying jobs. That said, the same claims
could be made for many sectors where a large base of employees earn low
wages, while the reverse is true for those at the top of the organisational pyramid or at the top of their profession. In 2011 16% of employed persons in the
sector were in a managerial or senior position whereas 49% were in elementary
occupations,which does not include those in sales and customer service occupations, (People 1st, 2013:27).

Discussions of wage levels in tourism rarely venture beyond the low pay characterisation. An analysis of data from the ILO's Laborsta database (Walmsley, 2012a) confirmed that overall at an international level wages in tourism were low, both in absolute (purchasing power) and relative (by comparison to other sectors) terms. The analysis also demonstrated variation in wage levels depending on occupations within the tourism sector itself, but also variations by country. Thus, although the analysis demonstrated that international wages in tourism are low by comparison to other sectors, within the broader notion of tourism employment considerable variation in wages exists.

Table 3.1 provides data on graduate and senior level salaries in tourism in the UK. According to the Association of Graduate Recruiters (AGR) the average graduate starting salary in the UK is £29,000 (US$ 44,300, based on the exchange rate of £1 = US$1.53 at the time of writing – end of May 2015). The data in 3.1 therefore further underpin the low pay status of the tourism sector, even at the graduate starting salary level where they are in the region of one third to almost one half lower than average the AGR graduate starting salary.

Table 3.1: Salaries in tourism and hospitality. Source: figures from Prospects (2014)

	Graduate starting / assistant (£)	Senior Level (£)
Accommodation manager	17,000 - 22,000	22,000 - 40,000+
Catering manager	15,000 - 21,000	25,000 - 40,000
Event manager	18,000 - 25,000	50,000 - 70,000
Hotel manager	From 21,000 for assistant GM	21,000 - 55,000
Public house manager	16,000 - 21,000	20,000 - 35,000
Restaurant manager	n.a.	20,000 - 40,000
Theme park manager	21,000 - 30,000	35,000 - 75,000
Tour manager	15,000 - 20,000	30,000+
Tourism officer	15,000 - 19,000	30,000 - 40,000
Travel agency manager	11,000 - 18,000	25,000 - 45,000

Although low wages in tourism tend to effect all employees regardless of age, young people are nonetheless particularly affected. First, although minimum wages now exist in many countries this is no guarantee of employers paying a minimum wage. On the 8th of June 2014, the UK government's revenue and customs office 'named and shamed' 25 employers who failed to pay the minimum wage. Five out of these 25 were in the hospitality sector. Young people who do not know their legal rights, and have fewer experiences when it comes to dealing with employers, may be more likely to be exploited in this regard. Ironically given their inception as a means to protect employees, minimum wages can result in lower wages for young people. Furthermore, the same minimum wage level does not apply to everyone. Young people are frequently not entitled to the same minimum wage as other employees. In Germany, for example, the minimum wage was introduced on 1st January 2015 at Euro 8.50. It is valid for all employees who are 18 years or older. Anyone under 18 years of age has no legal right to claim the minimum wage. In other countries there is greater variation of applicable minimum wage levels. In Australia, which is one of the countries with a relatively high minimum wage (Kane, 2015), employees who are under 21 years of age are classed as juniors. In the UK there are four different rates, one for individuals on apprenticeships, one of those under 18, one for those 18-20 and one for anyone 21 years and over. Based on a calculation of working a 38 hour week over 52 weeks at a minimum wage of £6.50 per hour (2014 figure) we arrive at an annual salary of £12,844. Immediately we can see (Table 3.1) that starting salaries for working in a travel agency must be based on a minimum wage calculation (for someone who is younger than 21 years of age and who therefore is entitled to less than the minimum wage for a 21 year old).

On the face of it, different pay for the same work appears unjust. However, one of the arguments for a differential minimum wage is that it is to prevent youth from quitting apprenticeships that are usually lower-paid than the minimum wage but that would give them better labour market prospects in the longer term. Another argument is based on the premise that young people are less productive. This is less convincing, certainly from a tourism perspective, when considering the low-skills requirements of many tourism jobs as claimed by employers themselves. To suggest that tourism employment is low skilled on the one hand but then argue that young people should not be paid as much as older employees because of the lack of skills on the other is a bit suspect.

The previous deliberations were underpinned by the notion of formal employment but as we have seen in Chapter 2, much tourism employment occurs outside of the formal economy, in fact in some countries informal employment in tourism is said to exceed its formal counterpart. The debate around wages in tourism employment, particularly youth employment as young people are more likely than older ones to be working informally, needs to recognise this. Harriss-White (2010:170) outlines a number of 'advantages' of informal economic activity in the short term, such as a reduction in an organisation's overheads, undercutting legal wage floors, labour may be controlled by avoiding the conditions where it might be organized in unions and the incorporation of new kinds of low-cost labour (e.g. rural, female and child labour). There are obvious incentives to the organisation for employing young people on an informal basis, which adds to the precariousness of youth employment, placing employment outside the boundaries of state regulation and protection.

Regulation does not guarantee fairness of course and earning a minimum wage may not protect against poverty. Results presented in July 2010 from an IFES (Institut für Empirische Sozialforschung) study on the labour climate index in Austria claimed that 15% of the tourism workers sampled responded that they couldn't live at all from their earnings, 46% mentioned they just about made ends meet. The Austrian trade union VIDA announced a minimum wage of Euro 1,400 1st May 2015, in accommodation and food services (VIDA, 2015). Calls for the payment of a living wage, i.e. a wage that covers basic needs, rather than a minimum wage, are getting louder and more employers are heeding this call. Politicians recognise that work must be a way out of poverty. In the UK in 2014 the living wage (outside of London) was just over a fifth higher than the minimum wage (£7.85 compared to £6.50). For young people who work in tourism on a statutory age-adjusted minimum wage of £3.79 (2014 figure) for an under-18 year old, this is less than half what is regarded as a living wage. Young people, generally, have fewer commitments in terms of supporting families and covering living expenses (for example by living at home) but for the exceptions that do, it is understandable that it may be virtually impossible to live off youth wages.

The experience of work

There are grounds for the poor image of tourism as an employer, although much evidence is anecdotal, which goes with the territory; given the sensitive, potentially damaging, nature of the issue, it is not something that employers, particularly poor employers, like to shout about. Accusations of poor working conditions in the sector continue to prevail, although obtaining data on working conditions can be problematic. At the outset it is necessary to be clear about this paucity of 'hard' data. Nonetheless, with the democratisation of information, notably the ease with which information can be created and disseminated (Friedman, 2005), it is becoming increasingly difficult for employers to hide poor employment practices as disgruntled employees take to social media platforms to air their grievances. While those making these grievances may be as partial in their claims as those responsible for poor working conditions, modern communication channels have undoubtedly provided a platform for disgruntled employees to air their views, although we are still far from a level playing field considering the power relationship between employee and employer.

The review of the nature of youth employment in this chapter has hitherto attempted to provide a discussion around objectively identifiable facets of youth employment in tourism and hospitality. Working conditions can be, for example, compared on the basis of contractual arrangements including working hours, leave entitlement, etc. However, the experience of work itself is socially structured, not 'natural' or 'inevitable' (Grint, 1991). In other words, objectively identical arrangements can be interpreted in a number of different ways by different workers, as Boon's (2006) analysis of resort work has shown. What shapes the experiences are on the one hand unique to the individual, as each individual brings his/her way of doing things/seeing things to the work-place, but also socially structured in that what we think, feel and act is shaped in part by social structures (see for example Bourdieu's notion of 'habitus').

The socially constructed experience and meaning of work are also reflected in the concept of work orientations, one of the earliest themes to emerge in the vast body of literature on the role of work in society (Lockwood, 1966). The theory of work orientations places workers in one of four different types, depending on how they view their role in society. Continuing with the social stratification theme, Fox (1976) suggests that the lower the occupational status of a job, the more likely its incumbents will be undertaking the job for extrinsic motives such as pay and security. If this hypothesis is true then many tourism jobs may be undertaken solely for these kinds of extrinsic rewards given the low status accorded to tourism employment (discussed further below).

In reality though, things are not this straightforward; the experience of tourism employment is complex and in many respects even incongruous. Korczynski (2009) explains in some detail the contradictory demands on the service employee. On the one hand the customer can be a source of satisfaction and pleasure, on the other the employee can be the cause of stress and frustration. This distinction reveals a further facet of the employment relationship in tourism and hospitality in that it does not consist of a two-way relationship between employee and employer, but also has a third party, the customer. The employee can then be torn between meeting contradictory demands as demonstrated in a quote from Weatherley and Tansik (1993:5):

> I'm damned if I do; damned if I don't. You just can't win. Either [the boss] is mad at me, or the customer is. If I don't get my work done, [the boss] is going to yell at me. But if I don't help the customers, they get pissed at me.

In Korczynski's (2009) analysis of service work, two conflicting forces that shape the experience of work are identified. The first is the drive towards efficiency via bureaucracy, whereby he draws on the work of Max Weber and Ritzer's McDonalidization theory. To survive, companies must become more efficient at what they do, and they do so by routinizing work processes. The customer is however an unpredictable entity, who does not ordinarily want to be treated like a number. Standardization does not always lead to high levels of customer satisfaction. Thus Korczynski (2009) has described the experience of service work as being determined by a customer-oriented bureaucracy.

Customer interaction and abusive behaviour

Much research now exists in the experience of work of customer service employees (CSEs) also known as boundary-spanners, i.e. employees who straddle the boundary between the organisation and its customers. One of the hallmarks of many tourism jobs is the direct customer interaction. Ironically, it is often precisely those that the organisation is trying to help, its customers, who negatively affect the experience of work. According to Grove *et al.* (2004) we are living in an *age of rage*. Volatile customer behaviour appears to be on the rise. Yagil (2008) describes occupations where the risk of being the target of aggression is traditionally high, such as in policing, the prison service or psychiatric nursing, but also notes that employees in what used to be considered low-risk service jobs, such as in sales, hotel work and even librarianship, are increasingly facing aggression. A report by the European Agency for Safety and Health at Work (2008) counts the hotel and catering sector as one of the most prone to violence, so the move from low to high risk should not be considered that recent. The impact on the employee of having to face customer abuse (both verbal and physical), notably stress, is well documented as are organisational consequences such as employee turnover (Poddar and Madupalli, 2012) and absenteeism (Grandey *et al.*, 2004).

One is inclined to consider whether a relationship exists between employee age and being the target of abusive behaviour. In effect, are young people more likely to face abuse from customers than older employees? Theoretically at least one may be able to answer this question in the affirmative. Customers may be less likely to 'hold back' when faced with someone who is their junior. Young people may be less confident in their role, something which a customer could well pick up on and exploit. This is also an explanation provided by Gilbert *et al.* (1998) who link the lack of confidence to low levels of formal education. As Yagil (2008) notes, perpetrator motives include levels of perceived risk, and it is possible that an aggressive customer perceives the risk of displaying abusive behaviour to a youth differently than to a mature adult. There also exists some evidence that young people do face more abusive behaviour than older workers in the sector. Scott's (1998) research suggests that almost half of hospitality graduates in his study had experienced some form of violence and that women and young employees were more likely to have been victims. That said, in certain environments such as bars, females are increasingly being employed in the role of bouncers as they are perceived at least to be better able to handle aggressive situations, although Roberts (2009) queries whether differences exist in the handling of aggressive incidents.

Akgeyik and Meltem (2008) cite a study by Mayhew and Quinlan (2002) that claims young workers are more likely to face violence in the workplace than older workers, especially in the fast food industry. In their own study Akgeyik and Meltem (2008) found that workers under 30 years of age were slightly more likely to face customer aggression than older workers. However, age seems to have played a greater role in counts of sexual harassment with those under 20 years of age reporting more incidents of this.

Sexual harassment is another form of abusive behaviour that has received a degree of attention in the tourism literature. Sexual harassment is not something that is confined to young people, but it does focus disproportionately on young women in particular (but not exclusively). Sexual harassment is difficult to define which makes it all the more insidious a scourge. The European Commission (EUR-Lex, 2015) defines sexual harassment as:

☐ conduct which is unwanted, unreasonable and offensive to the recipient;

☐ any conduct which is used explicitly or implicitly as a basis for a decision which affects that person's access to vocational training, access to employment, continued employment or salary;

☐ any conduct which creates an intimidating, hostile or humiliating work environment for the recipient,

Which makes it clear that this is a problem that affects both genders and is not confined to physical harassment alone.

Sexual harassment is regarded by many as endemic to the service sector (Woods and Kavanagh, 1994). The literature on sexual harassment in the hospitality sector in particular is replete with examples where the sexualisation of the service encounter is not just condoned but actively encouraged. Undoubtedly there is a sexualised element to many hospitality jobs. Gilbert *et al.* (1998:50) provide an anecdote from a 'young girl' who was starting a new job as a waitress and who was told to 'wear her skirt as short as she would feel it comfortable'. In this context it is instructive to compare three studies in three different geographical contexts that all focus on hospitality students' work placement experiences.

The first study (Mkono, 2010) draws on 77 guided interviews with placement students in Zimbabwe. The first paragraph of this paper makes reference to students' age as a potentially contributing factor to their victimisation. Although Mkono acknowledges the difficulty in generalising her study's findings to the wider hotel sector in Zimbabwe, it is still striking that 78% of the placement students in her sample said they had directly experienced sexual harassment. Of these 'only' 15% related to physical harassment. 44% of harassers were customers, the remainder either co-workers (34%) or managers (22%). An interesting aspect of Mkono's study was the relevance of tips as a blackmail tool. Because many waitresses relied on tips to make ends meet, they were pressured into accepting lewd behaviour by customers. This underlines another aspect of developing country employment, that of extremely unequal power relationships and dependence, that clearly impacts the work experience. Mkono (2010) explains that the high incidence of sexual harassment cases could be down to an absence of sound sexual harassment policies amongst other things, and yet even in countries where such policies exist sexual harassment may prevail as the next study demonstrates.

The second study, conducted in the UK by Ineson *et al.* (2013) broadens the issue of sexual harassment to sexual discrimination as well as harassment with a deliberate inclusion on sexual minorities such as lesbians, gay men, bisexuals and transgender. Of the sample of 101 UK domiciled placement students (mean age 22) 7% had witnessed sexual harassment and 4% had experienced it. A further 8% had experienced sexual discrimination and 4% had witnessed it. The context of the SH cases is one where an older, male employee harasses a younger, and inexperienced female employee. This confirms the relationship between age and victimisation. Ineson *et al.*'s (2013) study tells a powerful story about the personal experiences of sexual harassment in the hospitality workplace, and demonstrates that harassment is perpetrated by both customers and fellow employees, confirming Mkono's (2010) findings. Ineson *et al.* (2013) also explored eight cases in depth. Alas, in only one case was the matter resolved to the satisfaction of the harassed. In the other cases the matter was either not reported or when reported not dealt with appropriately (insufficient action or no action taken). It is evident then that having the right policies in place is not enough to remove sexual harassment from the workplace. The right policies are needed but without sufficient focus on implementation, and indeed a change in cultural values, the issue is not going to be resolved.

The final study was undertaken in Taiwan. Lin (2006) surveyed 301 students who had undertaken a practicum in the hospitality sector. As with the previous studies, sexual harassment is linked to youth. Referring to the survey's respondents, it is stated: '…since these individuals are often young… they are usually naïve and lack social experience' (Lin, 2006:53) which implies they are more at risk as less able to defend themselves against inappropriate behaviour. The same argument was made above in relation to young people accepting poor working conditions generally. The mean age of the 301 survey respondents was 20.41 years. The prevalence, but also difficulty, in defining sexual harassment is demonstrated by the fact that 97.3% of respondents answered at least one of the nineteen statements relating to sexual harassment positively (these ranged from being told suggestive or dirty jokes to rape), but 'only' 47.8% claimed to have actually been harassed. As with Mkono's (2010) study, harassers were grouped into three categories: customers, superiors and colleagues. Customers were responsible for only 25.4% of harassment demonstrating again that SH is not solely a boundary-spanner problem, i.e. relating to the customer-staff interface.

Surprisingly a small minority, predominantly males, declared their emotional reaction at being harassed as 'very happy' either to a mild (16.4%) or average degree (4.2%). Furthermore, although Lin's (2006) study confirmed that males were by far the most prevalent harassers, 28.6% of males in this sample reported having felt harassed at least once (by other males). Lin (2006:65) suggests that females were more likely to be harassed by strangers (i.e. customers) than men, and that those who harassed males "needed to spend more time testing their victim's limitations before they actually dared to challenge and harass them."

These three studies offer many similarities but also point to differences in the prevalence of sexual harassment as well as of sexual discrimination. Both the Taiwanese and Zimbabwean studies demonstrated higher levels of perceived sexual harassment than the UK study (where some respondents had spent their placements overseas). Measuring levels of sexual harassment is tricky however, as variations in levels of sexual harassment may in part be down to measurement differences. The relationship between sexual harassment and age is prevalent in all studies. One of the fundamental characteristics about SH is the underlying power imbalance between harasser and harassed. This has on the one hand to do with the nature of the service encounter and, as all studies argued, the problematic nature of the view that 'the customer is always right'. But this power imbalance is also aggravated by age and economic differences (certainly in Zimbabwe the latter also seems to have played a role). Finally, much sexual harassment originates with fellow workers and to a dispropor-tionate degree managers, again underpinning the role power imbalances play.

Aesthetic labour

In a discussion around the experience of work for young people in tourism, and perhaps fittingly after a review of work in the area of sexual harassment, attention now turns to immaterial aspects of labour, specifically emotional and even more so aesthetic labour. Emotional and aesthetic labour in tourism are not, of course, the exclusive preserve of youth *per se* and yet it is evident from lawsuits brought against airlines where the charge was ostensibly on grounds of age, one might conclude that in reality this was about aesthetics. Barry's (2007) book *Femininity in Flight* provides a chronology of female flight attendants—or *stewardesses* as they were known until the 1970s. From the 1930s through the 1960s airlines would only hire women who were white, single, young, slender, and attractive. Stewardesses could 'look forward to' forced resignation if they married (or turned 32 or 35) in many airlines. Segrave (2000:90) quotes an airline executive in the 1960s as stating: 'It's the sex thing. Put a dog on an airplane and twenty businessmen are sore for a month'. Although legislation now prohibits age-related discrimination in many countries, cases such as that brought against Virgin Atlantic in 2001 are recent enough to make one realise the issue has not simply gone away.

The common usage of the word aesthetic is 'concerned with beauty or the appreciation of beauty' (Oxford Dictionaries, 2015). Its origins in Greek have to do with perception and were adopted by Kant in the science of perception by the senses. There is nothing here that relates to which of the senses aesthetic specifically refers to although visual appeal is perhaps the most common under-standing of aesthetics; Kusluvan *et al.* (2010) certainly consider appearance the essence of an aesthetic labour approach. Despite the dominance of the visual, in relation to work aesthetic labour goes beyond the object, in a physical sense, of beauty but includes intangibles such as speech and comportment. Warhurst *et al.* (2000) write of aesthetic labour as embodied competencies (also capacities) that can be learned. In fact the distinction between generic skills, particularly communication, and aesthetic labour is not entirely clear-cut. Being able to communicate at an appropriate level with a customer, be that in a top-end restaurant or in a fast-food joint, could be classified as relying on communi-cation skills as much as aesthetic labour. Warhurst *et al.* (2000) acknowledge this when they refer to Torrington and Hall's (1998) use of competencies 'With some small overlap, competencies can be defined as the characteristics of an individual which produce a desired or optimum performance' (Warhurst *et al.*,

2000:5). It is not so much that aesthetic labour is new, it seems, but rather that its importance in providing a competitive edge has more recently been brought to the fore.

The extent of research into the experience of aesthetic labour is quite limited. Being able to embody a corporate ethos, convey a sense of style, or sophistication as mentioned in Warhurst *et al.*'s (2000) case study of a Glasgow boutique hotel, may instil a greater sense of confidence in the individual. The downside is that for those young people whose appearance is not deemed appropriate, or whose accents or manner of speaking do not fit the bill, the opposite might be the case. Warhurst and Nickson (2007) explored the experience of aesthetic labour, again in hospitality and looked briefly at employees' attitudes, rather than solely at how organisations incorporated aesthetic labour. Their findings resonate with this idea: those who passed 'aesthetic screening' generally thought it was a good idea, those who didn't clearly were aggrieved. Worse still, the requirements of certain types of aesthetic labour can represent a form of discrimination based on social class or geographical provenance. The word 'common' has pejorative connotations in British English referring to 'a lack of taste and refinement supposedly typical of the lower classes' (Oxford Dictionaries, 2015), ironically given the usage of the term 'common' as in 'frequently occurring' or 'most prevalent'. A 'common' accent may preclude work in certain roles or for certain companies in other words. Because tourism employment may provide a vital first step in employment due to low skills requirements, the inability of those from 'common' backgrounds to access certain jobs in tourism on the grounds of aesthetics would negate this virtue.

A further highly pertinent issue in relation to aesthetic labour is its classification as a skill. Warhurst *et al.* (2000, 2007) discuss, particularly in the later paper, how aesthetics are a key skill tourism recruiters are looking for. Clearly there is a debate to be had as to whether stretching the definition of skills to include appearance is in fact a step too far, an issue also acknowledged by Warhurst. Nonetheless, whether regarded as a skill or not, there is abundant evidence that appearance continues to play an important role as a desirable employee attribute in many tourism jobs. Warhurst and Nickson (2007) cite a study of nearly 100 human resource professionals in the USA who were responsible for hiring entry-level hospitality industry employees. The top two criteria were 'pride in appearance' and 'good attitude' (Martin and Grove, 2002, cited in Warhurst and Nickson, 2007:106).

Nickson himself (Nickson *et al.*, 2005) published a paper in this area which is telling in relation to the importance of aesthetics in tourism employment. Nickson *et al.* (2005) established that when hiring front line service staff employers thought appearance was either critical or important (33% and 57% respectively) while only 1% thought qualifications were critical and a further 19% felt they were important. It is not surprising therefore that Nickson *et al.* (2005:204) argue that individuals with social and aesthetic skills 'are at a distinct advantage in the recruitment and selection process, compared to those who lack such skills'. For many jobs in tourism the embodiment of an organisation's ethos may not be crucial; to be presentable most likely will. It is possible therefore to speak of varying degrees of aesthetic labour; the more is demanded by way of aesthetic labour, the more selective the recruitment process will be, the greater the chances of discrimination also, however.

The proliferation of writing on emotional labour since Arlie Hochschild first published *The Managed Heart* in 1979 predates the writing on aesthetic labour. One could say that aesthetic labour is a particular form of, or at least intersects with, emotional labour, if emotional labour is defined as 'the management of feeling to create a publicly observable facial and bodily display' (Hochschild, 1983:7). As discussed, aesthetic labour relates to the embodiment of competencies, competencies that relate to an organisation's aesthetics, style or ethos. Managing one's emotions to provide a performance aligned with the organisation's style demonstrates that aesthetic labour is a form of emotional labour.

Although there are negative connotations associated with aesthetic labour, this is possibly even more the case for emotional labour. One of Hochschild's key contributions was to suggest that managers' claims on the emotions of their employees, in other words the commoditization of emotions, was part of the capitalist labour process. The quasi-sale of emotions, be that as a result of surface or deep acting on behalf of the employee, appears as the ultimate claim of capital over the individual. At least this is the worst case scenario. Bolton and Boyd (2003), who like Hochschild researched cabin crew, do however point out that the employee also has a means to control their emotions according to their own agenda.

Work in an SME

Just as we have seen how the front line service worker in tourism is confronted with a complex mix of demands that shape the experience of work, a further aspect of youth employment in tourism relates to the structure of the industry, notably the predominance of small and medium-sized enterprises (Thomas, 1998). The question of the impact of organisational size on the experience of work in tourism has received scant attention. The fact is that most young people who find work in tourism will find themselves working in an SME (see also Chapter

6, p.161 ff). Here though, a certain degree of confusion reigns around the impact of organisational size on the experience of work. A prevailing view holds that large organisations with more formalised HR systems present more agreeable working conditions than those in small firms. Advances in the management of human resources spread more quickly in large organisations. However, evidence of lower levels of workplace satisfaction in small firms compared to large is hard to find. Indeed, it can be argued that a smaller, more personal working environment with increased levels of autonomy may be found in smaller firms. The experience of work in small organisations depends largely on the owner/manager who has direct control over working conditions (see for example Bacon *et al.*, 1996) as opposed to large organisations where there exist a multitude of systems and procedures set by HR that likewise determine the experience of work. Not all small business owners/managers need be despots after all. Indeed, Cobble and Merrill (2009:159) uphold the view that employment in small organizations differs from that in large organisations, and not necessarily in a negative way:

> employee-employer relations may be personal and collaborative rather than adversarial, formalized and highly bureaucratic. The employment relationship is not the classic one described by Marx, nor is it even the conventional us-versus-them world view that often prevails in large bureaucratically-run enterprises.

This assertion is not new as early considerations about small firm employment attest. Ingham (1970), for example, argues that a trade-off exists between economic and non-economic rewards in small firms. Based on his own survey, workers in small organisations accept lower wages for greater non-economic rewards, and Durkheim (1933) reflects that as firms grow (concentration of capital) employment becomes less harmonious. This view is expressed by Goss (1991) in the notion of the Green approach to small businesses as the antithesis to the concentration of capital. In hospitality and tourism itself Lucas (2004), drawing on the 1998 Workplace Employee Relations Survey, claims that work is harder and more stressful in large workplaces than in very small workplaces, but also warns about making blanket generalisations as the employment experience needs also to take individual characteristics into account. This was confirmed by Walmsley *et al.* (2012) with regard to tourism internships in SMEs, where some were akin to the harmonious environment described by Ingham (1970). The two quotations that follow relate to tourism SMEs from a study of internships in the sector, and provide a flavour of the potential for a family-orientated notion of working conditions (Walmsley, 2008:124):

"…the other owner…his family are very involved in the running of the business. His two sons work there part time, and…they kind of take you in, it's like a family. We went to his house for Thanksgiving. They bought us Christmas presents, they…you know, they treat us like a family…"

"It was basically a family business…and we were the family."

Furthermore, owner/manager priorities play a clear role in determining the development of a business, its size and working conditions. Particularly in the tourism and leisure industries the notion of non-economic imperatives in determining business performance are increasingly recognised and studied as they relate to SMEs (Byers and Slack, 2001; Ateljevic and Doorne, 2000; Morrison and Teixeira, 2004; Shaw and Williams, 2004; Di Domenico, 2005). A small lifestyle firm may differ considerably in its working conditions compared to a small firm that is 'reaching for the stars'.

This view that working conditions are more pleasant in SMEs is however not universally shared, neither generally (Rainnie, 1989:7, describes working conditions as 'brutal' in the printing and clothing industries) nor in the tourism and hospitality literature. Littlejohn and Watson (2004), who report on a round table event of tourism and hospitality stakeholders, claim that small tourism firms are often characterised by long hours and tough physical and mental work. In a similar vein, Doherty (2004) argues that the hospitality industry's poor reputation in human resource practices is mainly based on small employers. Baum (2007) also suggests that while much progress has been made in terms of remuneration and working conditions in the sector, in some small businesses working conditions can be borderline Dickensian. It is fair to suggest that employee relations in small firms vary considerably from one firm to another. Neither are all, or even the majority of, small firms necessarily beautiful, nor do employee relations necessarily conform to the Bleak House scenario. Having established that working conditions are related to styles of supervision and employer control, Goffee and Scase (1980) point to the dangers of 'size-reductionism' (see also Burrows and Curran, 1989) in assessing working conditions. Following this discussion it would be a gross oversimplification to lay the blame for tourism's reputation for poor working conditions on the doorstep of small employers.

Trade unions

Trade unions have traditionally played a weak role in tourism employment. There are a number of often-cited reasons for this:

☐ Because tourism is dominated by small firms, the organisation of workers across the sector is difficult.

☐ Tourism as a major economic force really only developed in the second half of the 20th Century. The roots of unionisation in the sector do not run deep in historical terms.

☐ The high levels of temporary and part-time employment do not favour union membership.

☐ Tourism draws on a diverse and often marginalised workforce which ironically may benefit most from union membership, and yet because of its fragmented, apolitical constitution, does not form strong union ties.

To these reasons Lee-Ross and Pryce (2010:15) also add 'a traditionally hostile and union-busting management style'.

In fact, unionisation in services more generally has been low, largely also for historical reasons. Although not entirely absent from labour and industrial scholars' purview, e.g. in studies of flight attendants or fast food workers, until the 1990s the theoretical frameworks underpinning labour studies were generally drawn from images of blue collar, factory floor workers in the manufacturing sector. Today service workers are receiving greater recognition in the academic literature and also in relation to labour standards, as well as in popular culture. An example of this greater recognition is a recently aired programme on UK television called *'The Call Centre'*, a fly-on-the wall reality television series about a call centre in South Wales, which aimed to provide an insight into the everyday life of call centre workers. It is now estimated (UNISON, 2015) that 1 million workers work in call centres in the UK (approximately 3% of all workers), 5 million in the USA (Witsil, 2014), which again equates to approximately 3% of all workers according to US Labor Force statistics (Rhode Island Department of Labor and Training, 2015).

Despite the challenges that trade unions face, especially in the service sector, they continue to play an important role in protecting workers' rights and function as an important partner in the tri-partite social dialogue between workers, employers and trade unions as promoted by the ILO's Decent Work Agenda. Examples abound where trade unions have stepped in to promote and safeguard tourism workers' rights, especially for frequently disadvantaged workers such as young people. The Austrian trade union VIDA (2013) has, for example, called on employers in the food and accommodation sector to respect workers' rights, in particular by adhering to legislation in the realm of providing sufficient periods of rest, and avoiding the misuse of 'all-inclusive contracts' (also professional contracts) that although originally envisaged for management are being applied across all job categories and which do not stipulate standard working hours. This can result in unpaid overtime which may then lead to wages that fall below the minimum wage. Apprenticeships are also a cause of concern for VIDA, specifically that employers are using them as a cheap source of labour by not then investing sufficiently in the education and training of apprentices.

VIDA itself is a member of EFFAT, the European Federation of Food, Agriculture and Tourism Trade Unions. EFFAT, similar to VIDA, has a strong record of bringing to light employer malpractices. At the end of May 2015 it, together with the IUF (International Union of Food, Agricultural, Hotel, Restaurant, Catering, Tobacco and Allied Workers' Associations) and the SEIU (Service Employees International Union) released a report on what it calls McDonald's worldwide abusive employment practices (EFFAT, 2015). McDonald's has not, as most readers will be aware, always benefitted from the most salubrious of reputations as an employer, especially since the coining of the term 'McJobs' which even has a dictionary definition. A McJob is, according to the Random House Dictionary Online (2015) 'an unstimulating, low-wage job with few benefits, especially in a service industry'. The report presents two employment scenarios employers can pursue, a high-road of taking responsibility for maintaining quality, family-supporting jobs, or a low-road strategy to suppress wages and circumvent labour legislation. The IUF, EFFAT and SEIU report is very clear that it believes McDonald's has chosen to take the low-road approach, although it recognises that this is not true for McDonald's in all countries.

Specifically, the report focuses on:

- ☐ The payment of low wages which frequently require topping up via the public purse in the form of benefits,
- ☐ Wage theft (the illegal underpayment of wages that are rightfully owed to workers),
- ☐ The lack of set work schedules (including zero hours contracts),
- ☐ Unsafe working environment,
- ☐ Exploitation of marginalized workers (including youth),
- ☐ Anti-union practices including fissured employment (i.e. using franchising to avoid responsibility for its workers).

Because of the sensitive, business-damaging nature of revelations about poor employment practices, very rarely do academics gain access to tourism workers. This is where unions can and do play an immensely important role in highlighting malpractices. They are, as is their remit, a mouthpiece for an all-too-frequently disenfranchised workforce. One needs only take a look at the IUF's website, specifically its hotel, catering and tourism news site, to discover a litany of alleged employer transgressions, arranged in chronological order. Particularly for young people, who may not have the cultural or social capital to bring about change, the strength a union provides in raising their concerns can be key in improving working practices. Despite claims that the days of unions are numbered, they do continue to play an indispensable role in promoting the rights of the young tourism worker.

Rather than succumbing to an inexorable decline, perhaps trade unionism has reached the bottom of the trough and will expand again, especially in an era of increased consumer consciousness about the responsibilities of business. The extent to which trade unionism is able to expand will also depend on legal frameworks, which vary at a national level. Thus, Cobble and Merrill (2009) argue that unionisation of service workers is hampered in the United States by a hostile social as well as legal environment where US labour law assumes a long-term, continuous relation to a single employer. As we know, many service workers, particularly in tourism and hospitality, and particularly young workers, move from job site to job site which hinders engagement in a worksite based system of organising. Such employees may simply not be with an employer long enough to utilize the conventional election procedures and card-signing associated with the National Labour Relations Act (Cobble and Merrill, 2009). If trade unions are to grow again it won't be an easy task to achieve.

Youth employment in developing countries

The rapid rise of international travel in the second half of the 20th Century, which has continued into the new millennium, may be one of the defining characteristics of our era. Tourism can be regarded as one key facet of a globalising world. In fact, advances in ICT which enable global communication and sharing of information has done nothing to dampen the desire to travel; if anything they have further boosted international tourism. International travel is predicted to continue to grow to 1.8 billion arrivals in 2030 (in 1950 international tourist arrivals stood at just 25 million) (UNWTO, 2014). While traditional destinations such as Europe and North America continue to attract the majority of international visitors, many new destinations are emerging to challenge this primacy, including those in developing countries. The UNWTO (2014:2) has forecast that:

☐ Between 2010 and 2030, arrivals in emerging destinations are expected to increase at twice the rate (+4.4% a year) of those in advanced economies (+2.2% a year).

☐ The market share of emerging economies increased from 30% in 1980 to 47% in 2013, and is expected to reach 57% by 2030, equivalent to over 1 billion international tourist arrivals.

Globally, the vast majority of young people are to be found in developing countries. This has led the UN World Youth Report (United Nations, 2003) to proclaim that 'this simple demographic factor alone is enough to define global youth policy as being fundamentally a question of development'. Fertility rates tend to be higher, sometimes much higher, in developing than in developed countries (although mortality rates are higher too). In time, the divergence in population demographics between more developed and less developed regions is predicted to decrease as the global population ages (United Nations, 2013). For now though, a comparison of population pyramids between less and more developed regions still shows marked differences (United Nations, 2013). Youth (un)employment is as relevant therefore to emerging economies as it is to developed economies, if not more so. Nonetheless, data sources on youth employment are more prevalent for developed than less developed economies which makes it all too easy, i.e. based on accessible data, to fall into the trap of making global claims based on localised observations.

It should not come as a surprise that academics frequently seek data close to home, which means empirical work in the area of tourism employment focuses heavily on data from North America, Europe and Australia/Australasia. This is changing as the recognition of tourism and hospitality as academic subjects in their own right is resulting in a steady globalisation of research in tourism. As yet however, this globalisation of scholarly activity, particularly in relation to employment studies, is still in its early phases. Taking a developing country perspective on youth employment is hampered by a lack of available data (see also the difficulties in trying to establish youth employment levels in tourism in Chapter 2).

At the outset it should be recognised that despite tourism's potential to improve lives, to provide opportunities for economic diversification particularly for least developed countries (LDCs) and to sustain livelihoods, tourism is rarely, if ever, a panacea. Nonetheless, tourism offers great potential in reducing poverty because it is consumed at the point of intervention and as such the low-skilled tourism worker in a far-flung corner of the planet can become an exporter of services to customers on the other side of the planet. As we have seen, tourism offers many forms of employment including work that require low skills levels. Furthermore, entry barriers to setting up tourism enterprises, particularly informal enterprises, are frequently low in terms of capital requirements. Tourism simply cannot be ignored as a vehicle to alleviate poverty and improve lives in disadvantaged regions.

That LDCs have long woken up to the potential for tourism to contribute to economic diversification and growth is recognised by the fact that in a review of 35 Diagnostic Trade Integration Studies (DTIS) 30 (86%) included a section specifically dedicated to tourism (UNDP, 2011). As the UNDP report, which is now referred to in more detail, suggests:

> …the presence of a tourism section is a reliable indication that the sector is a priority for the government and country as a whole. This is an important message for the development community, especially in view of the low priority traditionally assigned to the tourism sector in development cooperation. (UNDP, 2011:3)

This UNDP discussion paper analysed the 30 DTISs that prioritised the tourism sector, breaking the analysis down into interventions at three different levels: policy and regulatory framework, institutional support and supply-side (enterprise) response.

Overall the study concluded that there was insufficient emphasis placed on institutional support and that more needs to be done to translate policy measures into programmes. One aspect that at first glance causes some confusion is the DTIS' performance in providing vocational training and linking this with employment. Thus, the executive summary takes a positive perspective by claiming that:

> The DTIS performed well in showing how to better connect vocational training and skill upgrading efforts with local employment opportunities (UNDP, 2011:4)

but the discussion paper's findings, as well as its conclusions, suggest the opposite was the case:

> The DTIS have not adequately shown how to better connect vocational training and skill upgrading efforts with local employment opportunities.(UNDP, 2011:35)

The employment dimension clearly fell short in the DTIS. Of the thirteen criteria used in the analysis local employment was one of the three least covered categories. In fact the working paper is critical about the DTIS' lack of focus on employability:

> The DTIS rarely refer to local employment and almost no occurrences are found at the institution level. The DTIS also pay limited attention to gender participation in the tourism sector and quality of jobs and enforcement of labour conventions. All of these issues are fundamental to pro-poor tourism. (UNDP, 2011:31)

Furthermore the paper highlighted the need for training and skill development through domestic providers, but in partnership with global chains or regional vocational centres, as well as stressing the need to ensure opportunities for young people must be taken fully into account. One thing is certain, without an understanding of tourists' needs or a client-oriented culture (UNDP, 2011:36), and without an understanding of quality processes and standards, many destinations in LDCs will lose out in a very competitive global tourism marketplace.

It has been demonstrated in numerous studies that resident attitudes towards tourists and tourism vary depending on a number of factors, including the extent to which individual benefits are derived from tourism (Murphy, 1981, Harrill, 2004). At the same time, over-development and insensitive development of tourism can result in antipathy and even animosity towards tourists. Doxey's (1976) Irridex model with its hypothesised relationship between stages of tourism development and attitudes towards tourism set the scene for many of the ensuing studies that have explored resident attitudes. For many developing countries, as well as small island states, tourism is a major export earner. Attitudes towards tourism on the part of governments and policy makers can differ compared to those found in developed nations where tourism is often not taken seriously, or at least not as seriously as the tourism sector would like, which is then also reflected in attitudes towards tourism employment. Tourism employment is rarely held in high esteem (see also Chapter 4, page 83 ff.), and for many young people it represents a contingency career, an employer of last resort (Getz, 1994). That this is only a partial view is not solely reflected in attitudes towards tourism employment in developed, but certainly also in developing countries where tourism can provide prestigious, relatively well paid jobs. More generally, as Monterrubio and Espinosa (2013:56) have outlined:

> The specific role and contribution of tourism to employment varies from country to country, region to region, and location to location. The amount, type and quality of tourism employment are by no

means the same in all destinations; thus it is reasonable to suggest that the characteristics of tourism employment are not universal and are commonly dependent on local economic and sociocultural conditions.

Such an admission, though not entirely novel, is rarely acknowledged.

Tourism as a refuge sector

Cukier-Snow and Wall (1993) claim that many tourism jobs in developing countries pay better wages to the often only alternative, agriculture. Clearly, it is not just about absolute pay levels but pay relative to what is available in other sectors whereby Szivas and Riley (1999) mention a number of studies that argue that tourism draws heavily on employees from traditional sectors such as agriculture. Liu and Liu (2008) also support the notion that both working conditions in tourism and remuneration are often regarded favourably in developing countries. These thoughts are in part confirmed by Okumus *et al.* (2010) in a study of female employees in five-star hotels in Turkey. In contrast to the negative image of tourism employment, this group of employees expressed satisfaction with their employment, were positive about career progression opportunities and working conditions generally although dissatisfaction was expressed in relation to pay and heavy workloads. That tourism belongs to the lowest paying sectors globally has also been demonstrated by Walmsley (2012a) who compared relative wages across sectors for a sample of tourism and non-tourism jobs. If however the only alternative is an even worse paying, and potentially uncertain income from agriculture then tourism may be regarded as a more favourable form of employment (see also Monterrubio and Espinosa, 2013).

Data on the composition of the European workforce in tourism (measured as employment in accommodation and food services) during the recent recession showed the average age of tourism employees going up. As Figure 2.1 demonstrated, the proportion of young people in tourism employment in the European Union fell from 22% in 2008 to 20% in 2013. Although not evidence of tourism as a refuge sector, the data could certainly be interpreted this way, i.e. when traditional employment opportunities are limited tourism is turned to by older workers who then compete with young people for employment, thereby driving upwards the average employee age in tourism.

The issue of young people leaving rural areas in search of better employment opportunities, and therefore lives, in cities is a major issue in both developed and developing countries. Miller *et al.* (2012) describe how both tourism (and mining) are limiting youth migration from rural to urban areas in Australia, providing for a diversification of the economic base. In Bhutan high altitude farming is increasingly regarded as unappealing to young people. Tourism aside, there is little that is keeping them from turning to urban areas for employment (Brunet *et al.*, 2001). Mindo in Ecuador provides another example where tourism, here specifically adventure tourism, is providing a pull for young people to stay in the region (Widener, 2009). Widener contrasts this new form of tourism, i.e. adventure tourism, in the destination with eco- and resort-based tourism in Ecuador. These eco-and resort-based forms of tourism attract wealthy Ecuadorians and international tourists. Crucially, different forms of tourism will have differing impacts both on environmental protection as well as on employment. Trade-offs may need to occur between tourism's employment creation potential and its physical impacts. Essentially in this Ecuadorian example we are looking at fewer environmental impacts but also fewer tourism jobs for the community, particularly for young people, or more invasive forms of tourism, albeit with greater provision of work opportunities.

Tourism as a sector with growth potential and low entry requirements can, as Szivas and Riley (1999) have argued, offer a port in a storm when other sectors are contracting. They focussed on Hungary as it went through the transition from a former communist ally of the Soviet Union to a capitalist economy. For young people, it is not so much the contraction of other sectors that present a push into tourism employment, but individuals' low levels of human capital (lack of experience) which limits early employment opportunities. The underlying principle however is the same. What Szivas and Riley (1999) also found was that although the notion of a 'refuge sector' might be fitting for some who moved from other sectors into tourism, this does not hold for all. Levels of satisfaction with individuals' tourism employment were in fact quite high, despite data on wages in tourism compared to other sectors being quite low.

The ability of the tourism sector to provide jobs after political, social or economic turmoil is readily picked up by the United Nations Development Programme. So, for example, the UNDP is delivering phase two of a project that aims to empower young people economically in the Republic of Yemen (2014-2016). Yemen ranks 157th out of 174 countries on the Human Development Index (2013 data; UNDP, 2014a). Nearly half of Yemen's population is under 18 years of age and youth unemployment runs at almost 34 percent of the labour force. More than half the population is living on less than $2 per day. Broadly speaking, the project seeks to diversify the economy in terms of non-oil industries whereby fisheries, agriculture and tourism are mentioned specifically. The expected outcomes of the project are sustainable employment creation, greater community resilience and revitalization (UNDP, 2014b). The project consists of a number of phases with young people initially engaged in immediate income generating activities to build up seed capital, while they are simultaneously provided with personal and business skills training (capacity building). Young people who then come up with feasible business ideas graduate onto the next stage of the programme, where they are eventually supported in starting their own businesses.

A barrier to tourism development in many developing country scenarios is a lack of tourism know-how, or awareness of tourists' needs. If locals are to gain employment in tourism then capacity building is key (Liu and Wall, 2006). This capacity building does not need to focus only on customer service skills however, as Adam and Urquhart's (2007) study of the IT capacity building in the Maldivian tourism sector makes clear. In fact, Lee (2001) has argued that it is frequently the lack of human capital rather than physical capital in the area of IT that can hinder a country's or region's development. Rephrased, this means that were all countries to have the same level of technological infrastructure, differences in output and productivity would still result because of variations in the levels of human capital stock – a point widely recognised, of course, in economics (Becker, 1975). Adam and Urquhart (2007) claim that on the Maldives a lack of national IT policy and lack of national human resource development (HRD) policy for training and skills development continue to hamper tourism organizations in their efforts to build training and IT capacity. Despite the fundamental importance of the tourism sector to the Maldives, and the existence of a hotel school, no institute exists that trains individuals how to use hotel management software packages. Adam and Urquhart's (2007) case study of the Maldives at once shows the very individual nature of a country's or destination's human capital base, how it accumulates and transfers knowledge, and the role that training and education can play for young people to enhance tourism development.

Youth employment and responsible tourism

It is possible to frame a section on youth employment and its relationship to responsible tourism within the broader notion of youth employment in developing countries. However, to avoid confusion about the relationship of responsibility and tourism, specifically that this is an emerging economy or least developed country issue only, it is tackled separately here. The premise therefore of responsible tourism is that all forms of tourism, in all locations can become more responsible. For a more detailed discussion of this issue the reader is referred to Goodwin's (2011) text *Taking Responsibility for Tourism*.

Recently business, in particular big business, has come under a critical spotlight. There is a growing crisis of trust in organisations (Dietz, 2012). Spurred on by the 2007/08 global financial crisis, there is mounting scepticism that business, left to its own devices, will act responsibly. There is similarly continued negative press about tax evasion and tax avoidance schemes, and about rapid growth in earnings for those in the upper echelons of business (Srinivas, 2014) while the same increases in salaries are denied workers on the lower rungs of the corporate ladder.

This lack of trust towards business, in particular towards corporations, now extends into the political sphere also; movements worldwide continue to protest against current politico-economic models. Part of the protests are based around a growing questioning of the notion of trickle-down economics, i.e. that supporting the wealthy through incentives, leads to investment on their part, and this creates more wealth which then trickles down to all spheres of society. Authors such as Stiglitz (2002) and more recently Pickety (2014) question the prevailing economic system's ability to enhance the lives of all. The grassroots Occupy movement that began on Wall Street has spread to over 25 countries (Voigt, 2011). This movement did not appear in a vacuum as other social movements such as that of the Spanish *Indignados* were emerging (Halvorsen, 2012). The Indignados movement began when two collectives, *Juventud Sin Futuro* (Youth Without Future) and *Democracia Real! Ya!* (Real Democracy Now!) demonstrated in Madrid on 15th May 2011 (Stobart, 2014). At approximately 50%, Spain has one of the highest rates of youth unemployment in the EU (see also Chapter 2) so it is not that surprising that an increasing number of individuals, particularly young people, are beginning to voice their concerns about the status quo.

An interest in corporate social responsibility (and its sister concepts business ethics, corporate governance, corporate social performance, corporate citizenship and corporate social responsiveness) pre-dates the 2008 financial crisis, but the crisis has certainly stimulated further interest in this area. Companies' behaviour is coming under closer scrutiny and one of the areas that is, one might say at long last given what was said above, receiving more attention is labour relations.

Numerous research studies demonstrate that attitudes towards environmental protection are stronger amongst youth than for other age categories (e.g.Boeve-de Pauw and Van Petegem, 2010). Benckendorff *et al.* (2012) investigated environmental attitudes of a cohort of business and tourism students in

Australia. Using a multi-item scale, a strong degree of support was provided that this cohort of Generation Y students hold strong environmental attitudes. Benkendorff *et al.* (2012) went further than this however, comparing their results with twenty-one other studies that had used the same scale over thirty years. Contrary to expectations, they saw no increase in pro-environmental attitudes between 1992 and 2011. However, a number of explanations are provided for this unexpected result, including the proposition that with a growing awareness of environmental issues, responses to the scale have become more influenced by social desirability biases (Wise, 2010 cited in Benckendorff *et al.* 2012) and, furthermore, that attitudes towards the environment have become more complex and that the measurement scale was too broad to capture these nuances.

If today's young people do indeed hold stronger pro-environmental attitudes than previous cohorts, this implies that implementing environmental management strategies, or more broadly understood, sustainability initiatives is likely to resonate with them. It is frequently acknowledged in the change management literature, and in the vast literature on strategic management, that employee buy-in is required. Young people's generally greater awareness and more positive attitudes towards environmental protection could in essence make the task of becoming more sustainable within an organisation easier.

This relationship remains hypothetical however and levels of environmental awareness will differ on a country-by-country basis as Inglehart (1995) has argued. According to Inglehart, pro-environmental attitudes arise first in what he regards as a shift to post-materialist values. In societies with high levels of prosperity, individuals are driven less by the need to survive and can focus their attention on non-material issues such as political freedom, self-actualisation and environmental protection. However, Inglehart's application of his theory to data from the World Values Survey did not clearly support it. Inglehart found that a number of developing countries where affluence was low still displayed high levels of environmental concern. This was then explained on the grounds that local populations who were faced with concrete environmental problems were also likely to display high levels of pro-environmental attitudes. Thus he came up with the notion of 'objective problems, subjective values' explanation of pro-environmental attitudes that incorporates both explanations.

Whether societies are becoming increasingly post-materialist is contested, and Inglehart (1995) readily acknowledges this. The grass roots political movements mentioned above are an indication that values are changing, at least in certain parts of the population of developed economies. Youth values can be quite different to those of non-youth. Generation theory is based on this premise which has implications not just for pro-environmental attitudes but also for attitudes towards careers as discussed in Chapter 6. Recently Noreena Hertz, who has conducted extensive research on US and British teenage girls (13-20 years old), describes the age cohort as Generation K (after Katniss Everdeen, heroine of *The Hunger Games*). In an article in the *Financial Times* she describes how many twenty and thirty year-olds, the 'yes we can' generation, believed the world was their oyster but that for Generation K the world is 'less oyster and more Hobbesian nightmare'. Hertz writes that 75% of girls she surveyed were worried about terrorism; 66% worried about climate change; 86% were worried about getting a job and 77% about getting into debt. Trust was also an interesting feature, or rather the lack of it was. According to Hertz's study only 4% trusted large corporations to do the right thing (as opposed to 60% of adults), and one in ten trusted the government to do the right thing. This generation of young people's attitudes and values could have considerable implications for the future of politics and business.

In the previous section the example of tourism development in Ecuador drew attention to the issue that lies at the heart of any form of tourism development – that of reconciling a range of stakeholder interests. If tourism development invariably resulted in benefits to all stakeholders in a measure that was considered equitable by those stakeholders, then tourism development would hardly be a contentious issue. Early writings on the impacts of tourism (e.g. Krippendorf, 1987; Mathieson and Wall, 1982; Turner and Ash, 1975) demonstrate that tourism development is rarely uncontentious precisely because some may become winners, and others losers as a consequence of its development (all too frequently the losers were to be found, and often still are found, within the host communities). D'Sa (1999) has along these lines claimed that there is a fundamental schism in tourism between market values and community values and Fennell (2008) also points to tourism emphasising the value of one over the value of others. The growing awareness of tourism's negative impacts and the need to manage tourism, particularly in relation to its environmental impacts, was coupled with a growing notion of environmentalism in the 1960s, 70s and 80s as well as an increasingly critical stance towards traditional development theories. In this regard Jafari (2001) writes of a move in tourism development from an advocacy platform, where more development was simply better, to a cautionary platform, once the lessons of a fast and untrammelled development of tourism were understood. Today, firms' acknowledgement of their responsibilities is commonplace, even though the extent of these responsibilities and active engagement with them varies considerably (see for example Font *et al.*, 2012).

Writing around responsible (and sustainable) tourism rarely fails to draw attention to Elkington's (1994) three pillars of economic, social and environmental sustainability (occasionally also referred to as the three 'Ps' of people, profit and planet) the applicability of this view is not universally shared. One of the biggest criticisms levelled against the conceptualisation is that the drawing of artificial boundaries between economy and society may lead to a compartmentalised approach and the notion that trade-offs can be made, rather than asking questions about the nature of society itself (Giddings *et al.*, 2002). Thin (2002:25) is particularly critical of this 'triple bottom line' describing the three pillar model 'as two pins (the environmental and social critiques) bursting a balloon (naïve economism)'. DeKadt's (1979) early work on tourism development sees things in much the same light, protecting societies and cultures from the excessive economic focus that underpins much tourism development. Thin's (2002) critique returns, perhaps in a round-about way to the origins of corporate social responsibility (CSR) that reside in the question about businesses' responsibilities, not just to the owners and managers of firms but to wider society. Bowen (1953), one of the earliest writers about social responsibilities of business, argued that firms are not just producers of goods and services but also of social goods.

With the intention of better understanding labour relations Blair (1998) draws on Bowen's (1953) fundamental question in her article 'For whom should corporations be run?' Blair (1998) takes issue with traditional economic theory that states the owners of firms are entitled to the entirety of residual profits for the risks they assume. On this basis, employees are treated solely as a cost as any payments to employees result in a reduction of residual profit. Skirting around the issue of employee productivity and its relationship to HRM, Blair (1998) suggests that employees also bear a risk if the firm fails as they will have developed firm-specific human capital allowing them to demand a wage premium. They are in this sense more closely allied to a specific firm than traditional economic theory recognises. The extent to which this firm-specific human capital argument holds equally across all sectors is questionable, certainly in relation to tourism and hospitality where it can be argued there are less opportunities to create firm-specific human capital (Walmsley and Partington, 2014), which is one of the reasons for low pay in the sector and also questions the validity of the stepping-stone hypothesis relating to early work experiences in the sector. Nonetheless, Blair (1998) does raise an interesting issue when she equates employee wages to a firm's output rather than a cost, as this sheds an entirely different light on the employer-employee relationship, much in accordance with Bowen's (1953) notion of a firm's output of social goods.

The growth in the sustainable tourism literature, and more recently responsible tourism literature, did initially at least focus very heavily on environmental impacts. On the basis of an historical review of the development of sustainable tourism, Walmsley and Partington (2014) have argued that the environmental perspective has often taken precedence in tourism compared to tourism's social impacts, in practice as well as in the academic literature. Wunder (2000) concurs by suggesting that the literature in the area of eco-tourism has focussed strongly on environmental impacts rather than on the economic dimension. This set of circumstances is reflective of the management literature more generally according to Pfeffer (2010:35) who, with reference to Wal-Mart's CSR endeavours, queries why: 'polar bears…or even milk jugs are more important than people, not only in terms of research attention, but also as a focus of company initiatives?' This tongue-in-cheek remark still contains an important observation relating to how much emphasis has been placed on environmental protection rather than on the protection of individuals' rights and especially the rights of employees. Ironically, where discussions around businesses' responsibilities to society did not initially focus on environmental protection, in tourism the environmental aspects have received more attention and it is only recently that a real focus on employee rights has begun to feature in responsible tourism.

In practice some, albeit limited, progress has been made in relation to responsible employment in tourism. Baum (2007), for example, reviews the state of tourism employment providing the telling title to his paper 'Human resources in tourism: Still waiting for change' and indeed, despite changing research nuances, the bigger picture remains largely unchanged. It can therefore seem that working conditions and low pay are simply regarded as part and parcel of tourism, something that cannot be changed, a constant that we just have to live with. On the part of business, this view is very convenient as it removes pressure to improve working conditions for employees. At a policy making level, the focus is still very much on job creation rather than also on the characteristics of these jobs. That said, a greater appreciation of the complexities of the employment dimension of responsible tourism is beginning to emerge, one that has clear implications for youth employment. So, for example, the aforementioned (page 55) UNDP (2011) discussion paper on the contribution tourism can make to poverty reduction in LDCs draws attention to the characteristics of local employment where provision for young workers was also mentioned directly.

Education for sustainability

Whether young people's attitudes towards sustainability are changing or not, there is scope to influence attitudes (and underpin values) through education. Jithendran and Baum (2000) explore the role human resource development can have on sustainability in tourism, using India as a case study. At the heart of attempts to ensure businesses becomes more responsible is the recognition:

> considering the 'people dimension' of the tourism industry, the key to sustainability is the people who are involved in the tourism industry as guests, service providers and the hosts. (Jithendran and Baum, 2000:405)

From this follows the insight that human resource development (HRD) and education policy can play a crucial role in a move towards more responsible forms of tourism. It is the role of education to inculcate pro-sustainability attitudes therefore according to this perspective.

There exist a number of facets of how young people educated in the principles and practices of responsible tourism can drive the move towards a more responsible tourism sector. As previously mentioned, on the one hand it is about changing attitudes directly, or perhaps more fundamentally inculcating in youth the much-extolled notion of critical thinking (Pithers and Soden, 2000). This importance of including notions of responsibility or sustainability is discussed by Busby (2003:48) who articulates the rationale for the embedding of sustainability in the tourism curriculum as follows: 'Sustainable tourism, as a concept, is an important curriculum component since many of these graduates will become the managers of the future'. They will also become future consumers and may add to pressure for businesses to become more responsible.

Soltis (1968) has argued that it is common for educators to feel the need to have an ultimate aim and it is hard to imagine a course in higher education today not prefaced by a multitude of objectives and learning outcomes. In determining an aim for tourism education one could argue that, contrary to prevailing discourses (see the discussion around employability and the expansion of higher education in Chapter 5), industry has in fact held too much sway. Within the tourism literature, Tribe's (2002) reflections on the Philosophic Practitioner certainly point towards a refocussing of the tourism curriculum away from a single, uncritical acceptance of business imperatives, as do Belhassen and Caton (2011) by referring to how the tourism curriculum can be influenced by Critical Management Studies. These authors claim that 'rather than mindlessly reproducing the existing social order, academia is precisely the societal institution in which alternate futures can be envisioned' (Belhassen and Caton, 2011:1392) and they go on to describe current tourism programmes' instrumentalist approach as antediluvian.

Indeed, in practice a strong business focus is still very much present today in tourism programmes, according to Ring *et al.* (2009) who analysed 64 English-language undergraduate tourism courses and found that only 6% contained to a significant degree a liberal orientation. Flohr's (2001) analysis, drawing on data relating to the academic year 1999/2000, evidenced three postgraduate programmes in the UK with sustainability in the title, but a further nine indicating a 'sustainable orientation'. At the time Flohr (2001) identified 42 British universities offering 81 postgraduate courses in tourism. Today there are far more universities that offer tourism degrees (114 institutions were noted in an Association for Tourism in Higher Education report, Walmsley, 2012b) and one may expect that therefore more courses in sustainable or responsible tourism too. A search on the UCAS database that lists all undergraduate HE courses in the UK resulted in only one institution that offered a course in sustainable tourism specifically (University of Chichester: Sustainable Tourism Management). Canterbury Christ Church University offered three courses with tourism and ethics in their title. Judging solely on the basis of course titles at undergraduate level, there has not been an expansion of sustainable tourism-specific courses in the UK. In Australia the situation is somewhat different. Benckendorff *et al.* (2012) cite Sanders and Le Clus (2011) who suggest that of Australia's 26 tourism teaching universities 'only' nine offered tourism sustainability courses. Benckendorff *et al.* (2012) evidently see this as disappointingly low although by comparison to the UK this could quite equally be regarded as surprisingly high.

The inclusion of sustainability considerations in tourism curricula can take on a variety of forms, from an additional module(s) that look at sustainability, to a programme whose entire ethos is underpinned by sustainability considerations, or even an entire course on sustainable or responsible tourism. Busby (2003) writes of a continuum of approaches to sustainability in tourism degrees ranging from the holistic to the incidental. In the UK the Quality Assurance Agency (QAA) guidelines on hospitality, leisure, sport, tourism and events programmes are explicit in their recommendations that programmes need to look at sustainable development and social responsibility. It is suggested therefore that because of this issue's growing importance institutions should be encouraged 'to consider their corporate social responsibility by ensuring global sustainability and ethical positioning are clearly visible and appropriately supported across the entire student experience' (QAA, 2008:7).

It is clear from Tribe's (2002) writing that curriculum design in tourism can have very real implications on the ground in the sphere of tourism development. For Tribe, balancing the interests of business and those of wider society comes down to a balance between vocational and liberal ends of education. Tribe's (2002) and Belhassen and Caton's (2011) stances reflect ongoing wranglings between policy-makers, the business community and educators themselves as to the purpose of higher education. Another perspective, although admittedly infrequently mentioned, has emerged that questions the liberal-vocational dualism. For some commentators a liberal education is that which is most useful for business. By implication, a too vocationally driven education, at the expense of a liberal-humanist perspective, harms both business and society. Newman (1948 cited in Maskell and Robinson, 2001:31) maintained that left to pursue the good, the university will also supply the useful, a position that stands in contrast to more recent developments in HE:

> …That philosophical or liberal education, as I have called it, which is the proper function of a University, if it refuses the foremost place to professional interests, does but postpone them to the formation of the citizen, and, while it subserves the larger interests of philanthropy, prepares also for the successful prosecution of those merely personal objects which at first sight it seems to disparage.

Newman's (1948) is not a lone voice; others, (e.g. Morgan, 2004; Hesketh, 2000) share this view. Hesketh (2000:269) acknowledges that business may be rejecting aspects of higher education that 'furnishes the development of a more highly effective graduate labour force'. Acknowledging a certain level of irony, it appears that preparation for work, vocationalism in other words, is not best served by an exclusively vocational orientation to education.

A further point to note in this discussion about the role of the education of youth and its relationship to responsible tourism is the idea that rather than just developing in students a sense of the common good, tourism education must also provide the know-how and skills to add value to businesses in an era of increased environmental (and social) awareness. It is not enough to want to contribute positively to society, one should have the skills and capacity to do so. Sheldon *et al.* (2008:61) share this view:

> Amongst tourism educators there is a realisation that educators must be looking for ways to equip students with skills (knowledge of destination stewardship, ethics etc.) that will enable them to become future leaders in an industry 'that faces increasing pressures for responsibility and stewardship'.

We can see here that acting in a sustainable way may or may not be driven by a desire to do good, but for Sheldon *et al.* (2008) it simply makes business sense. Young people educated in the principles and practices of responsible tourism could in this regard provide companies that hire them with a competitive advantage.

Responsible tourism and competitive advantage

The notion that human capital can provide a competitive advantage based around the resource-based view of the firm (Barney, 1991) began to (re-)emerge at the same time as a shift was taking place away from seeing CSR as a reaction to a company's wrongdoings and towards seeing CSR as providing a competitive advantage for the firm. Empirically, the jury is still out on whether strong CSR performance leads to strong financial performance, despite a multitude of studies having investigated the issue (Margolis and Walsh, 2003, Vogel, 2005). A discussion of these studies goes beyond what is necessary here, but where the empirical evidence may be inconclusive (Lee, 2008) the theoretical case has been made quite convincingly: 'From a theoretical point of view, it is not an exaggeration to say that the coupling between CSR and CFP (corporate financial performance) has been made as tight as it can be' (Lee, 2008:64). One of the difficulties in establishing an empirical relationship between CSP and CFP relates to measurement issues, specifically :

- ☐ How to measure CSP
- ☐ How to establish causality when there are a multitude of intervening variables.

At a theoretical level, employing young people who have an awareness of the principles of responsible tourism can be justified on a number of counts. First, understanding the changing demands of consumers in relation to sustainability awareness would arguably enhance an individual's value in the marketplace as would it add value to the company that employs such an individual. Second, showing an understanding of how to run a business more efficiently in terms of resource use can result in significant cost savings. In an evaluation of ten global hotel chains' CSR behaviour Font *et al.* (2012) established that it was in the area of environmental management, and specifically a focus on the reduction of energy use where companies were most CSR active. A further competitive advantage for firms who employ young people with an awareness of responsible employment practices relates to responsible HRM. The premise here is that if you treat staff well they will display a number of positive behaviours in the areas of engagement, commitment, loyalty and productivity. Here again, the business case for responsible employment practices is very strong.

Not everyone agrees with the promotion of the enlightened approach to CSR (i.e. CSR serves corporate interest). It is but one of four approaches outlined by McGuire over 40 years ago (McGuire, 1963). The others are the neoclassical economic view that CSR has no role in business, the responsible view that CSR may or may not pay, but it is the right thing to do, and the confused which means justifying CSR ethically while expecting it to pay off for the company. Some consider there is currently an excessive focus on the business case for CSR (e.g. Lee, 2008) which can result in a focus only on elements of CSR that directly affect the bottom line – hence we see so many efforts in reducing energy and water use. Lee (2008) also argues that as more corporations become socially responsible, the marginal value of social responsibility will decrease. Here though one could argue that as an increasing number of firms engage in CSR there is even more pressure on those that do not to also become more responsible. Companies may need to display certain CSR behaviours just to 'be in the game'. Ultimately, young people who have benefitted from learning about the principles and means of improving a tourism firm's corporate social performance could offer a distinct advantage if given the opportunity to apply this knowledge.

Responsible tourism and hiring youth

A firm's responsible employment practices can also have a direct impact on the ability to hire young people. A question that arises in an era where many tourism firms complain of a lack of a suitable candidate pool is whether young people are more likely to want to work for a company that is socially responsible? Is there an immediate benefit to firms of conveying a positive image in relation to their corporate social performance? At least many companies think so, according to Sprinkle and Maines (2010). They are also more likely to be motivated by CSR behaviour: 'people are seeking meaning at work…and it has become clear that staff motivation is a powerful bottom-line benefit of corporate responsibility' (Murray, 2007:11).

Turban and Greening (1997) investigate the relationship between corporate social performance and attractiveness as an employer. As they explain, an organisation's HR policies can serve as a signal of general working conditions, thereby attracting or repelling applicants. In many countries we now find 'best places to work' awards, with those organisations receiving the awards extolling their virtues, particularly in graduate recruitment literature.

In the USA, for example, *Fortune* partners with Great Place to Work (www.greatplacetowork.com) to 'conduct the most extensive employee survey in corporate America' (Fortune, 2015). The first appearance of a tourism firm in the

2015 listings is at number 11: Kimpton Hotels & Restaurants (acquired in 2014 by Intercontinental Hotels Group). Its policies include the aim to staff new hotels to 50% with employees from existing hotels. It also offers fully-paid sabbaticals, paid time off for volunteering, and tuition reimbursement to employees. The voluntary turnover rate (full time) is just 19% in a sector notorious for high labour turnover rates, and on average there are 150 applicants per opening. A further four hospitality firms feature within the top 100: Four Seasons Hotels & Resorts at number 47, Marriott International at 53, Hyatt Hotels Corporation at 78 and the Cheesecake Factory Inc. at 88.

In the UK the *Sunday Times* publishes an annual 100 Best Companies to Work For and a 100 Best Small Companies to Work For list (in addition to two further lists relating to 'big companies' and not-for-profit organisations). In 2015 a hotel company came second in 100 Best Companies category. Red Carnation Hotel Collection which employs 872 staff at a number of hotels in the UK. Beatrice Tollman, the company's owner, believes that 'if you look after the employees they, in turn, will look after the guests'. Caring for the workforce in her view is simply good business practice (*Sunday Times*, 2015). Overall, eleven tourism and/or hospitality companies feature in the top 100, which demonstrates that poor employment practices are not an inevitable feature of tourism firms.

The aforementioned Great Place to Work organisation provides further lists for other countries ranging from Australia to Venezuela. Its mission it to 'Improve Society by Creating Better Workplaces'. It clearly supports the positive relationship between working conditions and firm performance arguing:

> We know that organisations that build trust and create a rewarding cycle of personal contribution and appreciation create workplace cultures that deliver outstanding business performance. (Great Place to Work, 2015)

Returning to Turban and Greening's (1997) study, an association was established between a firm's corporate social performance (CSP), its reputation and subsequently its attractiveness. Turban and Greening explain these results on the basis of social identity theory, which stipulates that an employee's self-concept is influenced by membership of an organization, and that the employee would have a more positive self-concept if they worked for an organisation with strong CSP. They also refer to the role of information sent out by the organisation, which, in a situation of incomplete information on the part of the potential applicant, serves as a signal about that organisation. Specifically, a company's CSP sends a signal about its values and these are seen to provide an indication of working conditions which in turn affects attractiveness.

Turban and Greening's (1997) study aside, many others have explored the relationship between a company's reputation, albeit not explicitly its CSP, and recruitment patterns with much empirical work now indicating the relationship between reputation and recruitment exists (e.g.Williamson *et al.*, 2010, Lemmink *et al.*, 2003). The most widely-cited benefit of a firm's reputation in recruiting individuals in this 'war for talent' (Rynes, 1991) is the increase in the size of the talent pool from which organisations can select.

Some studies have distinguished between a company's image generally and a company's employment image (CEI) (Lemmink *et al.*, 2003), that is the image of an organisation as a place to work. This is clearly a potentially very important distinction when it comes to recruitment, because individuals who evaluate a company image may do so for a range of reasons other than for employment purposes. Lemmink *et al.*'s (2003:5) study, which researched a sample of Dutch graduate business students' application intentions, suggested seven factors should be taken into account:

☐ The ability to attract, develop and keep talented people,

☐ Community and environmental responsibility,

☐ Financial soundness,

☐ Innovativeness,

☐ Marketing and communications,

☐ Quality of management,

☐ Quality of products/services.

Corporate social performance is therefore included within the general factors that shape corporate image but is only one amongst several. The extent to which it is important will vary at the level of the individual.

Lemmink *et al.* (2003) then operationalise CEI as consisting of the following dimensions:

☐ Advancement opportunities,

☐ Interesting job/function,

☐ International opportunities,

☐ Organisational culture,

☐ Pay,

☐ Training and educational possibilities.

As to be expected, it was hypothesised that both CI and CEI are positively related to intentions to apply to a specific firm. The study's findings confirmed that both CI and CEI appear to be strong antecedents of application intentions.

The data also suggest that CI forms the basis of CEI: 'Apparently companies are not capable of developing CEI without a sound basis of CI' (Lemmink *et al.* 2003:13). In interpreting this outcome it is suggested therefore that a tourism firm needs to have an overall positive image, not just in relation to its employment practices. Indeed, individuals will not necessarily be able to entertain a positive image of a potential employer, despite responsible employment practices if the firm is in other respects regarded as behaving irresponsibly. The study did not reveal how important CSR dimensions were compared to other image-forming factors, but as noted above, there is a growing concern with business ethics particularly among young people. If a similar study were to be conducted today it would be interesting to note just how important (or perhaps not) CSP is in the development of CEI and how this might affect application intentions.

References

Adam, M. S. & Urquhart, C. (2007) IT capacity building in developing countries: A model of the Maldivian tourism sector. *Information Technology for Development*, **13** (4), 315-335.

Akgeyik, T. & Meltem, G. (2008) Profile of victims of customer aggression: case of call-center and retail workers. *European Journal of Management*, **8** (4).

Ateljevic, I. & Doorne, S. (2000) Staying within the fence: Lifestyle entrepreneurship in tourism. *Journal of Sustainable Tourism*, **8** (5), 378-392.

Bacon, N., Ackers, P., Storey, D. J. & Coates, D. (1996) It's a small world: managing human resources in small businesses. *The International Journal of Human Resource Management*, **7** (1), 82-100.

Barney, J. (1991) Firm resources and sustained competitive advantage. *Journal of Management*, **17** (1), 99-120.

Barry, K. (2007) *Feminity in Flight: A History of Flight Attendants*, London: Duke University Press.

Battersby, D. (1990). Lifting the barriers. Employment and training in tourism and leisure. *Insights*, 1,D7-1–D7-8. English Tourist Board.

Baum, T. (2007) Human resources in tourism: Still waiting for change. *Tourism Management*, **28** 1383-1399.

Becker, G. (1975) *Human Capital: A Theoretical and Empirical Analysis, with special reference to education*, Chicago: University of Chicago Press.

Belhassen, Y. & Caton, K. (2011) On the need for critical pedagogy in tourism education. *Tourism Management,* **32** 1389-1396.

Benckendorff, P., Moscardo, G. & Murphy, L. (2012) Environmental attitudes of Generation Y students: Foundations for sustainability education in tourism. *Journal of Teaching in Travel & Tourism,* **12 (**1), 44-69.

Blair, M. (1998) For whom should corporations be run?: An economic rationale for stakeholder management. *Long Range Planning,* **31 (**2), 195-200.

Boella, M. & Goss-Turner, S. (2013) *Human Resource Management in the Hospitality Industry. A Guide to Best Practice,* London: Routledge.

Boeve-De Pauw, J. & Van Petegem, P. (2010) A cross-national perspective on youth environmental attitudes. *Environmentalist,* **30** 133-144.

Bolton, S. & Boyd, C. (2003) Trolley dolly or skilled emotion manager? moving on from Hochschild's Managed Heart. *Work, Employment and Society,* **17 (**2), 289-308.

Boon, B. (2006) When leisure and work are allies: The case of skiers and tourist resort hotels. *Career Development International,* **11 (**7), 594-608.

Bowen, H. R. (1953) *Social Responsibilities of the Businessman,* New York: Harper & Row.

Brunet, S., Bauer, J., De Lacy, T. & Tshering, K. (2001) Tourism development in Bhutan: Tensions between tradition and modernity. *Journal of Sustainable Tourism,* **9** (3), 243-263.

Burrows, R. & Curran, J. (1989) Sociological research on service sector small businesses: Some conceptual considerations. *Work, Employment and Society,* **3 (**4), 527-539.

Busby, G. (2003) The concept of sustainable tourism within the higher education curriculum: A British case study. *Journal of Hospitality, Leisure, Sport & Tourism Education,* **2** (2), 48-58.

Byers, T. & Slack, T. (2001) Strategic decision-making in small businesses within the leisure industry. *Journal of Leisure Research,* **33 (**2), 121-136.

Cobble, D. S. & Merrill, M. (2009) The promise of service worker unionism. *In* Korczynski, M. & MacDonald, C. (eds.) *Service Work: Critical Perspectives.* Abingdon: Taylor and Francis.

Cukier-Snow, J. & Wall, G. (1993) Tourism employment: Perspectives from Bali. *Tourism Management,* **14 (**3), 195-201.

D'Sa, E. (1999) Wanted: Tourists with a social conscience. *International Journal of Contemporary Hospitality Management,* **11 (**2/3), 64-68.

De Kadt, E. (1979) *Tourism: Passport to Development?*, Oxford: Oxford University Press.

Di Domenico, M. L. (2005) Producing hospitality, consuming lifesytles: Lifestyle entrepreneurship in urban Scotland. *In* Jones, E. & Haven-Tang, C. (eds.) *Tourism SMEs, Service Quality and Destination Competitiveness.* Wallingford: CABI.

Dietz, G. (2012). How to rebuild trust in business. *The Guardian*, 26th March 2012.

Doherty, L. (2004) Work-life balance initiatives: implications for women. *Employee Relations*, **26 (**4), 433-452.

Doxey, G. V. (1976) When enough's enough: the natives are restless in Old Nicaragua. *Heritage Canada*, **2 (**2), 26-27.

Durkheim, E. (1933) *The Division of Labour in Society*: Glencoe, Ill.

EFFAT (2015). McJobs: Big Mac, Small paychecks ! McDonalds' worldwide abusive employment practices exposed. Available: www.effat.org/en/ node/13957

Elkington, J. (1994) *Cannibals with Forks: the Triple Bottom Line of 21st Century Business*, Oxford: Capstone.

Eur-Lex (2015) *Protection of the dignity of women and men at work*. European Commission. Available: http://eur-lex.europa.eu/legal-content/EN/ TXT/?uri=URISERV:c10917a [Accessed 23.07.15].

European Agency for Safety and Health at Work (2008). Protecting workers in hotels, restaurants and catering. Available: https://osha.europa.eu/en/ tools-and-publications/publications/reports/TE7007132ENC_horeca

Fennell, D. (2008) Responsible tourism: A Kierkegaardian interpretation. *Tourism Recreation Research*, **33 (**1), 3-12.

Flohr (2001) An analysis of British postgraduate courses in tourism: What role does sustainability play within higher education? *Journal of Sustainable Tourism*, **9 (**6), 505-513.

Font, X., Walmsley, A., Coggoti, S., Mccombes, L. & Häusler, N. (2012) Corporate social responsibility: the disclosure-performance gap. *Tourism Management*, **33 (**6), 1544-1533.

Fortune (2015) 100 best companies to work for. Available: http://fortune.com/ best-companies [Accessed 30.04.15].

Fox, A. (1976) *The Meaning of Work. Unit 6. People and Work*, Milton Keynes: Open University Press.

Friedman, T. (2005) *The World is Flat: A Brief History of the Twenty-First Century.* New York: Farrar Straus Giroux.

Getz, D. (1994) Students' work experiences, perceptions and attitudes towards careers in hospitality and tourism: A longitudinal case study in Spey Valley, Scotland. *International Journal of Hospitality Management,* **13** (1), 25-37.

Giddings, B., Hopwood, B. & O'Brien, G. (2002) Environment, economy and society: Fitting them together into sustainable development. *Sustainable Development,* **10** (4), 187-196.

Gilbert, D., Guerrier, Y. & Guy, J. (1998) Sexual harassment issues in the hospitality industry. *International Journal of Contemporary Hospitality Management,* **10** (2), 48-53.

Goffee, R. & Scase, R. (1980) *The Real World of the Small Business Owner,* London: Croom Helm.

Goodwin, H. (2011) *Taking Responsibility for Tourism,* Oxford: Goodfellow Publishing Ltd.

Goss, D. (1991) *Small Business and Society,* London: Routledge.

Grandey, A., Dickter, D. & Sin, H.-P. (2004) 'The customer is not always right: customer aggression and emotional regulation of service employees'. *Journal of Organizational Behavior,* **25** (3), 397-418.

Graver, A. & Harrison, J. (2002). A skills development strategy for the tourism and cultural industries in South East England. 'Putting the Pieces Together'. Havant: Impact Research Limited.

Great Place to Work (2015) *About Us.* Available: http://www.greatplacetowork.com.au/about-us [Accessed 30.04.15].

Grint, K. (1991) *The Sociology of Work. An Introduction,* Cambridge: Polity Press.

Grove, S., Fisk, R. & Joby, J. (2004) Surviving in the age of rage. *Marketing Management,* **13** (2), 41-47.

Halvorsen, S. (2012) 'Beyond the network? Occupy London and the Global Movement'. *Social Movement Studies,* **11** (3-4), 427-433.

Harrill, R. (2004) Residents'attitudes towardtourism development: A literaturereview with implications fortourism planning. *Journal of Planning Literature,* **18** (1), 1-16.

Harris-White, B. (2010) Work and wellbeing in informal economies: The regulative roles of institutions of identity and the state. *World Development,* **38** (2), 170-183.

Hertz, N (2015) Generation K: what it means to be a teen, *Financial Times*, 17 April. Available: http://www.ft.com/cms/s/0/1642f9d2-e3ac-11e4-9a82-00144feab7de.html

Hesketh, A. J. (2000) Recruiting an elite? Employers' perceptions of graduate education and training. *Journal of Education and Work*, **13** (3), 245-271.

Hochschild, A. (1983) *The Managed Heart: Commercialization of Human Feeling*, Berkeley, CA: University of California Press.

Ineson, E., Yap, M. & Whiting, G. (2013) Sexual discrimination and harassment in the hospitality industry. *International Journal of Hospitality Management*, **35** 1-9.

Ingham, G. (1970) *Size of Industrial Organization and Worker Behaviour*, Cambridge: Cambridge at the University Press.

Inglehart, R. (1995) Public support for environmental protection: Objective problems and subjective values in 43 societies. *Political Science and Politics*, **28** (1), 57-72.

Iverson, R. D. & Deery, M. (1997) Turnover culture in the hospitality industry. *Human Resource Management Journal*, **7** (4), 71-82.

Jafari, J. (2001) The scientification of tourism. *In:* Smith, V. L. & Brent, M. (eds.) *Hosts and Guests Revisited: Tourism Issues of the 21st Century.* Cognizant.

Jithendran, K. J. & Baum, T. (2000) Human resources development and sustainability - the case of Indian tourism. *International Journal of Tourism Research*, **2** 403-421.

Johnson, K. (1981) Towards an understanding of labour turnover. *Service Industries Review*, 4-17.

Kane, L. (2015) *Minimum Wages around the World*. Business Insider UK. Available: http://uk.businessinsider.com/minimum-wage-around-the-world-2015-5 [Accessed 28.05.15].

Korczynski, M. (2009) Understanding the contradictory lived experience of service work. *In* Korczynski, M. & MacDonald, C. (eds.) *Service Work. Critical Perspectives.* New York: Routledge.

Krakover, S. (2000) Partitioning seasonal employment in the hospitality industry. *Tourism Management*, **21** (4), 461-471.

Krippendorf, J. (1987) *The Holiday Makers. Understanding the Impact of Leisure and Travel*, London: Heinemann.

Kusluvan, S., Kusluvan, Z., Ilhan, I. & Lutfi, B. (2010) The human dimension :A review of human resources management issues in the tourism and hospitality industry. *Cornell Hospitality Quarterly*, **51 (**2), 171-214.

Lashley, C. (2005). Student employment patterns in Nottingham's tourism sector: A research report for East Midlands Tourism. Nottingham: Nottingham Trent University Centre for Leisure Retailing.

Lee-Ross, D. & Pryce, J. (2010) *Human Resources and Tourism: Skills, Culture and Industry*, Oxford: Channel View Publications.

Lee, J. (2001) Education for technology readiness: Prospects for developing countries. *Journal of Human Development*, **2 (**1), 115-151.

Lee, M-D. P. (2008) A review of the theories of corporate social responsibility: Its evolutionary path and the road ahead. *International Journal of Management Reviews*, **10 (**1), 53-73.

Lemmink, J., Annelien, S. & Streukens, S. (2003) The role of corporate image and company employment image in explaining application intentions. *Journal of Economic Psychology,* **24 (**1), 1-15.

Lin, Y.-H. (2006) The incidence of sexual harassment of students while undergoing practicum training experience in the Taiwanese hospitality industry—individuals' reactions and relationships to perpetrators. *Tourism Management*, **27** 51-68.

Littlejohn, D. & Watson, S. (2004) Developing graduate managers for hospitality and tourism. *International Journal of Contemporary Hospitality Management*, **16 (**7), 408-414.

Liu, A. & Liu, H.-H. (2008) Tourism employment issues in Malaysia. *Journal of Human Resources in Hospitality & Tourism*, **7 (**2), 163-179.

Liu, A. & Wall, G. (2006) Planning tourism employment: a developing country perspective. *Tourism Management*, **27** 159-170.

Lockwood, D. (1966) Sources of variation in working class images of society. *Sociological Review*, **4 (**2), 249-267.

Lucas, R. (2004) *Employment Relations in the Hospitality and Tourism Industries*, London: Routledge.

Margolis, J. D. & Walsh, J. P. (2003) Misery loves companies: Rethinking social initiatives by business. *Administrative Science Quarterly*, **48** 268-305.

Maskell, D. & Robinson, I. (2001) *The New Idea of a University*, London: Haven Books.

Mathieson, A. & Wall, G. (1982) *Tourism: Economic, Physical and Social Impacts*, Harlow: Longman.

Mcguire, J. W. (1963) *Business and Society*, New York: McGraw-Hill.

Miller, E., Van Megen, K. & Buys, L. (2012) Diversification for sustainable development in rural and regional Australia: How local community leaders conceptualise the impacts and opportunities from agriculture, tourism and mining. *Rural Society, 22* (1), 2-16.

Mkono, M. (2010) Zimbabwean hospitality students' experiences of sexual harassment in the hotel industry. *International Journal of Hospitality Management, 29* 729-735.

Monterrubio, C. & Espinosa, B. (2013) Characterisation of ecotourism employment in a developing world destination. *GeoJournal of Tourism and Geosites, 11* (1), 54-65.

Morgan, M. (2004) From production line to drama school: Higher education for the future of tourism. *International Journal of Contemporary Hospitality Management, 16* (2), 91-99.

Morrison, A. & Teixeira, R. (2004) Small business performance: a tourism sector focus. *Journal of Small Business and Enterprise Development, 11* (4), 166-173.

Murphy, P. E. (1981) Community attitudes to tourism. A comparative analysis. *Tourism Management, 2* (2), 189-195.

Murray, S. (2007). Bottom-line benefits special award corporate social responsibility: Ethical concerns are a growing factor in staff motivation. *Financial Times*, 2 May 2007.

Nickson, D., Warhurst, C. & Dutton, E. (2005) The importance of attitude and appearance in the service encounter in retail and hospitality. *Managing Service Quality, 15* (2), 195-208.

Okumus, F., Sariisik, M. & Naipaul, S. (2010) Understanding why women work in 5-star hotels in a developing country and their work-related problems. *International Journal of Hospitality and Tourism Administration, 11* (1), 76-105.

Oxford Dictionaries. (2015) *Aesthetic*. Available: http://www.oxforddictionaries.com/definition/english/aesthetic [Accessed 16.02.15].

Pfeffer, J. (2010) Building sustainable organizations: The human factor. *Academy of Management Perspectives*, 34-35.

Pickety, T. (2014) *Capital in the Twenty-First Century*, Cambridge, MA: Harvard University Press.

Piore, M. J. & Sabel, C. F. (1984) *The Second Industrial Divide*, New York: Basic Books.

Pithers, R. T. & Soden, R. (2000) Critical thinking in education: a review. *Educational Research,* **42 (**3), 237-249.

Poddar, A. & Madupalli, R. (2012) Problematic customers and turnover intentions of customer service employees. *Journal of Services Marketing,* **26 (**7), 551-559.

Prospects (2014) www.prospects.ac.uk [Accessed 20.04.14]

QAA (2008) Subject Benchmark Statements for Hospitality, Leisure, Sport and Tourism. Quality Assurance Agency. Available: http://www.qaa.ac.uk/en/Publications/Documents/Subject-benchmark-statement-Hospitality-leisure-sport-tourism-2008.pdf

Rainnie, A. (1989) *Industrial Relations in Small Firms. Small Isn't Beautiful,* London: Routledge.

Random House Dictionary Online. (2015) *McJobs.* Available: http://dictionary.reference.com/browse/mcjob [Accessed 31.05.15].

Rhode Island Department of Labor and Training. (2015) *Labor Market Information.* Available: http://www.dlt.ri.gov/lmi/laus/us/usadj.htm [Accessed 30.05.15].

Riley, M., Ladkin, A. & Szivas, E. (2002) *Tourism Employment. Analysis and Planning.,* Clevedon: Channel View Publications.

Ring, A., Dickinger, A. & Wöber, K. (2009) Designing the idel undergraduate program in tourism: expectations from industry and edcuators. *Journal of Travel Research,* **48 (**1), 106-121.

Roan, A. & Diamond, C. (2003) Starting out: The quality of working life of young workers in the retail and hospitality industries in Australia. *International Journal of Employment Studies,* **11 (**2), 91-119.

Roberts, J. (2009) Bouncers and barroom aggression: A review of the research. *Aggression and Violent Behaviour,* **14 (**1), 59-68.

Rowley, G. & Purcell, K. (2001) 'As cooks go, she went': is labour churn inevitable? *International Journal of Hospitality Management,* **20 (**2), 163-185.

Rynes, S. L. (1991) Recruitment, job choice, and posthire consequences: A call for new research directions. *In* Dunnette, M. & Hough, L. (eds.) *Handbook of Industrial and Organizational Psychology.* Palo Alto, CA: Consulting Pscyhology Press.

Scott, B. (1998) Workplace violence in the UK hospitality industry: impacts and recommendations. *Progress in Tourism and Hospitality Research,* **4 (**4), 337-347.

Seagrave, K. (2000) *Age Discrimination by Employers*, Jefferson, NC: McFarland.

Shaw, G. & Williams, A. (2004) From lifestyle consumption to lifestyle production: Changing patterns of tourism entrepreneurship. *In* Thomas, R. (ed.) *Small Firms in Tourism. International Perspectives.* London: Elsevier.

Sheldon, P., Fesenmaier, D., Woeber, K., Cooper, C. & Antonioli, M. (2008) Tourism education futures: 2010-2030 building the capacity to lead. *Journal of Teaching in Travel & Tourism*, **8** (3), 61-68.

Soltis, J. (1968) *An Introduction to the Analysis of Educational Concepts*, Reading: Addison Wesley.

Sprinkle, G. & Maines, L. (2010) The benefits and costs of corporate social responsibility. *Business Horizons*, **53** 445-453.

Srinivas, S. (2014) *CEO pay rises at double the rate of workers* . The Guardian. Available: http://www.theguardian.com/money/2014/dec/05/save-jobs-numbers-companies-big-salaries-perks-executives [Accessed 26.07.15].

Stiglitz, J. (2002) *Globalization and its Discontents*, New York: WW Norton.

Stobart, L. (2014). Whatever happened to the Indignados? *Radical Struggle.*

Sunday Times (2015) *The Sunday Times Best 100 Companies*. Available: http://features.thesundaytimes.co.uk/public/best100companies/live/template [Accessed 30.04.15].

Szivas, E. & Riley, M. (1999) Tourism employment during economic transition. *Annals of Tourism Research*, **26** (4), 747-771.

Thin (2002) *Social Progress and Sustainable Development*, Bloomfield, CT: Kumarian Press.

Thomas, R. (1998) An introduction to the study of small tourism and hospitality firms. *In* Thomas, R. (ed.) *The Management of Small Tourism and Hospitality Firms.* London: Cassell.

Torrington, D. & Hall, L. (1998) *Human Resource Management*, London: Prentice Hall.

Tribe, J. (2002) The philosophic practitioner. *Annals of Tourism Research*, **29** (2), 338-357.

Turban, D. & Greening, D. (1997) Corporate social performance and organizational attractiveness to prospective employees. *Academy of Management Journal*, **40** (3), 658-672.

Turner, L. & Ash, J. (1975) *The Golden Hordes: International Tourism and the Pleasure Periphery*, New York: St Martin's Press.

Tyson, S. & York, A. (2001) *Essentials of HRM*, Oxford: Butterworth

Heinemann.

UNDP (2011). *Discussion Paper. Tourism and Poverty Reduction Strategies in the Integrated Framework for Least Developed Countries.* Geneva: United Nations Development Programme. Available: http://unwto.org/sites/all/files/pdf/undp_discussion_paper_tourism_and_poverty_reduction_strategies_in_the_integrated_framework_for_least_developed_countries.pdf

UNDP (2014a) *Human Development Index.* Available: hdr.undp.org/en/content/human-development-index-hdi-table [Accessed 18.04.15].

UNDP (2014b) *Republic of Yemen Project Report.* Available: http://www.undp.org/content/dam/undp/documents/projects/YEM/YEEP%20II%20-%20Signed%20Project%20Document.pdf [Accessed 17.04.15].

Unison (2015) *Call Centres.* Available: http://www.unison.org.uk/at-work/energy/key-issues/call-centres/the-facts/ [Accessed 16.02.15].

United Nations (2003). *World Youth Report 2003. The Global Situation of Young People.* New York: United Nations Department of Economic and Social Affairs.

United Nations (2013). *World Population Ageing 2013.* New York: United Nations Department of Economic and Social Affairs.

UNWTO (2014). *Tourism Highlights, 2014 Edition.* United Nations World Tourism Organisation.

Vida (2013) *Personalmangel im Tourismus. Schlechte Arbeitsbedingungen von Arbeitgebern verursacht.* Austria: VIDA. Available: http://www.vida.at/servlet/ContentServer?pagename=S03/Page/Index&n=S03_18.1.a&cid=1359977416554 [Accessed 22.09.13].

Vida (2015). Startschuss für ein modernes Entlohnungssystem. Available: http://www.vida.at/servlet/ContentServer?pagename=S03/Page/Index&n=S03_0.a&cid=1430965804456.

Vogel, D. (2005) *The Market for Virtue: The Potential and Limits of Corporate Social Responsibility,* Washington, DC.: Brookings Institution Press Inc.

Voigt, J. (2011) *Beyond Wall Street: 'Occupy' protests go global.* Available: http://www.edition.cnn.com/2011/10/07/business/wall-street-protest-global/ [Accessed 12.04.15].

Walmsley, A. (2004) Assessing staff turnover: A view from the English Riviera. *International Journal of Tourism Research,* **6** 275-287.

Walmsley, A. (2008) *The Impact of Tourism SME Placements on Career Intentions.* PhD, Leeds Metropolitan University.

Walmsley, A. (2012a) Decent work and tourism wages: An international comparison. *Progress in Responsible Tourism,* **1** (2).

Walmsley, A. (2012b). *Tourism Intelligence Monitor.* ATHE Report on Tourism Higher Education in the UK.

Walmsley, A. & Partington, S. N. (2014). A stakeholder approach to working conditions in the tourism and hospitality sector. 2nd International Hospitality & Tourism Conference, 2014 Penang, Malaysia.

Walmsley, A., Thomas, R. & Jameson, S. (2012) Internships in SMEs and career intentions. *Journal of Education and Work,* **25** (2), 185-204.

Warhurst, C. & Nickson, D. (2007) Employee experience of aesthetic labour in retail and hospitality. *Work, Employment and Society,* **21** (1), 103-120.

Warhurst, C., Nickson, D., Witz, A. & Cullen, A. M. (2000) Aesthetic labour in interactive service work: Some case study evidence from the 'New Glasgow'. *Service Industries Journal,* **20** (3), 1-18.

Weatherley, K. & Tansik, D. (1993) Tactics used by customer-contact workers: Effects of role stress, boundary spanning and control. *International Journal of Service Industry Management,* **4** (3), 4-17.

Widener, P. (2009) Oil tourism: Disasters and destinations in Ecuador and the Philippines. *Sociological Inquiry,* **79** (3), 266-288.

Williamson, I., King Jr, J., Lepak, D. & Sarma, A. (2010) Firm reputation, recruitment web sites, and attracting applicants. *Human Resource Management Journal,* **49** (4), 669-687.

Witsil, F. (2014). Call center jobs increase as more return from overseas. *USA Today,* 4th August 2014.

Wood, R. C. (1997) *Working in Hotels and Catering,* London: Routledge.

Woods, R. & Kavanagh, R. (1994) Gender discrimination and sexual harassment as experienced by hospitality industry managers. *Cornell HRA Quarterly,* **35** (1), 16-20.

Wunder, S. (2000) Ecotourism and economic incentives - An empirical approach. *Ecological Economics,* **32** 465-479.

Yagil, D. (2008) When the customer is wrong: A review of research on aggression and sexual harassment in service encounters. *Aggression and Violent Behaviour,* **13** (2), 141-152.

4 Barriers to Youth Employment

Aims of the chapter

This chapter explores barriers to youth employment in the tourism and hospitality sector. It addresses this issue from both supply and demand perspectives. The supply side discusses perceptions of tourism employment while the demand side takes the perspective of business, trying to better understand the nature of demand for tourism employees, skills gaps and shortages, and attitudes towards employing young people specifically. The chapter concludes by describing a range of initiatives that target the barriers to youth employment in tourism.

Supply side barriers

Supply side, as used here, relates to employees or potential employees who, in return for a wage, supply their labour, including their motivation, knowledge and skills, in other words their human capital. The point is stressed because occasionally those seeking work are referred to as *demanding* labour. It might seem peculiar to begin this chapter on barriers to youth employment by suggesting there is a supply-side dimension to this problem. Commonly the problem is solely regarded in terms of the unavailability of jobs, i.e. a shortfall in demand for labour in the economy. Nonetheless, as the next section will argue, some of the barriers to youth employment in tourism, relate to characteristics of labour supply.

Youth perceptions of tourism and hospitality employment

One of the areas where there appears to exist least contention with regard to youth employment in tourism is the generally low esteem in which tourism employment is held. The implications of this are of concern to educators (e.g. Jenkins, 2001) but also to employers and governments (Kusluvan and Kusluvan, 2000). In fact, this is an area that tourism firms have begun to take notice of and act upon. In 2013 the World Travel and Tourism Council (WTTC, 2013) published a study across three countries – China, the USA and the UK – into undergraduate perceptions of careers in tourism. The executive summary begins thus:

> There is pressing concern within the Travel & Tourism industry that companies are missing out on the best new talent due to negative perceptions of the career opportunities available in Travel and Tourism.

The results of the study in relation to perceptions of work in tourism were not as dire as might have been predicted based on other studies in this area, which we shall turn to in due course. The report suggests that overall the tourism industry is regarded as 'reasonably attractive' and that, presumably for those for whom this is not the case, it is 'an industry that appears to be still poorly understood'. There are in fact many reasons why tourism employment might be particularly attractive to young people, but first we shall review the predominant theme, in the scholarly literature at least, of negative attitudes and perceptions towards employment in the sector.

Despite much literature on youth employment, and on employment in tourism more generally, relating to developed, western economies there is a growing body of literature that has sought to understand attitudes of young people outside these areas (e.g. Aksu and Köksal, 2005; Kusluvan and Kusluvan, 2000; Roney and Oztin, 2007 in Turkey; Chang and Tse, 2012; Wan *et al.*, 2014 in Hong Kong and Macau respectively). In fact, in the sphere of tourism, Kusluvan and Kusluvan's (2000) study of undergraduate tourism students' perceptions provided the most developed, at that point certainly, attitude scale in this area. Kusluvan and Kusluvan propose that three groups of individuals' attitudes towards tourism employment are generally investigated: secondary or high school students, tourism employees and university students. Much of the literature on the perceptions of tourism employment relates to university students, who present an accessible source of data to tourism academics.

One of the most discussed detractors from entering the sector is low levels of pay. This negative perception largely reflects reality, where graduate starting salaries have been compared across different sectors (e.g. Chang and

Tse, 2012). Richardson and Butler (2012), whose study of Malaysian tourism and hospitality students' attitudes towards careers in the sector looked at the importance of factors as well as the extent to which respondents believed the sector can provide for these, highlighted the following areas where perceptions were weakest (see also Chapter 6, page 151, for a further discussion of this paper):

☐ A job that can easily be combined with parenthood,

☐ A good starting salary,

☐ A reasonable workload,

☐ High earnings over the length of a career

☐ Good promotion prospects.

According to this study, low earnings both now and in the future stand out as one of the weaker aspects of tourism employment. Low pay was also a concern for a cohort of Turkish students in Aksu and Köksal's (2005:440) study where 78.3% of respondents disagreed with the statement: 'I think that the salary for most tourism jobs is sufficient to lead a satisfactory life'. A study of tourism and hospitality students in Macau (Wan *et al.*, 2014) confirmed the importance of salary expectations in determining career intentions. Barron *et al.* (2007) conducted focus groups with predominantly Scottish hospitality students who also commented negatively on pay, particularly given the tough nature of much hospitality work. It is not solely about low pay in absolute terms, but low pay relative to the nature of employment. Again, this was something picked up on by Aksu and Köksal (2005:440) where 78% of students agreed with the statement: 'Considering the long working hours and work load, salaries are low in the tourism industry'.

Another major barrier to recruitment, as well as continued rather than temporary employment in the sector, is the perceived lack of career development opportunities. Although 'opportunities for advancement' are consistently ranked highly in surveys of tourism students' career preferences, Peters' (2005) research of apprentices in tourism SMEs in the Tyrol region of the Alps indicated their dissatisfaction with career progression opportunities. Young people's concerns over the absence of career development opportunities have been recognised in a number of further studies such as those by Chuang *et al.* (2007), Richardson and Butler (2012) and Hjalager and Andersen (2000).

Part of this recurring theme lies in the fact that many tourism firms are simply not large enough to offer much progression up the so-called corporate ladder. Tourism SMEs can however provide more autonomy and responsibility than large firms, at least in early stages of employment (Walmsley *et al.*,

2006), although the extent to which recent graduates are aware of this remains questionable. Turning again to Peters' (2005) study, here too satisfaction with tourism SME employment depended on the levels of autonomy provided, which were generally regarded as high. Despite the concerns around limited career progression opportunities, it is not uncommon for tourism employment to be promoted on the basis of its scope for rapid career progression. Ladkin's (2002) study of hotel general managers in Australia indicated that on average it had taken individuals just over 12 and a half years to become general managers after completing formal education, which would mean that the majority in the sample should have been younger than 35 years of age when they became general managers. Ladkin also points out that organisational hierarchies in hotels are becoming flatter which might indicate more rapid progression in the future, albeit for fewer people. It would appear that while within-organisation career progression is readily available in large tourism organisations, especially those with a dedicated HR function, the majority of small and medium-sized enterprises are unable to offer these opportunities.

It is regularly pointed out that young people regard tourism and hospitality employment as a short-term career option for the reasons previously cited, but also because of poor working conditions. Roan and Diamond (2003), for example, conducted interviews with young people in Australia who had undertaken an apprenticeship scheme in hospitality and concluded that for many, low quality of work life issues in the industry were accepted because this was only seen as a transitory phase in their working lives. In Aksu and Köksal's (2005) study, students enrolled on a tourism programme held predominantly negative views of tourism employment, and these included reference to physically demanding working conditions.

Usefully, Aksu and Köksal's (2005) study also explored the social status of tourism employment, whereby tourism's image was not considered to be held in high esteem across a number of measures. In another Turkish study of tourism students' perceptions of tourism employment (Roney and Oztin, 2007) the overall results were more mixed than in other similar studies, apart from in a few areas, including the perceived prestige of tourism jobs. Here only 25% of respondents agreed with the statement 'Tourism related jobs are more respected than the other jobs' although this could be interpreted as being quite a high proportion given the wording of the statement, which is not neutral but places tourism in an elevated position compared to other forms of employment. Occupational prestige and its relation to the self-concept are widely recognised in theories of career development, such as Super's (1957) work and also Gottfredson's (1981) theory of circumscription and compromise (see also Chapter 6). As such, understanding perceptions of tourism employ-ment as held by the general population is important as these are conveyed to prospective tourism students and employees in the sector (Walmsley, 2012). Certainly wider societal perceptions of tourism employment may function both as a barrier (Walmsley, 2012) as well as a conduit (Wan *et al.*, 2014) to youth employment in the sector.

A potentially positive aspect of much tourism employment that relates to working conditions, customer interaction, can on occasion nonetheless be turned on its head and result in frustration and disillusionment. This is picked up in a paper by Barron *et al.* (2007) as well as in an article by Korczynski (2009:76) where this dichotomy is summed up pithily as follows:

> The motif of service workers regarding customers as 'our friend, the enemy' is one with wide applicability in the contemporary service economy.

Interaction with customers, being able to assist them and being appreciated for one's efforts by customers, are among the most frequently-cited reasons for enjoying tourism employment. These customer interactions can also be one of the most trying aspect of tourism employment.

The frequent clash of reality with graduate expectations upon entry into the tourism workforce has been documented (e.g. Walmsley *et al.*, 2006, Collins, 2002; Raybould and Wilkins, 2005). The accepted wisdom is that it is the recent graduates' perceptions that are problematic, rather than actual working con-ditions, which it appears graduates will simply have to accept. The fact that, according to the literature at least, so many graduates are disappointed upon work entry could serve as a wake-up call to industry that employment prac-tices need looking into. There could be a mutual rapprochement as opposed to a 'one side must adjust while the other simply carries on as is' approach. Admittedly, employers are beginning to understand this, even if the reasons are driven by self-interest, i.e. attracting and retaining talent.

If we take the study by the WTTC (2013) on graduates' perceptions of tourism employment, we do not need to read beyond the first page to get an industry perspective on the issue. This study sets itself apart from many others by focussing a) on non-tourism graduates rather than those studying tourism, and b) its international scope comprising respondents from the United Kingdom, the USA and China. Thus the study's findings point to a differentiation of perceptions according to nationality (Chinese graduates were more positive, UK students less so). 87% of Chinese respondents said they would consider a career in Travel and Tourism. The figure for US students was still a relatively healthy 61% but in the UK it was just 49%. Airey and Frontistis (1997) also found that UK students had a more negative (or less positive) attitude towards tourism employment than their Greek counterparts.

With this swathe of literature painting a far from encouraging picture of perceptions of tourism employment, it would be all too easy to despair for the future of the sector. There are however studies that paint a more nuanced picture of youth perceptions of tourism employment. Barron *et al.*'s (2007) study of a sample of Scottish hospitality students' career expectations conforms to many others when it comes to highlighting what young people look for in tourism employment: its interactive, i.e. social, nature (see also Chuang and Dellmann-Jenkins, 2010), with some participants also recognising the sector's potential for swift promotion and global employment prospects. The aforementioned WTTC (2013) study mentions international opportunities, work life balance or the chance to speak languages as aspects of tourism employment that appealed to respondents.

Despite negative perceptions the sector continues to attract young people into its fold. To an extent this can be explained by the push of labour market circumstances, but for many young people the industry exudes an air of glamour and excitement – the image of a jet-set lifestyle (Busby *et al.*, 1997) prevails. Descriptions such as these are common:

> There really is no industry like travel and tourism to allow you to broaden your horizons and have great fun while developing a career. (Lucy Huxley, Editor in Chief, Travel Weekly Group, in the foreword of the 2015 publication *Take Off in Travel*).

The Australian-based Travel Industry Careers Association (2015) begins its explanation for why an individual might choose to work in the sector with the words: 'If you love travel then why not make a career of it'.

The fun-filled, adventurous and glamorous nature of tourism employment is certainly promoted in corporate promotions of working life in tourism. For example, a day in the life of a resort representative in a Thomas Cook 'Jobs Abroad' video (Thomas Cook, 2014) begins with an alarm going off at 7.00am followed by images of a laid back coffee on a sunny balcony, continuing with a range of situations where the resort worker deals with pleasant, smiling customers. At times it is difficult to discern the boundary between customers and employees, the two intermixing, sipping cocktails and eating sushi on a veranda as the sun sets, with a subsequent foray into the resort and its nightlife. The video ends with the alarm being set again for 7.00am the following morning. Based on this video, resort work might be described as exciting, lively, and above all fun. The tag accompanying the video summarises these thoughts as follows: 'There's no such thing as a typical day when working abroad with Thomas Cook. Every day is action-packed'.

It is not just employers who promote the glamour of working in tourism. Universities and colleges do so too (Fidgeon, 2010). To provide just one example of many, East Berkshire College (UK) which, it is important to stress, is not unique in this respect says the following on its website advertising its Travel and Tourism Courses:

> Thriving, fast-paced and sociable, careers in travel and tourism are highly sought after – and with good reason. Nothing beats the luxury of a foreign holiday, the glamour of a 'staycation,' or the excitement of a day trip. (East Berkshire College, 2015)

While it is true that the blurring of leisure and work is one of the attractions of much tourism employment (see for example Boon, 2006 who writes of ski resort employees in New Zealand or Adler and Adler, 2000, who write of *seekers* in Hawaii a predominantly young, white and from the mainland group of adventure and alternative-life-experience-seeking class of individuals), the balance between work and leisure is clearly skewed towards leisure in promotions of tourism employment. Untypical representations of tourism employment will only lead to disappointment when faced with the reality of daily chores, unreasonable customer demands, sales targets and such like. The importance of realistic job previews have long been promoted by HR specialists in trying to increased employee retention (Wanous *et al.*, 1992, Phillips, 1998). Thus, while much can be said for this type of resort work and many people do enjoy it, caution is nonetheless called for when promoting unrealistic images of tourism employment as this may ultimately result in disappointment, frustration and a loss of a recruit not solely for the individual firm, but also potentially for the entire sector.

Thus far the assumption has been that attitudes towards tourism apply to the sector in a broad, general sense. This is the angle that the majority of studies on attitudes towards tourism employment adopt. Although it is certainly possible to investigate and establish attitudes towards tourism employment, Airey and Frontistis (1997) also recognised in their comparison of Greek and British students' attitudes that these attitudes will vary depending on specific jobs within the sector. Indeed, other studies have recognised that young people hold varying attitudes towards different job roles or sub-sectors of tourism (Chuang *et al.*, 2007; Jenkins, 2001; Robinson *et al.*, 2015). This is not to say that the issue of attitudes towards tourism employment in a general sense is unimportant, but that when considering employment options, individuals will also focus on their perceptions of specific jobs rather than just on perceptions of the industry as a whole. There is clearly also the underlying assumption here that individuals make career choices based on attitudes towards certain sectors. The extent to which this holds true is explored in further detail in Chapter 6. Certainly, more work might usefully be undertaken in this area.

Demand side barriers

This section focuses on the business perspective; the demand for labour. Ultimately, a thriving tourism sector creates jobs and in times of high levels of youth unemployment one might imagine that sourcing skilled employees was unproblematic. The following discussion will demonstrate that this is not necessarily the case.

Skills gaps, skills shortages and the demand for tourism labour

Skills, this seemingly innocuous term, is the cause of much debate in practitioner and academic circles. Although the notions of *skills gaps* and *skills shortages* are frequently used interchangeably, as though they were synonymous, or simultaneously, as though where one exists the other must also, they relate to two distinct concepts with different implications for both firms and policymakers. Skills gaps refer to skills deficiencies internal to the firm, whereas skills shortages refer to such deficiencies in the external labour market (Schwalje, 2011). Should a firm discover a skills gap, it can either provide training for its employees or hire people with the requisite skills from the external labour market. Should however there exist a skills shortage as well as a skills gap then the productive capacity of the firm, and by implication other firms in the sector, is affected.

That this preamble to clarify the terms skills gaps and kills shortages was necessary is indicative of the fuzziness of the concept of skills itself. A further discussion of the concept is provided in Chapter 5 on education and training in tourism. What this section will address is the extent to which skills gaps and shortages exist, as this is fundamental to helping understand the supply of and demand for tourism labour.

The tourism trade press makes constant claims as to employers' difficulty in finding employees with appropriate skills, or about the lack of skills amongst current employees. This must come as a surprise to policy makers given continued levels of high unemployment, and the ongoing investment in vocational education taking place on a global scale. Articles with titles like 'Migrants and jobless youth key to stemming the hospitality skills gap' (Perkins, 2014) or 'Tourism minister warns industry to plug skills gap' (Griffiths, 2014) are indicative of a trend amongst employers to raise concerns about the lack of skills in their workforce.

People 1st, the UK's former sector skills council and now 'leading charity' for skills and workforce development for employers in the hospitality, tourism, leisure, travel, passenger transport and retail industries, continues likewise to focus on skills gaps and shortages in tourism and hospitality. Its *State of the Nation 2013* report is very clear in the foreword by its chief executive that skills gaps and shortages continue to hamper growth in the sector.

> Knowing that customer expectations will only continue to rise, and that customer tastes and preferences are changing, the industry must continue to address staff skills shortages in this area if it is to continue to grow. (Brian Wisdom, People 1st Chief Executive, 2013:4).

Similarly, Richardson and Butler (2012) taking a US perspective argue that labour and skills shortages are one of the greatest contemporary challenges faced by the sector. The demand for labour from employers is there, it is just that the desired level of human capital does not exist, or does not exist in sufficient quantity.

There is nonetheless a paradox here where statements such as these contrast with the reality of high levels of youth unemployment, of individuals who are over-educated or under-employed, and a continued, incessant expansion of vocational education (Wolf, 2011; Keep, 2012). This is the case not just in the UK but can be found in many nations. One may even be inclined to argue that to a large degree the bulk of jobs in tourism, particularly in accommodation and food services, have not changed that much in recent decades. This may be regarded as heresy in some circles, and yet without wanting to sound glib about this, it is arguable that labour processes have not really changed that much in many tourism jobs. Certainly, customers are more demanding today, more aware of their rights and less inclined to accept poor service, and yet in essence many jobs remain the same in their basic functions. This contrasts with the notion of a move to a knowledge economy that suggests low-skilled jobs are in decline as outlined previously (see also Goos and Manning, 2003).

Hjalager and Andersen (2000) who explored labour market structures in tourism in Denmark from 1980-1995 conclude that more people are being employed in the sector with formal qualifications. They note that tourism employment is increasingly based on qualifications. This is an indication that jobs in tourism today require more skills than in the past, but it is not proof. The value of a qualification in the labour market declines the more people have that qualification, but if entry requirements increasingly stipulate a specific level of education, then more individuals will try to attain it. Not all qualifications bear the same weight in the labour market, and indeed a proliferation of qualifications can serve to confuse employers. Where this is the case, employers are likely to stick with what they know. Wolf (2011) argues that those undertaking vocational qualifications below degree level, where there has been a proliferation of vocational qualifications, may in fact be being stigmatised by employers. With increasing numbers entering HE, those left behind run the risk of being stigmatised and therefore without a job. As Meyer noted, education not only socialises individuals but it provides a system of allocation, which itself is part of a broader system of legitimation. Education represents a sorting mechanism, conferring access to valued positions on some and removing it from others. As such, 'education is a central element in the public biography of individuals, greatly affecting their life chances' (Meyer, 1977:55). Meyer also points to the implications of allocation theory for those who are 'non-students'. Evidently, the more widespread and binding the allocation rules, the more convincingly are those individuals whose credentials are lacking assigned to increasingly limited positions in society.

Rather than just assigning individuals to a predetermined set of roles in society (allocation theory), education also changes the structure of society itself (legitimation theory). Thus, today Purcell et al. (2004) identify four categories of graduate occupations: traditional, modern, new and niche. The latter two categories are particularly relevant to tourism and hospitality employment, as these are arguably the types of positions that most tourism and hospitality graduates, if they find graduate level employment, will be entering. According to Purcell et al.'s (2004:6) description:

- ☐ New graduate occupations are in areas of employment, many new or expanding, where the route into the professional area has recently changed such that it is now via an undergraduate degree programme. Examples of such roles include: Marketing and sales managers, physiotherapists, occupational therapists, management accountants and countryside/park rangers.

- ☐ Niche graduate occupations are those occupations where the majority of incumbents are not graduates, but within which there are stable or growing specialist niches which require higher education skills and knowledge. Examples here include: Leisure and sports managers, hotel/accommodation managers, nurses, midwives and retail managers.

Table 4.1: Formal degree requirements in tourism employment

Position	No. of jobs advertised	Degree required
Retail Manager	4	0
PPC Executive	1	1[1]
Business Travel Supervisor	1	0
Business Development Manager	2	0
Reservations Manager	2	0
Product Manager	7	0
Ticketing Consultant	1	0
Specialist Consultant	1	1
Executive Jobs	4	1
Contracts Executive	2	1[2]
Travel Consultant	35	2[3]
Business Travel Consultant	49	0
Business Travel Manager	3	0
Account Manager	5	0
Retail Support Assistant	2	0
Product Executive	1	0
Hotel Consultant	1	0
Sales Manager	7	0
Contracts Manager	18	0
Travel Trade Recruitment	16	0
Sales Director	2	1[4]
Senior Business Travel Consultant	15	0
Conference and Events Consultant	4	0
Operations Manager	4	1[5]
IT Support	8	0
Marketing Manager	5	4
Retail Sales Consultant	2	0
Customer Service Executive	4	0
Homeworker	2	0
Total	**208**	**12**

Source: *Travel Trade Gazette* online 06.06.2014

1   Qualified to degree level or equivalent.
2   Ideally Tourism Management degree.
3   Education of degree level according to a job advert for 'luxury travel sales consultant'.
4   Degree from a top university
5   Candidates with a Tourism Degree / travel qualifications along with relevant work experience will also be considered.

In many respects formal requirements for higher levels of education have not filtered through to actual job advertisements in tourism. As is evident in Tables 4.1 and 4.2, which cover online job advertisements in a range of tourism trade publications, for what may somewhat lazily be called 'standard tourism employment', the formal requirements to have a higher level qualification is not a given.

The data in Table 4.1 are instructive in that 12 out of 208 jobs posted formally required a degree (or equivalent). Two out of the 12 mentioned a degree in tourism specifically (as desirable rather than essential), and one listing stipulated the degree should be from a 'top university', which, depending on how you define top may exclude many of the universities currently offering tourism degrees in the UK (i.e. former polytechnics). On the date the search was conducted in June 2014, *Travel Weekly*, another key trade publication, listed 859 jobs. Of these, 11 fell under the rubric of 'graduate jobs'. Surprisingly given the very limited stipulation of a degree for the jobs posted in Table 4.1, these 11 positions comprised roles as travel consultants, travel agents or reservations executive.

Just because degrees are not specified in the majority of job advertisements in Table 4.1 does not mean that degree level skills are not required. For some jobs, despite not stipulating a degree, higher level skills were in demand. For more senior positions it may have been the case that a degree was taken for granted. This is borne out by the fact that none of the 63 executive jobs posted on *Travel Weekly* (8th June 2014) stipulated a degree as a requirement. It could also be the case that the importance of having attained a degree wanes with time, as applicants are judged more on the basis of experience. It has been argued that one's work history and particularly success in one's work role are more important to individual's career success in mid-adulthood than formal qualifications (Wolf, 2011).

A similar analysis was conducted for jobs in hospitality. Table 4.2 summarises data for jobs advertised in a major UK hospitality trade publication, *Caterer and Hotelkeeper*, in June 2014. Here the degree requirements were even less evident than in tourism with 11 out of 656 jobs stipulating a degree (just 1.7%). The same caveats apply as mentioned for Table 4.1, specifically that despite not mentioning graduate requirements many jobs, arguably, demanded higher level skills. Furthermore, many large tourism and hospitality employers who may require candidates to have a degree do not necessarily advertise jobs in the *Travel Trade Gazette* or *Caterer and Hotelkeeper*. There was only minimal mention of graduate training schemes, for example, in any of the jobs posted.

This should also be borne in mind when interpreting the data in the tables. Nonetheless, the jobs included in both tables range from chief executives, operations managers to kitchen porters and bar staff, thereby covering a whole range of occupational levels.

Table 4.2: Degree requirements in hospitality employment

Position	No. of jobs	Count degree required
Conference and Event Jobs	30	0
Contract Catering Jobs	33	1
Education Jobs	12	0
Healthcare Jobs	5	2
Hotel Jobs	174	2
Leisure Jobs	17	1
Pub and Bar Jobs	45	0
Public Sector Jobs	2	0
Restaurant Jobs	334	5
Retail Jobs	4	0
Total	**656**	**11**

Source: *Caterer and Hotelkeeper* online edition, 7th June 2014

There have been many debates in recent years about graduates being over-educated for the work they do (e.g. Dolton and Silles, 2008; Battu *et al.*, 1999; Chevalier and Lindley, 2007). In other words these graduates are under-utilised as Mason (2001, 2002) would claim. Partly these debates have been stoked up by the continued expansion of vocational education (to include vocational courses such as tourism and hospitality in higher education). Unsurprisingly therefore the over-education (or underemployment) debate has also taken place in tourism and hospitality.

In many respects arguing that a skills gap or a skills shortage exists in what is repeatedly claimed as being a low-skilled industry is in itself surprising. In the figure adapted from (Green *et al.*, 2003) below it is quite feasible, as has often happened, to place tourism employment in the low-skills equilibrium quadrant. This implies that poorly skilled managers and workers deliver low quality products and services, and furthermore that a self-reinforcing system exists which stifles the demand for improvements in skills levels (see for example Finegold and Soskice, 1988).

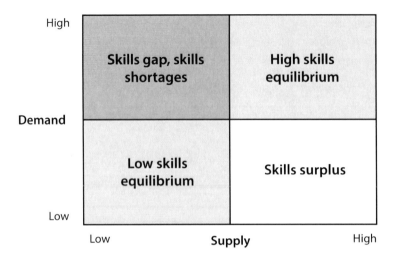

Figure 4.1: Supply of and demand for skills

Different views prevail amongst those who argue that tourism employment is characterised by a low skills equilibrium and others who suggest skills gaps and skills shortages exist. A rarely-mentioned although important point is noted by Froy (2013:351) in that what are often termed skills shortages or gaps 'are in fact labour shortages as employers are unable to find people who are willing to accept the work available at a given level of wages and working conditions'. As wages for many jobs in tourism are low, employers' lamentations about skills gaps and shortages may well be down to an unwillingness to pay staff more; certainly this is a thought seldom expressed but worth entertaining. In fact, poor working conditions more generally are also highlighted by the People 1st (2013) report where nearly one in five employers cites unsociable hours and shift work as reasons why they struggle to recruit to some positions, along with poor terms and conditions. Rather than the existence of a simple skills shortage, different levels of shortages exist then contingent upon pay and working conditions offered. This is further corroborated by data that explain that 43% of skills shortage vacancies in the sector are in elementary occupations (People 1st, 2013). Are the data that underpin this statistic really suggesting that among all the unemployed youth, including those with college and university qualifications, none can be found to fill these vacancies?

A possible answer to this paradox is Yorke's (2006) contention that employers have in general been satisfied with the subject-specific skills developed by HE, but it is in the area of 'generic skills', such as communication, teamworking and time-management where graduates have been found wanting.

This theme of poor work-readiness of recent graduates is widely discussed. A solution around some of the paradoxes of skills shortages in the sector may also be explained in part by a more detailed look at where these stated shortages are most acute. Skills shortages, where they exist, tend to apply to certain occupations in the sector more than others. People 1st (2013) notes that there is an ongoing challenge in the UK to recruit trained chefs, partially as the result of an expanding restaurant sector as opposed to a decline in the number of people with chef's skills.

A further issue to review in relation to skills gaps and shortages is employers' inability to make use of their workforce's skills. Again, this is something that has received only limited attention. With regard to skills shortages, Froy (2013) does not solely mention wages as a means to hire more skilled employees, but also points to this issue of firm's inability to make best use of their staff's skills. While she admits that a large focus of UK policy has been on getting technology firms to better utilise the skills of their workforce, particularly in relation to production processes, she is at pains to point out that at all skills levels there is room for improving skill utilisation, much of which will depend upon providing employees with autonomy when dealing with customers' needs. A quote from Jacobs (1969) is worth drawing attention to in this regard:

> when humble people, doing lowly work are not also solving problems, nobody is apt to solve humble problems.

This quotation implies that improvements can occur at all levels of a business, and furthermore be driven by all employees. However, for this to occur employees must be provided with some degree of empowerment. Having skilled employees does not inevitably mean these will apply their human capital. It takes a strategic approach to HRM to ensure that the organisation not only hires suitable candidates, but actually makes most use of their abilities (see for example Oakland and Oakland, 2001).

An encouraging study in terms of the benefits of upskilling, which then leads to greater value added in the hospitality industry, is provided by Verma (2012). Verma's study focussed on two hotels in Toronto, Canada, both of which aim to deliver a distinct service to their guests. The value chain both hotels have developed follows the adage that a better trained employee will deliver a high quality and unique experience to the guest, which in turn leads to higher levels of customer satisfaction and ultimately shareholder value.

The progressive nature of both hotels' HR practices can be seen in the detailed formal recruitment and selection process, which contrasts with an often informal approach to recruitment in the sector. Because both hotels have built up a reputation as good employers there is a surfeit of candidates for advertised jobs, enabling the businesses to recruit the best candidates from the talent pool available to them. Once recruited, both hotels emphasize internal promotions, provide internal training as well as encourage employees to pursue education and training of formal courses external to the organisation. One of the hotels has begun to participate with its union, UNITE-HERE, in a joint training centre. The other hotel (which is part of a larger chain) has a dedicated full time learning manager in each of its establishments, and each hotel is measured on its learning (e.g. number of training hours undertaken per employee). Labour turnover in both businesses ranges between 8-12% which is far lower than the industry norm. Importantly, it is not wages that keep the individuals in the hotels as these are not much higher than elsewhere in the industry, but the way staff are treated, specifically the training and develop-ment opportunities provided to them.

A final but important point to note in relation to the existence of skills gaps and shortages is perhaps the surprising contention that the tourism sector is not low skilled at all. Much common wisdom would fly in the face of this assertion, and it certainly conflicts with the prevailing discourses around tour-ism employment. The basis for a questioning of the low-skills view of tourism employment lies in the under-appreciation of soft skills, which, because they are hard to quantify are easily overlooked. Burns (1997) provides perhaps the most critical voice in this debate. For Burns, the classification of tourism employment as unskilled (the term 'unskilled' is used rather than 'low skilled') primarily can and in fact should be questioned on the grounds that the typical tourism employee must display a range of soft skills in responding to customer needs. Burns quotes Poon (1993:213) who reiterates that most common of wis-doms, that employees are the key to competitive advantage in tourism. If this is indeed so, then how can one simultaneously argue that tourism work is largely low-skilled (Burns, 1997)? For Burns, owner/managers have a vested interested in perpetuating the low-skills myth as it provides a justification for keeping labour costs down, and indeed Burns presents an historical, and thereby culturally-grounded explanation for the segmentation of the workforce into, low-, semi- and high-skilled individuals. Herein lies the problem however, as wages do not depend solely on skills content of a given job, but also on the supply of the required skills and the demand for them. Nonetheless, Burns' thoughts (and others' e.g. Grint's (1991) who also questions the top-down clas-sification of employees according to skills levels, albeit not within a tourism context) provide a refreshing perspective, even though voiced some time ago, that further demonstrate the socially constructed discourses surrounding tourism employment.

To summarise the discussion thus far, the continuing clamour about skills shortages may well overstate the issue. There are undoubtedly some skills shortages, particularly in certain occupations. However, the extent of skills shortages appears to be overstated and employers may be facing difficulty in recruiting workers with required skills due to poor working conditions and a low wage offer. In other words, the skills are there, but they just need to be properly valued. In one sense there is some positive news here for young people seeking employment, in that vacancies in the sector clearly exist, on the other hand however, young people may not be willing to accept some of these vacancies, as discussed above.

Attitudes towards employing young people

It has been suggested that conflicts exist between generations. Bourdieu, for example, treats generation as a social construct which is produced by conflict over resources (economic and cultural) within a specific field (Turner, 1998). Turner points to the contest between generations over access to labour markets, income and occupational prestige, arguing that the development of retirement legislation was at least in part brought about by increasing life-expectancy constraining the availability of work for younger workers. One does wonder to what extent beliefs about youth's attitudes, ability and work ethic are the result of generational prejudices. A Prince's Trust report referred to in People 1st's (2013) *State of the Nation* report identifies employers' beliefs about young people as a barrier to youth employment:

> Seven in 10 of (sic) respondents said they believe jobless young people face stigma from employers in general, while two thirds… admitted they could be more open-minded about recruiting unemployed young people in their own business.

Following James' (1995, 18 cited in Foster, 2013) prescription that 'our beliefs are really rules for action' the belief that young people are unskilled, work-shy and so forth is going to find repercussions in employment decisions, as well as in discourses around young people's skills levels.

Where to start when attempting to summarise employers' concerns about the employability of young people? So much has been written in this regard that the task is truly a daunting one. To begin with there appears to be a general consensus that at all educational levels, i.e. including recent graduates, young people are lacking important skills as well as in appropriate attitudes. To cite just one such study, *The Times* and the *Sunday Times Good University Guide* report on a YouGov survey that claims 52% of graduate employers said none or few graduate recruits were work ready (News UK, 2013). The issue of unpreparedness is not unique to any particular geographical location. Chang and Tse's study in Hong Kong suggests that recent graduates entering the sector needed to improve their technical skills and product knowledge as well as most importantly acquiring 'the correct attitude to service' (Chang and Tse, 2012:10).

Although it would be churlish to brush aside such concerns as entirely unfounded, a generational discourse is apparent in the way young people are portrayed. With reference to the YouGov study it was also claimed, for example, that many graduates expect to 'get rich quick' after being 'damaged' by fame culture, and are more interested in 'what a job can do for them, not what they have to offer an employer'. These portrayals display a degree of hostility, or at least disappointment and surprise. These attitudes may curtail youth employment opportunities and are certainly not conducive to them. A practical consideration, for example, relates to an issue that has not been researched in tourism, as far as the author is aware, but that he has heard mentioned by some tourism employers. This relates to a preference to hire older workers because their lives are more stable. As outlined above, there are costs related to staff turnover and a fear for some employers when hiring young people is that they are more likely to leave than older employees, partially because they demonstrate less commitment but admittedly also because they have fewer family and financial commitments tying them to specific locations.

Initiatives to foster youth employment in tourism and hospitality

Because the youth employment agenda is so important, and the consequences of failing to provide young people with transitions into employment are so dire, the substantial efforts of policy makers to assist in this regard are understandable. Many of these initiatives involve collaboration between education institutions and employers and examples will now be provided of such initiatives.

People 1st, the previously-cited UK workforce development charity for tourism and hospitality, works closely with employers in an attempt to ensure that the sector has the talent it needs. At the time of writing (2015) it was working with 19 key industry bodies committed to the development of skills in the sector (Hospitality Guild, 2015). Taking one of these bodies as an example, Springboard is a charity that 'helps young people achieve their potential; nurtures unemployed people of any age into work; and helps alleviate poverty by supporting disadvantaged and underprivileged people into sustainable employment within hospitality, leisure and tourism' (Springboard, 2015). Springboard provides a range of specialist careers information and advice, and various Into Work programmes relating to the industry. It achieves this via placement, mentoring, training and employment. According to Springboard's figures, 174,000 people have been provided with careers information and 15,000 work experience and taster sessions have been provided.

The private sector is also active in promoting youth employment opportunities in tourism. Hilton Hotels, for example, has partnered with the International Youth Foundation (IYF) to provide employment opportunities globally for youth through initiatives such as *Bright Blue Futures* and *Passport to Success*.

> 'We have a tremendous opportunity to prevent a lost generation of young people by helping them acquire the life skills and job training they need to be successful in the workplace and beyond', says Christopher Nassetta, president and CEO, Hilton Worldwide. 'As a global citizen and a leader in one of the largest industries in the world, we have a business imperative and responsibility to develop solutions that preserve our collective futures.' (Hilton Hotels, 2015)

Bright Blue Futures and *Passport to Success* (PTS) are examples of collaborative IYF and Hilton initiatives seeking to support youth employment. PTS is in fact the signature life skills program of the International Youth Foundation which has been implemented in 28 countries and has had an impact on the lives of 63,500 young people. PTS is based on hands-on, practical learning and utilizes a combination of interactive learning strategies to engage different types of learners. The programme covers four core competencies: professional development, problem solving, healthy lifestyles and workplace success (International Youth Foundation, 2015).

Examples from the *Bright Blue Futures* initiative include human resource managers and other team members who have assisted young people in gaining job application skills, from writing CVs, to how to present oneself at an interview via mock interviews at Hilton Munich Park and Hilton Munich City. At Hilton Columbus at Easton (USA) secondary school students have been given the opportunity of job shadowing at the hotel for a day and at the Hilton Adelaide a chef apprenticeship programme aims to develop kitchen staff between the ages of 14-25 who have prior hotel experience. Clearly, some effort and creativity can go a long way to create valuable opportunities both for employers and for young people seeking to gain a foothold in the labour market.

Collaboration to assist youth transitions into employment can take on a variety of forms, frequently relying on a whole range of collaborative partners. An example of this is the Youth Career Initiative (YCI) which is delivered by the International Tourism Partnership and Business in the Community. It teaches life and work skills to at-risk young people using hotels as its learning platform. YCI is based on a unique partnership model, where participating full-service hotels provide the human, operational and training resources to deliver the programme, and a local non-profit partner identifies and recruits eligible candidates who can benefit from the programme. YCI is an intensive 24-week education and employability programme that combines classroom-based and practical training with experienced hotel staff acting as mentors to YCI students. The aim of the programme is to enable young participants to make informed career choices and to help them appreciate the range of options available to them. YCI has been running for over twenty years and has assisted more than 3,000 individuals. Its ambitious Strategy and Growth Plan 2015-2019 is to annually assist over 2,500 graduates and involve over 400 hotels. It is clearly focusing on upscaling its operations whereby it will also achieve greater economies of scale (examples of success stories can be found on the website www.youthcareerinitiative.org).

YCI has recently been working closely with the US Department of State in support of the reintegration of rehabilitated survivors of human trafficking. An example of how critical these kind of programmes can be to assisting at-risk young people, not just in providing meaningful employment but also in raising self-confidence and independence, is Asha's story (BITC, 2015). A survivor of human trafficking, Asha received training and then found permanent employment at The Westin Mumbai Garden City hotel. She says of the programme: 'Working here is second nature now. I've been working in the laundry department for a year, so I'm able to talk to people with confidence, and I've earned the respect of those around me'.

In Jordan a three-way public-private-NGO collaboration of USAID, the Jordanian Government and the aforementioned International Youth Foundation has been established to assist vulnerable young people to find long-term work in tourism. The Youth for the Future (Y4F) initiative's broad goal is to create an enabling environment with a greater capacity to serve Jordan's youth at risk (Youth for the Future, 2015). Two core programmes seek to deliver Y4F's services: ensuring successful transitions to work and building sustainable community youth hubs. The International Youth Foundation's Passport to Success scheme is again critical for achievement of the former.

Y4F counts numerous success stories, such as that relating to Tarek, one of eight siblings, who at the age of 18 was in and out of temporary work in retail sales and auto mechanics. Via a friend's mother he then found out about the PTS programme, applied and was accepted on a training programme through the Jordanian Hospitality and Tourism Education Company. As his training was drawing to a close he was able to secure a job as a waiter at a café. Three months later an international franchise, Café Coffee Bean and Tea Leaf, asked Tarek to join their company. Tarek accepted the offer and a week after the training was promoted to assistant manager, then to store manager. Tarek comments: 'In one year, my life turned upside down. I transformed from an underemployed, hopeless person to a store manager at a world famous café franchise'.

Examples such as these may be anecdotal – it is impossible to judge the success of this and other initiatives based solely on this kind of anecdotal evidence. What this does show however is how tourism can provide pathways out of dead-end, low skilled jobs, thereby setting young people on track to make more of their potential, benefitting them, the tourism sector and ultimately society. Individual businesses may on occasion train and then lose employees to other companies, but if they are good employers, in a broad sense of the term, then this does not have to happen and similarly they will be in a stronger position to attract staff too.

The list of public-private sector partnerships that aim to assist transition into the tourism sector is extensive. Other examples include Baristas Life & Job Skills Training Program for At-Risk Youth (Pacific Community Resources, 2015). This initiative based in Surrey, British Columbia, Canada, comprises a partnership between PCR, the Surrey School District and Starbucks Coffee Canada. It aims at helping at-risk youth enter the workforce by building their confidence and skills via a work placement programme. Specifically, this consists of five weeks of employability and life skills training, five weeks of work experience at a Starbucks location and one week of job search.

Additional aims of the programme are to:

- ☐ Provide young people with life skills and the enhancement of self-esteem designed to improve their long-term employment prospects
- ☐ Provide workshops designed to introduce young people to workplace health and safety practices as well as an introduction to retail service standards

☐ Assist young people not only in the development of employability skills but also towards becoming empowered and contributing citizens.

Sometimes increased youth employment is a side-effect of other aims. The Rwandan Government in recognising the potential contribution tourism can make to the economy also recognises the issue of a lack of service quality in many Rwandan tourism firms. It therefore assisted in the creation of the Romero Hospitality Academy. The academy helps young people who already have employment in the sector to improve their customer service skills. Students go through training programmes that last for over 240 notional learning hours (approximately 9 weeks) in technical skills, underpinning knowledge and customer care at the academy (Murag, 2012). The World Bank through IDA credits works in partnership with the Rwandan Government in providing further training initiatives in tourism that assist youth transitions into employment as well as improving skills levels of those already employed.

References

Adler, P. & Adler, P. (2004) *Paradise Laborers. Hotel Work in the Global Economy,* New York: Cornell University Press.

Airey, D. & Frontistis, A. (1997) Attitudes to careers in tourism: an Anglo Greek comparison. *Tourism Management,* **18** (3), 149-158.

Aksu, A. & Köksal, D. (2005) Research in brief. Perceptions and attitudes of tourism students in Turkey. *International Journal of Contemporary Hospitality Management,* **17** (5), 436-447.

Barron, P., Maxwell, G., Broadbridge, A. & Ogden, S. (2007) Careers in hospitality management: Generation Y's experiences and perceptions. *Journal of Hospitality & Tourism Management,* **14** (2), 119-128.

Battu, H., Belfield, C. R. & Sloane, P. J. (1999) Overeducation among graduates: a cohort view. *Education Economics,* **7** (1), 21-38.

BITC (2015) Asha's Story, http://www.bitc.org.uk/blog/post/giving-hope-survivors-human-trafficking-through-yci---asha [Accessed 16.08.15]

Boon, B. (2006) When leisure and work are allies: the case of skiers and tourist resort hotels. *Career Development International,* **11**(7), 594-608.

Burns, P. (1997) Hard-skills, soft-skills: undervaluing hospitality's 'service with a smile'. *Progress in Tourism and Hospitality Research,* **3** (3), 239-248.

Busby, G., Brunt, P. & Baber, S. (1997) Tourism sandwich placements: an appraisal. *Tourism Management,* **28 (**2), 105-110.

Chang, S. & Tse, E. C.-Y. (2012) Understanding the initial career decisions of hospitality graduates in Hong Kong: Quantitative and qualitative evidence. *Journal of Hospitality & Tourism Research.* Available at http://jht.sagepub.com/content/early/2012/10/09/1096348012461544

Chevalier, A. & Lindley, J. (2007). Overeducation and the skills of UK graduates. *Discussion Paper No.79.* Centre for the Economics of Education, London School of Economics.

Chuang, N.-K. & Dellmann-Jenkins, M. (2010) Career decision-making and intention: a study of hospitality undergraduate students. *Journal of Hospitality & Tourism Research,* **34** (4), 512-530.

Chuang, N.-K., Goh, B., Stout, B. & Dellmann-Jenkins, M. (2007) Hospitality undergraduate students' career choices and factors influencing commitment to the profession. *Journal of Hospitality & Tourism Education,* **19** (4), 28-37.

Collins, A. B. (2002) Gateway to the real world, industrial training: dilemmas and problems. *Tourism Management,* **23 (**1), 93-96.

Dolton, P. & Silles, M. (2008) The effects of over-education on earnings in the graduate labour market. *Economics of Education Review,* **27** (2), 125-139.

East Berkshire College (2015) Travel & Tourism courses. www.eastberks.ac.uk/courses/travel-and-tourism.html [Accessed 16.01.15]

Fidgeon, P. (2010) Tourism education and curriculum design: a time for consolidation and review? *Tourism Management,* **36 (**1), 699-723.

Finegold, D. & Soskice, D. (1988) The failure of training in Britain: Analysis and prescription. *Oxford Review of Economic Policy,* **4 (**3), 21-53.

Foster, K. (2013) Generation and discourse in working life stories. *British Journal of Sociology,* **64**(2), 195-215.

Froy, F. (2013) Global policy developments towards industrial policy and skills: Skills for competitiveness and growth. *Oxford Review of Economic Policy,* **29 (**2), 344-360.

Goos, M. & Manning, A. (2003). Lousy and lovely jobs: the rising polarization of work in Britain. Working paper. Centre for Economic Performance, London School of Economics and Political Science

Gottfredson, L. S. (1981) Circumscription and compromise: A developmental theory of occupational aspirations. *Journal of Counseling Psychology Monograph*, **28** (6), 545-578.

Green, A., Hasluck, C., Hogarth, T. & Reynolds, C. (2003). East Midlands FRESA Targets Project—Final Report for the East Midlands Development Agency. University of Warwick: Institute for Employment Research, and Pera.

Griffiths, S. (2014). ITT 2014: Tourism minister warns industry to plug skills gap. *Travel Trade Gazette Digital*.

Grint, K. (1991) *The Sociology of Work. An Introduction*, Cambridge: Polity Press.

Hilton Hotels. (2015) *Global Corporate News*. Available: http://news.hiltonworldwide.com/index.cfm/newsroom/detail/22722 [Accessed 26.03.15].

Hjalager, A.-M. & Andersen, S. (2000) Tourism employment: contingent work or professional career? *Employee Relations*, **23** (2), 114-129.

Hospitality Guild. (2015) *Our hospitality partner organisation*. Available: http://www.hospitalityguild.co.uk/partners/ [Accessed 23.03.15].

International Youth Foundation. (2015) *Library*. Available: http://library.iyfnet.org/sites/default/files/library/PTS_HW_Fact_Sheet.pdf [Accessed 26.03.15].

Jacobs, J. (1969) *The Economy of Cities*, New York: Random House.

Jenkins, A. K. (2001) Making a career of it? Hospitality students' future perspectives: an Anglo-Dutch study. *International Journal of Contemporary Hospitality Management*, **13** (1), 13-20.

Keep, E. (2012). Youth Transitions, the Labour Market and Entry into Employment: Some Reflections and Questions. *SKOPE Publications*. Cardiff: SKOPE.

Korczynski, M. (2009) Understanding the contradictory lived experience of service work. *In* Korczynski, M. & Macdonald, C. (eds.) *Service Work. Critical Perspectives*. New York: Routledge.

Kusluvan, S. & Kusluvan, Z. (2000) Perceptions and attitudes of undergraduate tourism students towards working in the tourism industry in Turkey. *Tourism Management*, **21** (3), 251-269.

Ladkin, A. (2002) Career analysis: a case study of hotel general managers in Australia. *Tourism Management*, **23** (4), 379-388.

Mason, G. (2001). *Mixed fortunes: Graduate utilisation in service industries*. London: National Institute of Economic and Social Research.

Mason, G. (2002) High skills utilisation under mass higher education: graduate employment in service industries in Britain. *Journal of Education and Work,* **15** (4), 427-456.

Meyer, J. (1977) The effects of education as an institution. *American Journal of Sociology,* **83** (1), 55-77.

Murag, D. (2012) *Remera hospitality academy officially launched.* Available: http://www.wda.gov.rw/node/50285 [Accessed 25.07.13].

News Uk (2013). *The Times and The Sunday Times Good University Guide*: New recruits are not job ready according to survey. *News UK.*

Oakland, S. & Oakland, J. (2001) Current people management activities in world-class organizations. *Total Quality Management,* **12** (6), 773-788.

Pacific Community Resources (2015) Baristas. Available: http://pcrs.ca/baristas [Accessed 04.04.15]

People 1st (2013). *State of the Nation Report 2013.* An analysis of labour market trends, skills, education and training within the UK hospitality and tourism industries. Uxbridge: People 1st.

Perkins, C. (2014). Migrants and jobless youth key to stemming the hospitality skills gap. *Big Hospitality.* Available: http://www.bighospitality.co.uk/Trends-Reports/Hospitality-skills-gap-migrants-youth

Peters, M. (2005) Entrepreneurial skills in leadership and human resource management evaluated by apprentices in small tourism businesses. *Education + Training,* **47** (8/9), 575-591.

Phillips, J. (1998) Effects of realistic job previews on multiple organizational outcomes: A meta-analysis. *Academy of Management Journal,* **41** (6), 673-690.

Poon, A. (1993) *Tourism, Technology and Competitive Strategies,* Wallingford: CAB.

Purcell, K., Elias, P. & Wilton, N. (2004). Research paper no. 3 - Higher Education, Skills and Employment: careers and jobs in the graduate labour market. Warwick: Employment Studies Research Unit, University of the West of England, & Warwick Institute of Employment Research

Raybould, M. & Wilkins, H. (2005) Over qualified and under experienced. Turning graduates into hospitality managers. *International Journal of Contemporary Hospitality Management,* **17** (3), 203-216.

Richardson, S. & Butler, G. (2012) Attitudes of Malaysian tourism and hospitality students towards a career in the industry. *Asia Pacific Journal of Tourism Research,* **17** (3), 262-276.

Roan, A. & Diamond, C. (2003) Starting out: The quality of working life of young workers in the retail and hospitality industries in Australia. *International Journal of Employment Studies*, **11** (2), 91-119.

Robinson, R., Ruhanen, L. & Breakey, N. (2015) Tourism and hospitality internships: influences on student career aspirations. *Current Issues in Tourism* 03/2015.

Roney, S. A. & Oztin, P. (2007) Career perceptions of undergraduate tourism students: A case study in Turkey' *Journal of Hospitality, Leisure, Sport and Tourism Education,* **6** (1).

Springboard. (2015) *Making a difference to people's lives.* Available: http://www.charity.springboard.uk.net/ [Accessed 26.03.15].

Super, D. (1957) *The Psychology of Careers,* New York: Harper.

Schwalje, W. (2011). What is the Difference Between a Skills Gap and Skills Shortage? NORRAG NEWS, Towards a New Global World of Skills Development? TVET's turn to Make its Mark. **46**, 44-46. Available: http://www.norrag.org

Thomas Cook (2014) www.youtube.com/watch?v=lY9tL5VuxLI [Accessed 29.11.14]

Travel Industry Careers Association. (2015). Why travel and tourism? Available: http://www.travelindustrycareers.org/why-travel-and-tourism.html [Accessed 11.01.15].

Turner, B. (1998) Ageing and generational conflicts: a reply to Sarah Irwin. *The British Journal of Sociology,* **49** (2), 299-304.

Verma, A. (2012). Skills for competitiveness: Country report for Canada. *OECD Local Economic and Employment Development (LEED) Working Papers,* OECD.

Walmsley, A. (2012) 'Pathways into tourism higher education'. *Journal of Hospitality, Leisure, Sport and Tourism Education,* **11** 131-139.

Walmsley, A., Thomas, R. & Jameson, S. (2006) Surprise and sense making: undergraduate placement experiences in SMEs. *Education + Training,* **48** (5), 360-372.

Wan, P., King, Y., Wong, A. & Kong, W. H. (2014) Student career prospect and industry commitment: The roles of industry attitude, perceived social status, and salary expectations. *Tourism Management,* **40** 1-14.

Wanous, J. P., Poland, T. D., Premack, S. L. & Davis, K. S. (1992) The effects of met expectations on newcomer attitudes and behaviors: A review and meta-analysis. *Journal of Applied Psychology*, **77** (3), 288-297.

Wolf, A. (2011). Review of Vocational Education. - The Wolf Report. Department for Education and Department for Business, Innovation and Skills. Available: https://www.gov.uk/government/uploads/system/uploads/attachment_data/file/180504/DFE-00031-2011.pdf

WTTC (2013). *A Career in Travel & Tourism*. London: World Travel and Tourism Council.

Yorke, M. (2006). *Employability in higher education: what it is – what it is not.* Learning and Employability, Series One. York: The Higher Education Academy.

Youth for the Future. (2015) *Youth Work Jordan*. Available: www.youthworkjordan.org [Accessed 27.03.15].

5 Education, Employability and Youth Employment

Aims of the chapter

This chapter explores in more detail the nature of the relationship between education and youth employment in tourism. It reviews the development of tourism and hospitality higher education with a particular focus on perceptions of the purpose of education from policy makers' standpoint. It extends the discussion around skills begun in the previous chapter within the context of employability, reviewing the role employers, universities and policy makers play in the provision of a skilled tourism workforce. The chapter concludes by outlining the potential advantages of hiring a young workforce.

Nature and expansion of tourism and hospitality education

Data demonstrate that an increasing proportion of young people worldwide are in formal education. Data from UNESCO indicate that in 2010 there were approximately five and a half times more people enrolled in tertiary education than in 1970 (the global population increased by a factor of 1.8 between 1970 and 2010).

Table 5.1: Global enrolment in tertiary education (millions)

	1970	1980	1990	2000	2010	1970-2010 Compound annual growth rate
Arab States	..	1.58	2.39	5.04	8.66	--
Central and Eastern Europe	8.76	10.04	9.84	14.02	21.54	1.0227
Central Asia	..	1.48	1.54	1.48	2.07	--
East Asia and the Pacific	3.58	7.04	13.77	24.97	54.8	1.07
Latin America and the Caribbean	1.58	4.67	7.02	11.2	21.5	1.067
North America and Western Europe	14.06	20.15	25.03	27.77	37.72	1.025
South and West Asia	2.68	4.0	6.34	12.16	28.47	1.061
Sub-Saharan Africa	0.21	0.57	1.3	2.55	5.78	1.086
World	32.69	49.73	67.54	99.53	181.05	1.04

Source: UNESCO

Wolf (2011) draws on three UK studies that focus on cohorts born in 1958, 1970 and 1991. When aged 18 ,the proportion of young people from these cohorts in full time education or training was 17%, 25% and 45% respectively. Changes in tertiary education go beyond a simple expansion. They have also been far-reaching in relation to its purpose, with a vocational orientation ever more present. Subjects such as tourism and hospitality are indicative of this reorientation, which is also reflected in the preferences of students, who view higher education today more in vocational terms than as a source of liberal education (Tarrant, 2006, in Baron and Corbin, 2012).

Table 5.2 presents data that relate to the percentage of graduates graduating from social sciences, business and law (SSBL) in a select number of advanced economies. Business and Law may be seen as a proxy for vocational orienta- tion. As these data show, there was almost a uniform increase in the proportion of graduates in SSBL graduations between 2000 and 2006, but since then the development has been mixed. Although largely speculative, given the focus only on the UK, data from ATHE point to a plateauing of the popularity of tourism courses in higher education (Walmsley, 2012), which would mirror the current trends in SSBL more generally.

Table 5.2: Percentage of graduates from tertiary education graduating from social sciences, business and law

	2000 (%)	2006 (%)	2012 (%)
Denmark	24.9	31.9	35.7
Finland	22.8	23.4	25.3
France	37.4	40.9	41.5
Germany	20.6	24.2[1]	23.4
Japan	25.1	27	27
United Kingdom	27.5	30.5	31.6[2]
USA	40.8	38.1	36.4[2]

1 2005 data
2 2011 data

Source: UNESCO

The history of tourism and hospitality higher education is relatively recent. While earliest aspects of tourism and hospitality education pre-date the Second World War, it was not until the rapid growth of tourism subsequently and the concomitant growth of professionalism in the sector that led to its expansion and increased vocationalism (Fidgeon, 2010). While it is true that tourism education and training varies in the extent of its vocational orientation (Hudson, 2005), most would agree it is primarily a vocational subject. One imagines therefore that prior to any formal tourism education, individuals learnt about tourism on the job, or were specialists in other areas albeit with knowledge that could then be applied to the sector (e.g. accounting, general management, psychology etc.).

Global expansion of tertiary level tourism and hospitality higher education: Examples from seven key countries

UK

According to Busby and Fiedel (2001), the first undergraduate degrees in tourism in the UK were offered in 1986. Cooper *et al.* (1994) then note that the number of degrees increased ten-fold between 1986 and 1991. The number of HE institutions offering undergraduate tourism education stood at around 114 in 2012 (Walmsley, 2012). Hospitality education at HEIs has a longer pedigree with the 1960s seeing the delivery of the first hospitality programmes (Knowles *et al.*, 2003).

India

According to Mishra and Rana (2012) the inception of hospitality education started with the Institute of Hotel Management, Catering Technology and Applied Nutrition, Mumbai, the first of its kind in South East Asia, founded in the year 1954. By the year 2012 the All India Council for Technical Education and Hospitality Education-approved hotel management institutes in India numbered 134 with a total of 9,716 seats in various hotel management programmes.

Australia

The first tourism degrees in Australia were offered in the 1970s (Richardson 1999, cited in Wang, 2008). After slow growth in the early 1980s, at the end of the eighties and early nineties tourism higher education is described as explosive by McKercher (2002). Wang (2008) suggests tourism higher education was fully recognised by the late 1980s with the establishment of the first Chair in Tourism Management at James Cook University.

Malaysia

Bin Mohd Yusof's (2010) review of tourism and hospitality education in Malaysia describes how tourism and hospitality programmes in Malaysia have proliferated in the last 30 years. According to Ibrahim (2007) it is one of the fastest growing post-secondary education pathways in the country with hotel and catering programmes being offered in 1967 at Universiti Teknologi MARA. The first tourism administration programme was offered here in 1975.

Brazil

The beginnings of tourism higher education in Brazil can be dated to 1970 but since then, especially in the 1990s, it has witnessed dramatic growth, and by 2004 there existed approximately 600 programmes (to include hospitality, Leal, 2004). Similar to the UK, hospitality programmes began earlier in the 1960s (Knowles *et al.*, 2003).

Turkey

Roney and Öztin (2007) briefly describe, as the basis of their study into tourism students' perceptions of tourism employment, the development of tourism education in Turkey. Following the rapid development of tourism in Turkey in the 1990s the Turkish Government developed a strategy to strengthen the provision of tourism education. Two- and four-year courses were established at Vocational Schools affiliated with a number of universities. Roney and Öztin's (2007) article suggests that at the time of writing there were 31 universities in Turkey that offered a four-year programme, and there existed 92 two-year programmes.

North America

Hudson (2005) reviews the development of tourism education in North America. Despite the first courses appearing in the 1940s it was not until the 1980s that the subject area really started to develop. Hudson (2013) highlights that the growth in tourism education went hand-in-hand with expansion of the industry, and also because of the exciting career opportunities the sector offers. In the 1970s there were roughly 40 four-year tourism-related programmes in the U.S. but by 2005 there were 170 granting degrees and over 800 programmes offering associate degrees, certificates or diplomas. (Hudson's review of tourism education in North America is one of a handful focussing on a range of countries in Airey and Tribes' book *An International Handbook of Tourism Education*.)

Is tourism education too vocational?

Whether tourism education is too vocational or not vocational enough is impossible to answer definitively of course, not least because educational values change over time. As the previous discussion has shown, there are those who feel it needs to focus less on the demands of business, and take a broader societal orientation. Others, notably in the business arena, but not exclusively so, believe students are ill-prepared for work and that tourism programmes should increasingly remove those aspects which are not directly vocational. A danger resides in unintended consequences of ill-considered changes to curricula that are supposed to better prepare students for the world of work. To provide one example, the traditional final year research project at undergraduate level, the dissertation, with its focus on the collection and interpretation of primary data is regarded by some as too academic, certainly not vocational enough to be included in modern tourism curricula. On reflection though it is difficult to see how the skills inherent in the compilation of dissertations such as critical analysis, project management, and synthesis, to name but a few, are somehow skills that employers would not want. The point is that the academic-vocational distinction needs to be treated with caution, the boundaries are not clear cut and as was outlined previously, what is good for academia may also be good from a vocational perspective (see page 67).

Education and economic growth

An article in *The Economist* suggests 'The Whole World is Going to University' (The Economist, 2015) but posits that there is little evidence to suggest whether it is worth it. The reason provided by the article is that universities are failing to properly educate their students. The article refers to poor student scores, suggesting that employers frequently choose employees based on institution attended rather than what they have actually learnt. 'In short, students could be paying vast sums merely to go through a very elaborate sorting mechanism' as the article states.

Notwithstanding regular critiques such as this, the global expansion in education is promoted by policy makers as it is regarded as key to economic growth. Drawing on the UK as a case in point, successive UK governments continue to adopt 'upskilling' as a means to increase the country's competitiveness. Today, it is almost as though there is no other purpose to university education than to contribute to economic growth, report Maskell and Robinson (2001) in a scathing attack on UK higher education policy. Occasionally the subjugation of education to economic concerns is thinly veiled. The 1997 *Dearing Report* (official title: *Higher Education in the Learning Society*) in its introduction to Chapter 1 begins: 'The purpose of education is life-enhancing: it contributes to the whole quality of life'. The tone quickly changes however: 'This recognition of the purpose of higher education in the development of our people, our society, and our *economy* is central to our vision'. The subsequent sentence then reveals the true reasoning underpinning the report: 'In the next century, the economically successful nations will be those which become learning societies'.

Almost a decade later the Leitch Review was tasked with investigating the UK's skills needs. Here too it was established that prosperity depends on developing the human capital base (Leitch, 2006:27):

> The Review found that fundamental changes under way in the global economy mean that the future prosperity of advanced economies increasingly depends on their skills bases... Just as being at the forefront of the Industrial Revolution determined prosperity in the previous century, so making the most of these changes through the skills of the people will determine prosperity in this century.

The development of skills was then not left solely to schools and colleges, but also to universities. Indeed all educational establishments have a responsibility to develop skills for the purposes of fostering economic growth. According to Wolf (2011) the Leitch Review perpetuates a wider assumption that advanced economies will need to employ more and more 'knowledge workers' ultimately leading to the disappearance of unskilled employment. The distribution of jobs by skills levels resembles more of an hour-glass, with a large number of jobs requiring high skills levels but where there is an equally large (if not larger) base of low skilled jobs. This polarisation of jobs is widely documented (Autor *et al.*, 2006; Goos and Manning, 2007).

Things may be changing now, however, in higher education in the United Kingdom. On the face of it, the education for economic growth maxim still prevails. Thus, the foreword to the Browne Report (2011) which aimed to explore HE funding in the UK boldly claims:

> Graduates go on to higher paid jobs and add to the nation's strength in the global knowledge based economy

and elsewhere in the foreword:

> A degree is of benefit both to the holder, through higher levels of social contribution and higher lifetime earnings, and to the nation, through higher economic growth rates and the improved health of society.

Having on numerous occasions stipulated that a) the nation needs graduates for economic growth and b) graduates are better off than non-graduates as they earn more than the latter, the report then clarifies that the burden of funding of higher education should be placed on graduates, but only if they earn sufficient income from their employment. There is open acknowledgement here that a degree may not result in higher earnings for some graduates, or at least not earnings sufficiently high to permit paying of student debt. This differs markedly from what was delivered in the Dearing Report:

> Society benefits from higher education to the extent that a graduate pays taxes, as well as earning a greater amount post-tax...

The 'graduate bonus' varies considerably from one nation to another. For example, the earnings premium for 25-to-64-year-olds with tertiary education, relative to those with upper secondary education, ranges from 15% in New Zealand to 119% in Hungary (OECD, 2008). The benefits of education need to be weighed against its costs and these, for the individual, rise rapidly in many countries for post-compulsory education. Furthermore, the distribution of wages across individuals with similar levels of educational attainment must also be heeded, as it is an indication of risk associated with investing in education. While for statistical purposes all individuals who have tertiary education are put into one category, the distribution of wages across these individuals is far from even.

Furthermore, if remuneration is to be equated with productivity, low graduate earnings are a sign for low graduate productivity. Statistics suggest that an increasing number of graduates will be unable to repay their student loans. According to the Institute for Fiscal Studies (*The Economist*, 2014) 73% of graduates will not repay their loans in full. The UK government expects to recover just 55% of its costs, against an estimate of 72% in 2010. Brown *et al.* (2011:116) discuss the decline in graduates' real term salaries in the United States and the UK. Average starting salaries in the US declined in real terms between 1973 and 2005. In the UK one third of students who took-up government loans from 1998 onwards had still made no repayments in 2010 because their earnings had remained beneath the (modest) level that triggered repayments. In terms of a policy double-whammy this is surely a hit. Not only do graduates not earn enough, which means the public purse is likely to be worse off than prior to the changes in funding arrangements, if graduates are not earning enough they are unlikely to be employed in work for which their graduate-level skills are required. This then raises concerns as to whether a wholesale upskilling the workforce is really benefitting the economy.

The view that upskilling itself necessarily leads to increased competitiveness can be queried on a number of grounds. Firstly, HE participation rates in the UK have risen beyond 45% (DfBIS, 2014). There has been a similar increase in the uptake of tertiary education throughout OECD countries. In almost all OECD countries, 25-to-34-year-olds have higher tertiary attainment levels than the generation about to leave the labour market (55-to-64-year-olds). On average across OECD countries, 33% of the younger cohort has achieved a tertiary education, compared with 19% among the oldest cohort (OECD, 2008). The same OECD report that furnishes the above statistics posits that despite an increase in skilled jobs, the increase in the uptake of tertiary education has exceeded the rate of growth in skilled jobs. The ONS explains that the proportion of recent graduates in lower skilled jobs has increased from 26.7% in 2001 to 35.9% in 2011 (ONS, 2012). Whether all these highly skilled graduates are using their skills is something that is frequently asked and yet often quickly put to one side.

Sharma (2014) with reference to the rapid expansion of higher education in China and India questions what to do with these 'millions of extra graduates'? Sharma (2014) quotes Indian Labour Ministry figures that indicate that one in three graduates up to the age of 29 are unemployed. In China, the number of graduates has expanded sevenfold in the last fifteen years. There is a risk that a generation of highly educated and yet un- or under-employed is being created. According to Sharma's (2014) report Craig Jeffrey professor of Development

Geography at Oxford University warns:

> In the past, India was seen as the country of the bus conductor with a BA. Now it is the country of the MA manual labourer. It has got so much worse.

A phenomenon has arisen which sees young people waiting for opportunities that never arrive. Prof Jeffrey describes this phenomenon as the *timepass* generation.

At a macro level, the evidence that any increases in a nation's human capital stock forcibly lead to greater competitiveness and growth are far from proven. A strong attack on the education for growth position is provided by Alison Wolf in her book *Does Education Matter?*. Wolf (2002) berates policy makers' continued unquestioning support for the expansion of education per se. The relationship between education and growth is complicated, and is not simply a question of more is better. Ramachandran (2004) similarly queried the blanket treatment of education as a homogenous concept and using economic modelling theorised how different types of education (primary, secondary and tertiary) influence the overall economic development process. His results, which point to the need for more research, align with Wolf's (2002) position that the difficulty in finding significant correlations between educational attainment and economic growth is at least in part due to measurement difficulties.

Whereas Ramcharan (2004) focuses his critique on traditional ways of measuring educational attainment, Wolf (2002) focuses on using wages as a proxy for levels of economic output at the level of the individual: The higher the wage, the greater the individual's productivity. It does not take much convincing to see that the relationship between education, wages and productivity is problematic. Wolf (2002) draws on the example of lawyers, but given the recent turmoil in the financial sector we could refer to bankers' bonuses. Many people would question the notion that an investment banker who enjoys, say, a $1m bonus is twenty-five times more productive that a nurse earning $40,000. While there is evidently a relationship between education and earnings, making predictions about future economic growth on the basis of educational levels alone is difficult.

As Wolf (2002) furthermore argues, at a societal level, measuring the impact of education, the so-called social returns on education, is even more difficult due to additional calculations in relation to costs associated with the provision of education, a quasi cost-benefit or return on investment type analysis. As we have seen, education is a signal for earnings, but not necessarily a signal for economic growth. This in itself is not an original insight. Collins (1971 cited in Meyer, 1977) has argued that if education functions solely as an allocation mechanism then there is no effect on 'the aggregate product'. Recruiters may be using education as a sorting mechanism to sort people according to ability, not necessarily according to skills, so Wolf (2002) suggests. In an increasingly competitive labour market, one now frequently needs a degree simply to get on a short-list (not necessarily in tourism though as we have seen, e.g. Table 4.1 and Table 4.2), whether the skills gained on the degree are actually required on the job is another matter entirely (Maskell and Robinson, 2001). After removing any notion of a liberal education from the purpose of higher education, we are now left with a situation where the education-economic growth link is not as strong as policy-makers initially believed.

It is not enough to educate and train people, to embed employability skills (see also section below) into curricula, to provide placements, internships and apprenticeships to ensure economic growth. A further matter to consider is whether employers themselves are actually making most use of the skills of the workforce. This is an issue discussed in some detail by Payne and Keep (2011) who criticise the then UK's coalition government for its over-emphasis on supply side skills policy, instead of also questioning how to raise employers' demand for, and utilisation of, skills. The issue has also been recognised by others, e.g. Froy (2013). There is no guarantee that the tourism or hospitality graduate who enters a firm actually goes on to employ his/her skills although to do so would be beneficial to the organisation.

Although this chapter, and indeed this book, place a strong emphasis on tertiary education, it is worthwhile pointing to vocational education at lower levels of the educational hierarchy. Here Wolf (2011) in her report on vocational education for the UK government is even more critical of recent educational policy. Instead of improving their lot, vocational qualifications are often detrimental to individuals' career development. The then UK Secretary of State for Education acknowledges:

> Far too many 14-16 year olds are doing courses with little or no value because performance tables incentivise schools to offer these inadequate qualifications. As a result between a quarter and a third of young people between the ages of 16-19 are, right now, either doing nothing at all or pursuing courses which offer no route to higher levels of education or the prospect of meaningful employment. She is correct to say these young people are being deceived and that this is not just unacceptable but morally wrong'.

These are quite remarkable admissions.

Employability

Employability has become something of a holy grail of higher education policy as it delivers on at least two counts: first, the employment of graduates should lead to economic growth, and second it also addresses youth unemployment. This is certainly true in the UK (see preceding section and also Jackson, 2009) but similar developments are evident in many countries (e.g. Cumming, 2010; Kreber, 2006) seeking to strengthen their national competitiveness in the light of increased levels of global competition. Faced with what may at times appear to be an overwhelming employability discourse expounded by policymakers and industry, frequently seconded by leaders in HE, occasional voices that offer a counter-discourse can still be heard. Within a Canadian context (Axelrod, 2002:3-4) claims:

> More than ever, higher education is expected to cater directly, quickly, and continually to the demands of the marketplace ... Preparing graduates for employment is undeniably part of the university endeavour . . . but in the race for riches, symbolized by endless rhetoric about the need for Canada to become globally competitive, technologically advanced, and proficient at churning out 'knowledge workers' for the twenty-first century, something significant is being lost.

Kreber's (2006:7) is just one voice among many in the academic community that fear traditional values such as curiosity-driven research, social criticism, and preparation for civic life are being lost in the instrumentalism pervading HE policy. The critical voices are not new either. Lyotard in 1984 suggests: 'the goal (*of education*) is no longer truth, but performativity – that is, the best possible input/output equation' (Lyotard, 1984:46). The demonstration of this instrumentalist approach to higher education is reflected in the notion of value which it seems is simply reduced to whether one lands a graduate job or not. Wilson (2014) expresses a view that is increasingly marginalised in HE discourse where impact needs to be immediate:

> The mysterious thing about having had a university education is that its benefits only begin to show years afterwards. You realise that particular abilities – to think for oneself above all – would not have developed so fully without the three years spent studying for a degree, however time-wasting they seemed at the time.

The idea that results or the impact of education have to be immediate is picked up by Price with reference to the teaching of strategic management and employers' calls for 'soft' skills:

> Intriguingly, however, employers consistently ask for practical business skills such as presentation and teamwork – not strategic thinking. Essentially, strategy is for senior managers. In a time of mass higher education few students will ever become senior managers, and those who do will not achieve such jobs for at least a decade. (Price, 2007:258)

Maskell and Robinson whose harsh critique of UK HE policy and its attempts to undermine traditional educational values with its uncompromising focus on employability go even further. These authors lament that, in their view, 'the new university' has been reduced to a place where individuals supposedly receive training in skills. They promote the idea that wisdom as traditionally promoted by liberal education may in fact stand at odds with a utilitarian focus of HE. Their work leaves no stone unturned in criticising the 'new managerial regime' in UK higher education and unsurprisingly questions the proliferation of courses in 'those new dubiously vocational subjects like Leisure and Tourism' (Maskell and Robinson, 2001:18).

Arguably then, the extent to which the debates around the purpose of higher education and the current focus on employability are considered beyond the confines of the academic community is a questionable matter. For some it would appear that HE managers all too willingly accept the brave new world of HE, where any attempt to query the economic imperative is met with incredulity, as though education for economic gain were akin to the laws of physics. This is confirmed by Holmes (2013:539):

> Whilst those who would wish to hold to a liberal-humanist view of higher education may lament this increasing focus on the role that higher education can and does have in enhancing post-graduation employment, there seems to be little doubting this as the current reality.

In light of the current employability discourse, and the high levels of youth unemployment, the calls for a re-orientation of HE policy away from this economic imperative may simply be the last-ditch flailing of a bygone era, one consigned to the annals of educational history. At present, the shift in the role of education from its liberal-humanist ideals to become but the handmaiden of industry is undeniable. This also has implications for the relationship between student and educational institution. Noting the tensions between student expectations and staff educational objectives, James and Beckett (cited in Baron and Corbin, 2012:766) observe that these tensions are being played out on a number of fronts, major and minor, and 'amount to an unplanned renegotiation of the higher education curriculum, driven by new student preferences and the willingness of students to exert these preferences', a point also recognised by Tarrant (2006).

It is of course easy to stand on the side-lines and bemoan this focus on employability, but the young person who seeks work may have very different and immediate concerns. The policymakers faced with disastrously high levels of youth unemployment likewise will have their own concerns, as will the tourism managers seeking to ensure the profitability of their enterprises. This is where the aforementioned notion of the philosophic practitioner (Tribe, 2002), itself drawing on earlier debates around the relationship between education and society (e.g. Schön, 1991), provides an attempt at compromise between seemingly countervailing forces. But even if there was agreement around the utilitarian notion of the purpose of education, this does not mean that what ensues in terms of policy objectives is appropriate to meet desired ends.

Employability skills

The dominance of the employability agenda should not detract from the fact that the concept of employability itself is swathed in a blanket of confusing definitions and terminology. Tymon (2013) suggests that three stakeholders, employers, higher education institutions and students, are present in the employability agenda, each with its own approach and understanding of the term which clearly complicates matters.

Perhaps the most fundamental problem with the concept of employability is its frequent reduction to a set of skills. The notion of skills that features so heavily in discussions around employability is incredibly ambiguous, but this has not prevented the use of the term by policymakers, employers and HE. As Atkins (1999) points out, terms such as enterprise, core, key, common, transferable and generic have all been used in different ways to describe skills. Cashian *et al.* (2015) nonetheless believe a consensus has emerged, in business schools at least, of what constitute employability skills.

The following list is taken from the CBI report (2009) *Future fit: preparing graduates for the world of work*:

- ☐ Team working
- ☐ Business and customer awareness
- ☐ Problem solving
- ☐ Communication and literacy
- ☐ Application and numeracy

☐ Application of information technology (now often replaced by 'digital literacy').

Admittedly, today, many definitions extend beyond skills and, as Harvey (2005) has suggested, there has been a move away from defining employability as a narrow set of skills. The skills discourse is still very much in evidence however, and the term has simply been extended to incorporate just about anything anyone wants it to comprise. If there ever was a fuzzy concept in HE, it is that of skills.

For Harvey (2005:13-14), a prolific contributor to the academic literature on employability, there are two fundamental aspects to graduate employability:

☐ The ability of a graduate to obtain a job, and then
☐ The ability to progress in that job.

This is also the definition provided by two further frequent contributors to the employability arena (Yorke and Knight, 2006:3) who suggest employability is:

> a set of achievements – skills, understandings and personal attributes – that make graduates more likely to gain employment and be successful in their chosen occupations, which benefits themselves, the workforce, the community and the economy.

The distinction between getting a job and then progressing in it is important in tourism and hospitality, where access to jobs is less of an issue than career development once employed.

Becoming employed

Staying momentarily with Harvey's (2005) first aspect of employability, the ability to obtain a job, this is very much something that educational institutions can assist with. This is about the ability to convince a prospective employer of one's suitability for a specific role. This takes the matching view of recruitment and selection (also called the 'right person' approach, Price *et al.*, 2007), which suggests that the organisation defines the characteristics and abilities it needs and then matches applicants against these characteristics and abilities, both personal and technical. This is the gold standard approach to recruitment and selection, and is evidently the approach accepted in much of the discourse surrounding employability and employer needs. According to this view, employability is a level playing field where applicants are selected based on merit. In reality of course, employability extends beyond the person and relates to social structures. Cashian *et al.* (2015:2),who review perspectives on employability, propose that class of degree and work experience aside, the third most crucial factor affecting a student's employability 'are a range of social and biographical factors which may impact on a student's initial success in the graduate labour market'.

While it is commendable of these authors to recognise the impact of social structures on career paths, the suggestion that social structures only play a role in a graduate's initial quest for success in the graduate labour market is plainly wrong. As was highlighted in the introduction, early employment experiences can have long-term implications. Despite the discourse around *protean* and *boundaryless* careers (see also next chapter), not having had a 'normal' career can place one at a distinct disadvantage in the labour market. In tourism, but in other sectors too, many jobs are not advertised openly. In many instances the mantra of 'who you know rather than what you know' still holds true. This latter point is possibly less applicable in tourism and hospitality than in other sectors such as finance, banking, PR and advertising although internal labour markets are generally regarded as weak in tourism (Riley, 1996; Baum, 2006), which includes informal and unspecific recruitment practices. The transition into work will be reviewed in more detail in the next chapter but the point to note here is that employability extends beyond personal agency. One's employability is determined by a host of factors, some of which are beyond the control of the individual or the educational institution that the individual has attended.

The rise in the requirement to undertake unpaid placements in sectors such as journalism and the media is further recent evidence of social structures determining employment outcomes and reinforcing existing social structures (Kimball, 2012). Tourism and hospitality are less affected by this, and are more meritocratic in this regard, thereby strengthening their appeal as an employment destination for many young people who do not have the social or financial capital to access graduate positions in other sectors.

Despite the acknowledgement that employability extends beyond finding employment, HE statistics focus largely on early graduate destinations in their attempts to demonstrate graduates' employability. Thus in the UK the Destination of Leavers from Higher Education survey administered by HESA asks graduates about their employment status six months after graduation, and in a further survey about their employment approximately 40 months after graduation. Some of these data are then presented on the UK government-approved Unistats website where prospective students are able to compare institutions by subject area, using ostensibly objective 'key information sets', including information on employment prospects. The six month survey presents data on salary and whether the job is 'professional or managerial'. This does a disservice to tourism and hospitality graduates given career paths in the sector that require hands-on practical experience before graduates progress into managerial, i.e. 'graduate' positions (see Table 4.1) and even here hands-on work is often required. What these HESA statistics further fail to disclose is the second facet of employability, career progression. The tourism and hospitality sector is often promoted on the basis of providing opportunities for rapid career progression. The only data provided relating to the later survey, i.e. after 40 months, is average salary. The benefit of focussing only on salary is its simplicity, but as a proxy for career opportunities or achievement of graduates it is a very crude measure. It reduces career progress only to a measure of earnings. The need for prospective students to have information to make informed career choices is important, but this information needs to encompass more than just earnings. Reducing career opportunities or progression solely to a measure of earnings disadvantages tourism where earnings relative to other sectors are low, but where the non-financial rewards can be equally if not more attractive.

Tymon's (2013) notion that employers have a different understanding of employability, that they focus on a different employability agenda to students and HE institutions is reflected in the common disappointment of employers with graduates' ability to 'hit the ground running', which is well documented (see also Chapter 4). The current employer perspective is seemingly one where the graduate is supposed to contribute to the company's bottom line almost from day one in the organisation. The apparent adjustment period required, i.e. the graduate's adjusting to the new organisation is, so Harvey (2005) maintains, a cost that graduate employers are no longer able or willing to bear. Harvey does not explain whence this sudden change comes from. A time did then presumably exist where it was accepted that a new employee would have time to adjust to the new organisational setting and where the organisation could cope with this transition/adaptation period. Harvey's description of the employer's approach to employability is uncritical and has profound implications, for it implies that it is not the employer's responsibility to train and develop their staff. Industry needs work-ready graduates and it is society's (policy makers and HE institutions') responsibility to provide them. Of course, this view sits comfortably with the instrumentalisation of education discourse, and indeed, it is integral to it.

The view that young people lack the necessary skills required to work in industry extends beyond those graduating from higher education and is certainly not new or confined to the UK. For example, Roan and Diamond (2003) describe a number of schemes the Australian Government undertook in the

1990s that sought to train young people in preparation for labour market entry. Roan and Diamond (2003) provide an example of the Australian Traineeship Scheme which targeted fifteen to nineteen-year-olds, lasted one year in most cases and provided an accredited qualification. This was followed by the New Apprenticeship Scheme in 1998. At the same time a number of vocational qualifications were introduced in government-sponsored vocational colleges. In developing countries, skills gaps are particularly acute, although this is frequently the result of individuals not engaging in education beyond primary school. A UNESCO (2015) report suggests that 20% of young people in developing countries fail to complete secondary school.

The role of employers in training

Placing the burden of education, or rather training, on the shoulders of higher education has not entirely escaped critical voices. Yorke (2006) suggests preparation of the 'oven-ready' graduate who needs no further training, who can hit the ground running and is therefore in a position to fulfil his/her role is too much to ask from education providers. The reason he provides for this is that some skills, certainly knowledge, is very context-specific. We should then expect:

> a discrepancy between what employers would ideally like (a graduate perfectly attuned to their needs) and what higher education can reasonably supply. The corollary is that the employer has to expect that the graduate will need to be inducted into the particular organisational culture and given the support to succeed. (Yorke, 2006:11)

Gracey and Kelly (2010) also place a stronger emphasis for smoothing the education to work transition on the shoulders of employers. The difficulties lie downstream (inside the labour market) rather than just upstream (inside the education and training system) although the latter is where much of the focus has been. Froy (2013) discusses this issue, noting that employers often have a short-term perspective when it comes to training, citing the example of apprenticeship schemes in Italy and France. In critiquing the over-reliance on employers to set the educational agenda, Wolf (2002) comments that while individual employers may have a perspective on what skills their particular workforce requires, they are as a whole, no better at determining skills needs than policy-makers or higher education institutions. This point has not escaped policy makers who have begun to take a more bottom-up, locally steered, and industry-specific approach to educational policy (Froy, 2013). The idea is to move away from a bureaucratic, centralised system, in other words.

A slightly different, and worrying, perspective relates not to the ability of young people to perform flawlessly, but to an inability to undertake relatively simple tasks (see for example the previously-mentioned YouGov survey, News UK 2013). According to the CBI and NUS (2011) there are a set of employability skills that all employers desire of graduates. But then the CBI and NUS (2011) propose that employability is about more than skills and also includes personal attributes, foremost of which is the notion of 'a positive attitude'. To these attributes is then added knowledge – not knowledge in the sense of information but the 'capability to apply maths for practical purposes and the ability to structure a piece of written work logically, with correct use of grammar and spelling' (CBI and NUS, 2011:11). While HE should further hone numerical and writing skills, one would imagine that someone who qualifies for higher education may already be sufficiently adept at applying (basic) maths for practical purposes and is able to write logically, adhering to basic grammatical and spelling conventions.

If not attuned to the needs of employers when entering HE, tourism and hospitality graduates when they leave HE should find it relatively easy to meet employers' needs. In the United Kingdom, the Quality Assurance Agency (QAA) subject benchmark statement for hospitality, sport, leisure and tourism on curriculum content cover a vast range of skills (in a narrow definition of what a skill is, i.e. not including personal attributes such as diligence, honesty, flexibility etc.). From being able to 'research and assess paradigms, theories, principles, concepts and factual information, and apply such skills in explaining and solving problems' to being able to 'recognise and respond to moral, ethical, sustainability and safety issues which directly pertain to the context of study including relevant legislation and professional codes of conduct' the tourism and hospitality graduate should in theory be more than adequately prepared for employment.

An additional perspective on employability is the organisational fit approach to recruitment, which focuses not so much on specific skills or knowledge but more on applicants having the right attitude or mind-set, which harks back to the CBI's notion of having a positive attitude. The underpinning idea here is that the individual might not have the expertise or skills required at time of organisational entry, but these can then be developed as long as the individual displays the right attitude. This appears to be a common approach in tourism, certainly at the more informal end of the employment spectrum. Even where recruitment and selection practices are more formal, there is frequently an emphasis on demonstrating personal attributes and generic skills rather than being able to undertake job-specific tasks. This is evident where applicants are required to have obtained a certain level of qualification, e.g. a degree, but further subject specificity is not mentioned. Drawing on Elias and Purcell's (2003) typology of graduate occupations, this would apply to many jobs in tourism which are neither traditional graduate occupations nor modern graduate occupations, but rather niche or new graduate occupations.

The contribution of young people to the achievement of organisational objectives

The academic and practitioner literature is replete with statements that point to the role human resources play in providing competitive advantage. For example, Band *et al.* (1994:22) offer: 'The ultimate competitive asset of any organisation is its people'. Intercontinental Hotels Group (IHG) corporate website explains the importance of people to its success as follows:

> We're a company which passionately believes that it's our people who have brought us to where we are today and our people that will help us grow. (IHG, 2015)

It is not unique in this regard, other global hotel chains do not fail to explain the importance of their staff to organisational success.

Specifically with regard to tourism, the link to competitive advantage is often associated with service quality/excellence, which again depends on people to deliver the required level of service (Lashley, 2001). Kusluvan *et al.*'s (2010) review of human resources management issues in the sector provides a useful discussion of the service quality-HRM link. The underlying premise with all of the above associations is outlined in one of the earliest foundations of what was later to become the resource-based view of organisational strategy, Penrose's (1959) acknowledgement that a firm is essentially a collection of resources. Even though subsequent authors in the field of strategic management (e.g. Andrews, 1971) reiterated the importance of a firm's resource position, much writing on strategy traditionally focussed on the product-market, i.e. environmental opportunities perspective (Wernerfelt, 1984). Interest in the resource-based view (RBV) of the firm and competitive advantage then re-emerged with papers by Barney (1991), Conner (1991) and Kogut and Zander (1992). Simultaneously in the field of employment there were a number of shifts in perspective from personnel to human resource management to strategic human resource management (SHRM). There is an evident link between the resource-based view of the firm and SHRM in that a refocussing on a firm's resources almost inevitably raises the standing of its employees as a key organisational resource. As Wright *et al.* (2001:702) explain:

> Growing acceptance of internal resources as sources of competitive advantage brought legitimacy to HR's assertion that people are strategically important to firm success…the integration of the resource-based view of the firm into the SHRM literature should surprise no one.

In the knowledge that human resources are key to providing competitive advantage to firms, we might say especially to the tourism firm via the notion of service quality, the immediate question is whether there are any characteristics of young people that provide an advantage for the firm? What follows is necessarily speculative, given the absence of research that addresses this issue. There is furthermore a very real danger of drawing inferences at the level of the individual based on (perceived) general traits in a population. We would strongly advise against this of course, but despite these caveats consider an exploration of this issue of considerable interest and thus it merits inclusion here.

According to Eurofound (2004) working conditions in hotels can require physical endurance. Many jobs in hospitality and restaurants entail long periods of standing (for women often in uncomfortable shoes), carrying, repetitive movements and working in painful positions. The European Agency for Safety and Health at Work (2008) emphasises both the high degree of youth employment in the sector as well as its physical demands. From a purely physical perspective young people may therefore have youth on their side when it comes to enduring these kind of working conditions. There exists research on the impact of age on fatigue but not, to the author's knowledge, in tourism. Winwood *et al.* (2006) looked at the relationship between age, domestic responsibilities (being partnered and having dependents), recovery from shiftwork-related fatigue and the evolution of maladaptive health outcomes among full-time working female nurses. The results suggest that the impact of age on fatigue is equivocal. Although the youngest cohort actually demonstrated the greatest amount of fatigue this could have been down to the older cohort working fewer multiple and night shifts. More generally, this paper's review of the literature on age and fatigue demonstrates the underlying complexity of factors. So, on the one hand family responsibilities, likely to be more prevalent in older populations rather than younger, might at first blush be associated with increased levels of chronic fatigue. However, the positive value of companionship has also been linked to lower levels of fatigue.

It was already outlined why young people and other segments of the population (females and migrants) are overrepresented in tourism employment. One of the explanations was their greater flexibility in terms of accepting irregular work patterns. The issue of zero-hours contracts is indicative of a growing desire for a flexible workforce. This quotation by Sean Wheeler, Area Director of Human Resources at the Dorchester Collection explains the move towards greater flexibility:

> On a positive note I think there will be a lot more requirements for flexibility in the workforce. Currently about ninety-five percent of our employees are full time permanent employees, but the business is changing quite significantly… so we do need a lot more flexibility in our workforce. That can be a positive thing because then we can go out to markets we are not necessarily focussing on at the moment, such as part-time workers, women returners, casuals, students. (cited in People 1st's *State of the Nation Report*, 2013)

Youth is generally regarded as a time of fewer commitments which may permit greater flexibility in relation to irregular work patterns although economic necessity can force people into jobs that do not necessarily suit them. There is increased demand for employee flexibility in relation to working patterns, evidenced not only in the above quotation by Sean Wheeler, but also by official statistics. The UK's Office for National Statistics (ONS, 2015) presents data that indicates that the number of people employed on a zero-hours contract in their main job was 697,000 for October to December 2014, representing 2.3% of all people in employment. In the same period in 2013, this was 1.9% of all people in employment (586,000). The difference could be down to more individuals recognising the term in 2014 than as a result of an actual change, however, this 19% increase does suggest that there has been a real increase in the number of people on zero-hours contracts. The same ONS press release suggests that people on zero-hours contracts are more likely to be women, in full-time education or working part-time, or young people (i.e. those aged under 25) or those aged 65 and over. Over half of employers in Accommodation and Food Services made some use of no guaranteed hours contracts in August 2014. These data underline the fact that youth employment in tourism is in large part affected by flexible working patterns.

It is frequently suggested that young people are more open to new ideas, have 'passion, determination, ambition and drive' as a government-sponsored website for Newfoundland and Labrador (Canada) suggests, continuing that young people:

☐ Bring new ideas and perspectives to the workplace;

☐ Are eager and willing to learn;

☐ Are enthusiastic, energetic and physically active;

☐ Are creative, adaptable, open-minded and learn quickly

☐ Not afraid of technology or change;

☐ Are a wealth of knowledge;

☐ And are comfortable in a diverse workplace (NL HR Manager, 2015).

This characterisation sits at odds with employers' views in relation to youth employability – one could say these two views sit at opposite ends of a spectrum. What the above description does provide though is a view into the potential of young employees.

Aesthetic labour is increasingly important to organisational success where the image or brand of a company needs to be represented, indeed embodied (Witz *et al.*, 2003), by employees as well as more traditionally by the fixtures and fittings of an establishment. Whereas the pros and cons of aesthetic labour with regard to working conditions can be debated (see Chapter 3, page 46), the aesthetics of service provision are becoming increasingly important. In Kusluvan *et al.*'s (2010:172) words:

> services are made tangible in the personality, appearance, attitudes, and behavior of the service provider; thus, employees become part of the product, represent the organization, and help to form the image of the organization.

There is undeniably an age factor associated with 'looking good and sounding right' as Nickson *et al.* (2005) call it. Nickson *et al.* explain further that companies employ people with certain capacities and attributes that favourably appeal to customers' visual or aural senses. Evidently then, in certain resorts, in certain restaurants, clubs and bars clientele expect to see staff that embody youth values (recognising that this is a broad notion). In equal manner, there will be other establishments where age might not be a barrier but certainly where the embodiment of youth culture and values are avoided. Age, while not a sufficient condition for certain forms of tourism employment, is then still a necessary condition.

References

Andrews, K. (1971) *The Concept of Corporate Strategy,* Homewood: Dow Jones-Irwin.

Atkins, M. J. (1999) Oven-ready and self-basting: taking stock of employability skills. *Teaching in Higher Education,* **4** (2), 267-280.

Autor, D. H., Katz, L. F. & Kearney, M. S. (2006) The polarization of the US labor market. *The American Economic Review,* **96** (2), 189-194.

Axelrod, P. D. (2002) *Values in Conflict: The University, the Marketplace and the Trials of Liberal Education,* Montreal: McGill-Queen's University Press.

Band, D. C., Scanlan, G. & Tustin, G. M. (1994) Beyond the bottom line: gainsharing and organizational development. *Personnel Review,* **23** (8), 17-32.

Barney, J. (1991) Firm resources and sustained competitive advantage. *Journal of Management,* **17** (1), 99-120.

Baron, P. & Corbin, L. (2012) Student engagement: Rhetoric and reality. *Higher Education Research and Development,* **31** (6), 759-772.

Baum, T. (2006) *Human Resource Management for Tourism Hospitality and Leisure. An international perspective.,* London: Thomson.

Bin Mohd Yusof, M. F. (2010) The issues of hospitality and tourism education in Malaysia. Available: umkeprints.umk.edu.my/397/1/Paper%203.pdf.

Brown, P., Lauder, H. & Ashton, D. (2011) *The Global Auction,* Oxford: Oxford University Press.

Browne Report (2011). *Securing a Sustainable Future for Higher Education.* London: Department for Business, Innovation and Skills.

Busby, G. & Fiedel, D. (2001) A contemporary review of tourism degrees in the United Kingdom. *Journal of Vocational Education and Training,* **53** (4), 501-522.

Cashian, P., Clarke, J. & Richardson, M. (2015). *Perspectives on: Employability is it time to move the employability debate on?* Chartered Association of Business Schools.

CBI & NUS (2011). *Working towards your future. Making the most of your time in higher education.* Confederation of British Industry and the National Union of Students.

Conner, K. (1991) A historical comparison of resource-based theory and five schools of thought within industrial organization economics: "Do we have a new theory of the firm?" *Journal of Management,* **17** (1), 121-154.

Cooper, C., Shepherd, R. & Westlake, J. (1994) *Tourism Hospitality Education*, Guildford: University of Surrey.

Cumming, J. (2010) Contextualised performance: reframing the skills debate in research education. *Studies in Higher Education*, **35** (4), 405-419.

Dearing, R. (1997). *National Committee of Inquiry into Higher Education. Higher Education in the Learning Society, Report of the National Committee*. Norwich: HMSO.

DFBIS. (2014) *Participation Rates in Higher Education 2006 to 2012*. Department for Business Innovation and Skills. Available: https://www.gov.uk/government/publications/participation-rates-in-higher-education-2006-to-2012 [Accessed 16.05.14].

Elias, P. & Purcell, K. (2003). *Research Paper No.1 - Measuring Change in the Graduate Labour Market*. Employment Research Services Unit, University of the West of England, & Warwick Institute for Employment Research.

Eurofound (2004). *EU Hotel and Restaurant Sector: Work and Employment Conditions*. Dublin: European Foundation for the Improvement of Living and Working Conditions.

European Agency for Safety and Health at Work (2008). Protecting workers in hotels, restaurants and catering. Available: https://osha.europa.eu/en/tools-and-publications/publications/reports/TE7007132ENC_horeca

Fidgeon, P. (2010) Tourism education and curriculum design: a time for consolidation and review? *Tourism Management*, **36** (1), 699-723.

Froy, F. (2013) Global policy developments towards industrial policy and skills: Skills for competitiveness and growth. *Oxford Review of Economic Policy*, **29** (2), 344-360.

Goos, M. & Manning, A. (2007) Lousy and lovely jobs: The rising polarization of work in Britain. *The Review of Economics and Statistics*, **89** (1), 118-133.

Gracey, S. & Kelly, S. (2010). *Changing the NEET Mindset: Achieving More Effective Transitions Between Education and Work*. London: LSN Centre for Innovation in Learning.

Harvey, L. (2005) Embedding and integrating employability. *New Directions for Institutional Research*, **2005** (128), 13-28.

Holmes, L. (2013) Competing perspectives on graduate employability: Possession, position or process? *Studies in Higher Education*, **38** (4), 538-554.

Hudson, S. (2005) North America, Airey, D. & Tribe, J. (eds.) *An International Handbook of Tourism Education*. Oxford: Elsevier.

Ibrahim, Abdul-Hamid (2007) Open Learning and Hospitality and Tourism Education: Perspectives in Malaysia, http://asiapacific-odl.oum.edu.my/C33/F552.doc

IHG (2015), Who is IHG? Available: http://careers.ihg.com/about-ihg [Accessed 14.06.15]

Jackson, D. (2009) Profiling industry-relevant management graduate competencies: The need for a fresh approach. *International Journal of Management Education,* **8 (**1), 85-98.

Kimball, A. (2012). Who gets to be a journalist if the route in depends on money and class? *The Guardian*, 5th September 2012.

Knowles, T., Teixeira, R. M. & Egan, D. (2003) Tourism and hospitality education in Brazil and the UK: A Comparison. *International Journal of Contemporary Hospitality Management,* **15 (**1), 45-51.

Kogut, B. & Zander, U. (1992) Knowledge of the firm, combinative capabilities, and the replication of technology. *Organization Science,* **3 (**3), 383-397.

Kreber, C. (2006) Setting the context: The climate of university teaching and learning. *New Directions for Higher Education,* **2006 (**133), 5-11.

Kusluvan, S., Kusluvan, Z., Ilhan, I. & Lutfi, B. (2010) The human dimension: A review of human resources management issues in the tourism and hospitality industry. *Cornell Hospitality Quarterly,* **51 (**2), 171-214.

Lashley, C. (2001) *Strategies for Service Excellence,* Oxford: Elsevier.

Leal, S. (2004). Is tourism education in Brazil sustainable? *In:* Tribe, J. & Wickens, E. (eds.) *Critical Issues in Tourism Education.* Great Missenden: Association for Tourism in Higher Education.

Leitch, S. (2006). *Prosperity for all in the global economy : world class skills : final report.* London: Her Majesty's Treasury.

Lyotard, J.-F. (1984) *The Postmodern Condition: A Report on Knowledge,* Manchester: Manchester University Press.

Maskell, D. & Robinson, I. (2001) *The New Idea of a University,* London: Haven Books.

McKercher, B. (2002) The future of tourism education: An Australian scenario? *Tourism and Hospitality Research,* **3 (**3), 199-210.

Meyer, J. (1977) The effects of education as an institution. *American Journal of Sociology,* **83 (**1), 55-77.

Mishra, L. & Rana, V. (2012) Undergraduate hospitality education and its challenges: Special reference to Uttarakhand. *International Journal of Basic and Advanced Research,* **1 (**1), 6-10.

Nickson, D., Warhurst, C. & Dutton, E. (2005) The importance of attitude and appearance in the service encounter in retail and hospitality. *Managing Service Quality,* **15 (**2), 195-208.

NL HR Manager (2015) *The Benefits of Hiring Youth.* Available: www.nlhrmanager.ca/index.php?option=com_content&view=article&id=85&Itemid=88 [Accessed 14.06.15].

OECD (2008). *Growing Unequal? Income Distribution and Poverty in OECD Countries*. Paris: OECD

ONS (2012). *Graduates in the Labour Market, 2012*. Office of National Statistics. Available: http://www.ons.gov.uk/ons/dcp171776_259049.pdf [Accessed 14.06.15].

ONS (2015) *Contracts with No Guaranteed Hours, Zero Hour Contracts, 2014.* Office of National Statistics. Available: http://www.ons.gov.uk/ons/rel/lmac/contracts-with-no-guaranteed-hours/zero-hour-contracts--2014/index.html [Accessed 14.06.15].

Payne, J. & Keep, E. (2011). One Step Forward, Two Steps Back? Skills Policy in England under the Coalition Government. *SKOPE Research Paper No. 102*. Cardiff: SKOPE, Cardiff University.

Penrose, E. (1959) *The Theory of the Growth of the Firm,* Oxford: Oxford University Press.

People 1st (2013). *State of the Nation Report 2013*. An analysis of labour market trends, skills, education and training within the UK hospitality and tourism industries. Uxbridge: People 1st.

Price, A. (2007) *Human Resource Management in a Business Context,* London: Thomson Learning.

Price, R., Thornton, S. & Nelson, S. (2007). *The Social Cost of Carbon and the Shadow Price of Carbon: What They are, and How to Use Them in Economic Appraisal in The UK*. Available: https://www.gov.uk/government/uploads/system/uploads/attachment_data/file/243825/background.pdf London: DEFRA.

Ramcharan, R. (2004) Higher or Basic Education? The Composition of Human Capital and Economic Development. *IMF Staff Papers,* **51 (**2), 309-326.

Riley, M. (1996) *Human Resource Management in the Hospitality and Tourism Industry,* Oxford: Butterworth-Heinemann.

Roan, A. & Diamond, C. (2003) Starting out: The quality of working life of young workers in the retail and hospitality Industries in Australia. *International Journal of Employment Studies,* **11** (2), 91-119.

Roney, S. A. & Oztin, P. (2007) Career perceptions of undergraduate tourism students: A case study in Turkey. *Journal of Hospitality, Leisure, Sport and Tourism Education,* **6** (1).

Schön, D. (1991) *The Reflective Practitioner. How professionals think in action.* Aldershot: Ashgate.

Sharma, Y. (2014). Rising unemployment – Are there too many graduates? University World News. Available: http://www.universityworldnews.com/article.php?story=20140213153927383

Tarrant, J. (2006) Teaching time-savvy Law students. *James Cook University Law Review,* **13** 64-80.

The Economist (2015). The whole world is going to university. *The Economist.*

Tribe, J. (2002) The philosophic practitioner. *Annals of Tourism Research,* **29** (2), 338-357.

Tymon, A. (2013) The student perspective on employability. *Studies in Higher Education,* **38** (6), 841-856.

UNESCO (2015). *Education for All. Achievements and Challenges.* Paris: United Nations Educational, Scientific and Cultural Organization.

Walmsley, A. (2012). *Tourism Intelligence Monitor.* ATHE Report on Tourism Higher Education in the UK, 2012.

Wang, X. (2008) *Is tourism education meeting the needs of the tourism industry? An Australian case study,* University of Canberra.

Wernerfelt, B. (1984) A resource-based view of the firm. *Strategic Management Journal,* **5** (2), 171-180.

Wilson, A. N. (2014) A university education is priceless. *The Telegraph.* Available: http://www.telegraph.co.uk/education/universityeducation/10872696/A-N-Wilson-A-university-education-is-priceless.html [Accessed 17.07.14].

Winwood, P., Winewood, A. & Lushington, K. (2006) Work-related fatigue and recovery: the contribution of age, domestic responsibilities and shiftwork. *Journal of Advanced Nursing,* **56** (4), 438-449.

Witz, A., Warhust, C. & Nickson, D. (2003) The labour of aesthetics and the aesthetics of organization. *Organization* **10** (1), 33-54.

Wolf, A. (2002) *Does Education Matter? Myths about Education and Economic Growth,* London: Penguin.

Wolf, A. (2011). *Review of Vocational Education. The Wolf Report.* Department for Education and Department for Business, Innovation and Skills.

Wright, P., Dunford, B. & Snell, S. (2001) Human resources and the resource based view of the firm. *Journal of Management,* **27** (6), 701-721.

Yorke, M. (2006). *Employability in higher education: what it is – what it is not.* Learning and Employability, Series One. York: The Higher Education Academy.

Yorke, M. & Knight, P. (2006). *Embedding employability into the curriculum.* Learning and Employability, Series One. York: Higher Education Academy.

6 The Education to Work Transition

This chapter discusses a number of perspectives on the transition to work, including a review of the increasingly important notion of self-employment. It begins by outlining recent discussions around the notion of career. It then reviews a selection of dominant theories relating to career decision-making and development, using these to improve understanding of transition from education to work in tourism and hospitality. It discusses attitudes towards work among youth as well as early work and placement experiences and how these facilitate or hinder the transition into tourism employment. The chapter closes by looking at the role of SMEs and graduate entrepreneurship as relatively unexplored but important destinations for graduate (self) employment.

The importance of a successful transition

The education to work transition, sometimes casually referred to as 'from learning to earning', constitutes a major step for young individuals on their journey into adulthood. Successfully taking this step used to be taken for granted for the majority of young people. Today however, and not just because of the recent economic turmoil, this step provides a challenging task for many. In what Bendit and Miranda (2015:183), with reference to Argentina, call 'post-modern contexts', that is economic modernisation processes, labour market restructuring and the downscaling of social policies, the challenges relating to the transition to adulthood is an issue affecting many modern economies. The transition into work is regarded as critical by policy makers in addressing a wider set of problems confronting young people (Bynner, 2001). Because of the importance of work in addressing a range of social problems, facilitating successful transitions into employment is a policy priority.

Difficulties in the transition into work effect young people at all levels, not just those with low educational attainment. In the UK in 2012, for example, one in five new graduates, i.e. those who graduated within two years, available for work in the UK were unemployed (ONS, 2012). Sharma (2014) with reference to East Asian economies highlights rising levels of graduate unemployment across a number of nations, from South Korea, to Singapore and China. The problem is not confined to advanced economies. In Nigeria it is estimated that graduates of tertiary education institutions make up about 20% of youth unemployment and often remain unemployed for upward of five years after graduation (Akande, 2014).

The meaning of 'career'

'Perhaps the primary issue in the study of career is, what we do mean by career?' This question, as posed by Herr (1990:1), signals that the study of careers is anything but uncontested. Some commentators, including researchers in tourism and hospitality, have tried to provide relatively value-free, 'factual' definitions of career. Thus Riley and Ladkin (1994) suggest that, at its simplest, a career can be regarded as a series of jobs arranged in a sequence over time. Based on this definition, most people who work will have a career, and it does not matter what kind of jobs they are, how many jobs the individual has held, how long they were held for, or whether progress in terms of skills, salary and prestige played a part. In comparison to what Collin (1998) regards as the most frequently cited definition of career: 'a succession of related jobs, arranged in a hierarchy of prestige, through which persons move in an ordered, predictable sequence' (Wilensky, 1960:554) we can see Riley and Ladkin's (1994) attempts at democratising the concept of career, with a move from the view that only certain people have careers (Collin, 2001), i.e. those with certain types of jobs, who demonstrate progression along a predetermined career path. Riley and Ladkin's (1994) neutral perspective is mirrored by Arthur, Hall and Lawrence (1989:8) who define career as 'the evolving sequence of a person's work experience over time' whereby it is recognised that as an experience, careers are inherently subjective. The same sequence of identical jobs may mean progress to one person and failure to another. It is simply not possible to provide a meaningful definition of career without straying into the realm of values. It is worthwhile in this regard to focus in more depth on Collin's (2001) work because one of the primary concerns in relation to youth employment and the youth labour market relates to the extent to which graduates find jobs or whether they find careers. Not only is this then a question of 'to be in employment or not to be in employment', but 'to have a career or not to have a career'.

Returning to Riley and Ladkin's (1994) definition of career, it reflects certain assumptions about the human condition in post-modernity. A traditional notion of career may include the idea of progress, linearity, focus and masculinity (Collin, 2001). An analogy is made here by Collin (2001) to the literary notion of the Homeric epic with its singularity of focus and unified world view, in contrast to the modern notion of career, open to numerous interpretations and therefore likened to a novel. Based on Collin's (2001) distinction, the traditional idea of having a career would not apply to many young people employed in tourism, and certainly not to those moving in and out of the sector in jobs where there is limited or no progression.

A change in the meaning of career in modern societies from continuous employment in one organization, underpinned by the image of a ladder (Sennett, 1998), or corporate pyramid (Hall, 1996) and by the individual's subordination to the needs of the organization (Whyte, 1956) is well documented, most notably in concepts such as the 'boundaryless career' (Arthur and Rousseau, 1996) or the 'protean career' (Hall, 1996). For Hall, the careers of the 21st Century will be driven by the person, not by the organization, and will furthermore require reinvention from time to time. Hall presents a convincing case that a changing organisational environment leaves the individual with a greater need to take control of their career development:

> The new career contract is not a pact with the organization; it is an agreement with one's self and one's work. (Hall, 1996:10)

This was in fact also reflected in a UK study of business leaders' attitudes towards graduate employment, where it was argued that graduates were more interested in what the organization could do for them, rather than what they could do for the organization (News UK, 2013).

Littleton, Arthur and Rousseau's (2000:101) discussion around the future of the boundaryless career makes the same point:

> The new environment suggests a shift from pre-ordained and linear development to perpetually changing career paths and possibilities.

Where Hall (1996) nonetheless recognises that much writing on these new careers is overdone, something that appears to be accepted also by Littleton *et al.* (2000:101) in that many individuals 'never really played by the traditional rules anyway', there is also the assumption that in the future the vast major-ity of careers will be boundaryless. The absence of boundaries is not solely an objective, i.e. physical, issue. Of the six meanings of the boundaryless career laid out in their work (Arthur and Rousseau, 1996) only two are physical, the others psychological (e.g. rejecting existing career opportunities for personal or family reasons, or careers that draw validation – and marketability – from outside the present employer). Sullivan and Arthur (2006) conclude that the majority of empirical studies have focussed on the physical aspects of the boundaryless career, rather than on the psychological, but that commentators should not neglect the psychological dimension. The distinction is certainly one that may usefully be considered in light of youth employment in tourism.

We know, for example, that job mobility in tourism is higher for young people than for other age groups and to add to this, job mobility in tourism is itself high. On the face of it then the notion of the boundaryless career seems very applicable to youth employment in tourism. The salient issue is however whether this physical state of flux in young people's careers is matched by a psychological change in career orientation. Sullivan and Arthur (2006:23) pro-pose a two-by-two matrix along physical and psychological dimensions that serves to illustrate different combinations of both. They provide furthermore two examples of hospitality employment, which they map onto this matrix, and these are worth citing. First is Colin, a young individual 'bent on seeing the world', who offers his skills as a waiter or bartender in a series of jobs that provide the opportunity to travel. The second is Karl, a chef who works his way through a series of jobs, gaining additional experience which ultimately leads to setting up his own business. Colin is held up as an example of a high physical-low psychological boundaryess career, whereas Karl's is a high physical-high psychological boundaryless career. What is neglected in this discussion is the extent to which the individual actually desires, or at least accepts, the ongoing flux, which for some commentators is actually the meaning of psychological mobility (Marler et al., 2002). Although both Colin and Karl do accept it, there may be many young people in tourism employment who would prefer a career in a more traditional sense. Constantly moving into and out of jobs may physi-cally be equated with a boundaryless career and yet not be what is ultimately desired.

Career decision-making and development

There are many controversies surrounding the nature of career decision-making. Before we seek to explore how key career development theories may be applied to youth employment in tourism it is worth initially drawing attention to one of the great dilemmas of career decision-making: the role rationality plays in the process. It seems that most studies in tourism which look at student/graduate careers in a broad sense do so from the perspective of recent graduates being rational decision-makers. At least lists of tourism students' career preferences imply that somehow these preferences are critical to their career decision-making. While this may, at first glance, appear to be a reasonable assumption to make, literature on career decisions provides grounds to question it.

The UK graduate employment website Propects (www.prospects.ac.uk) suggests 'Choosing a career is the most important part of any job search'. But this statement is prescriptive, and it does not conform to how the majority of young people make career decisions. Many graduates do not systematically choose a career but instead go for jobs that are available at a particular time and place. The idea that individuals in general, particularly young people and recent graduates, make career decisions according to some long-term career plan is not a given. It is a traditional view of career decision-making, but one that falls short of describing reality (Hodkinson, 2008).

Historically a choice for a career meant a choice for a particular occupation and it is probably the case that for many people this aligns with their understanding of what a career is. Ginsberg *et al.* (1951:3) suggested:

> In modern society practically every individual, surely every male and an increasing number of females, must choose an occupation. In fact, most individuals confront the problem at least twice: once for themselves, and again, as parents, for their children.

This view of career decision-making begins with a decision for a particular occupation. Some individuals clearly still make occupational decisions and it would be a gross oversimplification to suggest that the meaning of career and allied to this the meaning of early career decision-making, have changed so much that there is no common ground between theories of career developed in the 1950s and those that have been offered more recently. However, occupational structures have changed considerably in modern times and many of the jobs that exist today do not conform to what might be regarded as an occupation ('occupation' is used here as meaning more skilled trade than simply a job). Thus when Ginsberg *et al.* (1951) wrote about individuals having to make occupational choices they were not presumably writing about the call centre workers who make up 3% of the UK and US workforces.

The recognition of the limits of rationality in decision-making has generated a burgeoning literature in behavioural economics which marries the insights from psychology with traditional economics. Behavioural economics provides a major critique of classical economic theory and its notion of the rationality underpinning decision-making (Wilkinson, 2008). Parsons (1909) wrote of 'true reasoning' as the mechanism that results in a career decision. Just what this true reasoning entails is not obvious but it is recognised today that the purely rational models of career decision-making are normative rather than descriptive. They outline how an individual should go about making a rational decision as opposed to how decisions are actually made.

A study that combines both rational and intuitive elements in the career decision-making process, thereby moving beyond a simplistic either/or perspective of career decision-making, is offered by Krieshok *et al.* (2009). Rather than throwing the proverbial baby out with the bathwater, these authors offer a perspective on career decision-making that acknowledges that rationality does still play a role but that it is just one element of career decision-making. Krieshof *et al.* describe two approaches to career decision-making:

☐ System 1 is 'habitual, implicit, associative and heuristic, often emotionally charged'

☐ System 2 is typically 'deliberate, explicit, deterministic, systematic, and not generally subject to emotion' (Krieshof *et al.* 2009:278).

Career decision-making draws on both, with individuals placing different emphases on one system or the other.

The shortcomings of a purely rational approach to career decision-making, in describing how career decisions in tourism are made, has received some, albeit limited, attention in the literature on tourism careers. In fact, more generally little research exists on how tourism and hospitality students actually make career decisions (Chuang and Dellmann-Jenkins, 2010, Kim *et al.*, 2010). Kusluvan and Kusluvan (2000) established a more intuitive approach to career decision-making for undergraduate students in Turkey. Walmsley (2012a), who looked at pathways into tourism higher education, described four such paths that demonstrated a decision was made at different times in individuals' career paths and with varying degrees of forethought. Some decisions were clearly considered, others may best be described as spur-of-the-moment decisions. To illustrate, some participants in the study were not prepared for the impending career decision as they were nearing the end of secondary education. This led to a hasty career decision then being made both in relation to whether to attend HE and, indeed, what to study. In such situations prospective students may make career decisions based on very limited information, and in a manner that is more intuitive than rational.

The career decision-making of tourism students reflects therefore a range of further difficulties relating to career decision-making which are outlined by Gati *et al.* (1996). Gati *et al.* provide an initial distinction of a) a lack of readiness and b) a lack of information (or inconsistent information). It would go beyond the scope of this text to explore the difficulties that Gati *et al.* describe in more detail, and indeed it would be difficult to relate these issues to tourism because there is scant literature in tourism that draws on it. Largely, the investigations of tourism and hospitality students' career decision-making has been a-theoretical. This does provide avenues for further research and, using Gati *et al.*'s framework one may query the extent of tourism students' preparedness for career decision-making, as well as the extent of labour market knowledge.

Our attention now turns to the notion of career development. Although sometimes both career decision-making and career development are used synonymously, the use of the term 'career development' in the literature suggests a more long-term orientated perspective, career development being the outcome of multiple individual career decisions. According to Collin (1998) the North American approach to the study of careers has largely taken a psychological perspective, whereas in the UK and Europe societal influences on careers have stood to the fore, thereby demonstrating her point that:

> Career arises from the interaction of individuals with organisations and society. (Collin, 1998:143)

Indeed, at a most fundamental level, human behaviour results from person-environment interaction (Lewin, 1951) and so it is not too surprising that career theorists have developed their approaches to understanding career development on this basis. In fact, although theories of career development tend to either be more psychological (individual traits) or sociological in orientation (influence of social structures and institutions) predominant career theories do not entirely neglect either perspective.

Which are the dominant theories of career development is debatable, although Holland's theory of vocational personalities in work environments and Super's career development theory would probably be included, according to most commentators. Leung adds work adjustment theory, Gottfredson's theory of circumscription and compromise and social cognitive career theory to these in his list of the 'big five career theories' (Leung, 2008). These theories have all, as Leung points out, been developed by North American scholars and as such there is more of an individual orientation contained within them, as opposed to a focus on societal influences as we might find in the European literature (Collin, 1998).

Despite numerous studies on tourism and hospitality students' career preferences and early career development, very few have availed themselves of the theoretical foundations offered by these that may help us better understand and make sense of the transitions into youth employment and its characteristics. A summary of these theories, along with tourism-related examples, will be provided to demonstrate their relevance to youth employment in tourism.

The theory of work adjustment

The theory of work adjustment, seeks to explain career outcomes such as satisfaction and tenure on the basis of person-environment correspondence. Where individual and organisational needs overlap, and importantly where subsequently expectations are met, satisfaction and tenure increases. Neither the individual, nor the environment (organisation) are fixed entities, hence the individual and to a lesser extent the organisation can adjust in an attempt to achieve greater levels of correspondence. The individual may not have the skills required by the employer, leading to the need to adjust if a greater degree of person-environment correspondence is to be achieved. Thus the individual can attempt to develop the required skills in a number of formal (e.g. training) or informal (e.g. observation of work practices) ways. Incongruence between employer and employee can also relate to work attitudes. Here the individual who does not demonstrate sufficient commitment to a job can either increase levels of commitment or accept incongruity between person and organisational requirements. Whether the employer would then adjust their expectations is another matter, of course, and will at least to a degree depend on labour market conditions. As we have seen above (Chapter 5) employers frequently complain about the lack of skills in the graduate population which in terms of the theory of work adjustment would be interpreted as a lack of person-environment correspondence. Although the prevailing discourse seems to suggest that the education system is in deficit in not providing work-ready graduates, and the obvious solution appears to be adjustments to the education system, the theory of work adjustment reminds us that adjustment can take place on both sides. To an extent this happens via placements or internships but a closer engagement between employers and the education system could prove beneficial in this regard.

The theory of vocational personalities in work environments

Holland's theory of vocational personalities reflects strongly the North American approach to understanding vocational behaviour and career development, with its focus on personality traits or types. Parsons (1909), who is often regarded as having laid the foundations for modern career guidance (Brown, 2002), stipulated that choosing a vocation involved three steps:

1 being aware of one's interests and abilities,

2 understanding the requirements of different jobs,

3 and finally 'true reasoning' between these first two.

Holland similarly postulates that career interests reflect personality types of which six career types exist:

☐ Realistic (R)

☐ Investigative (I)

☐ Artistic (A)

☐ Social (S)

☐ Enterprising (E)

☐ Conventional (C).

Individuals can adopt more than one type but usually there is a primary type and two secondary types, i.e. people are characterised by three letter combinations from the six types. Vocational environments can likewise be separated into different types. Where there exists a high degree of congruence between career interest type and vocational environment type job satisfaction and stability are likely to be higher. In this regard there are many similarities between the theory of work adjustment and Holland's theory of vocational personalities. A possible research avenue could be to view the extent to which individuals working in tourism belong to a specific type. One may surmise that if many jobs require people skills, individuals with at least a primary type S (Social) might frequently be found working in the sector. A major problem with this type of trait approach to careers is its inability to take into account changes in people and work environments which makes matching unrealistic (Hodkinson, 1998).

Career development theory

Super's theory of career development (originally 1953) further developed by Savickas (2002) explains career development in the context of the development of an individual's self-concept. For Super, career development can be regarded as the individual's progression through a number of career development phases:

☐ Growth

☐ Exploration

☐ Establishment

☐ Maintenance

☐ Disengagement.

Whereas Super's original theory laid more emphasis on the personal construct theory, Savickas' (2002) theory placed more emphasis on the development of vocational self-concepts as determined by the complex interplay of person and environment. Although vocational self-concept should become more stable through the course of a career, it is not a static entity (Leung, 2008). Indeed, if the notions of boundaryless and protean careers are valid then vocational self-concepts are likely to be more fluid than ever before as individuals move from one form of employment to another. Super's understanding of career development phases can be quite instructive in making sense of fickle and fluctuating career aspirations of young people. They are in a position where self-concepts are still being developed (at least more so than in later years), in a period of exploration and therefore one should not be all too surprised when tourism students' interest in careers in the sector wax and wane (see also Walmsley *et al.*, 2012).

The theory of circumscription and compromise

Gottfredson's (1981, 2002) theory of circumscription and compromise is, relatively speaking, a new theory of career development. It also emphasises the interplay of person and environmental factors. According to her theory, individuals first circumscribe possible career options (occupations) that match their vocational self-concepts, before then compromising in terms of personal proclivities and abilities, labour market circumstances and other factors that prevent the uptake of their desired occupational choice. The process of circumscription is influenced by person and environmental influences, e.g. occupational prestige and personal preferences. Occupations are not value-neutral but bound up in meaning fostered by society and social institutions. There is a clear relationship here to discussions around the prestige associated with work in tourism (or, the lack of it; see also Chapter 4). The effect of negative attitudes towards tourism and their impact on seeking tourism employment are explained in part by Gottfreson's theory.

The social cognitive career theory

The fifth and last of the key career theories expounded by Leung (2008) is social cognitive career theory (SCCT). This was initially presented by Lent *et al.* (1994) and is based on the work around Bandura's (1986) social cognitive theory. Self-efficacy beliefs, 'people's judgement of their capabilities to organise and execute courses of action required to attain designated types of performances' (Bandura, 1986:391), outcome expectations and goals, lie at the heart of social cognitive career theory's attempts to explain the development of career interest, choice and performance. Self-efficacy beliefs are in part derived from personal experience, which is the behaviour one has engaged in. This behavioural dimension provides a novelty to the person-environment interaction, where behaviour is regarded solely as a by-product rather than as a constituent element (Brown and Scase, 1994). Bandura (1986) terms this 'triadic-reciprocality'. Within youth employment in tourism, social cognitive career theory provides a theoretical explanation for what is often observed, specifically in relation to young people's early work experience in the sector, and the consequent development of self-efficacy beliefs. Within Walmsley's (2012a) four pathways into tourism higher education, one pathway highlighted the critical role early work experiences play in providing individuals with greater levels of confidence and self-efficacy beliefs. Other studies in tourism that have looked at the role of placements/internships equally find growth in confidence a key outcome (see page 157). As many young people's early work experiences are in tourism and especially hospitality, if these experiences are positive, this may positively impact levels of confidence and self-efficacy beliefs. SCCT helps explain how this then directs individuals to pursue careers in tourism, including opting to study tourism in further or higher education.

Changing attitudes to employment and career

Uncertainty is a condition of modern, globalised, society. In the past social norms laid down clearer guidelines about the 'right' way to direct one's life (Guichard *et al.*, 2012), today there is more freedom, more choice, but greater uncertainty. The complexity and fluidity of modern societies (Sennett, 1998; Bauman, 2000; Giddens, 1991) is reflected in the world of work. The notions of protean or boundaryless careers (Arthur and Rousseau, 1996; Hall, 1996) are, as we have seen, now regularly encountered in the careers literature, pertaining to the flexible nature of modern careers and the need for individuals to define their own career paths. Occupation as a clear identity marker is being challenged by the notion of individuals having to reinvent themselves in relation to their work (Heggli *et al.*, 2013).

For career decision-making, and consequently development, having too many options can pose a dilemma. Schmitt-Roedermund and Silbereisen (1998) compared East German and West German youth's career decision-making just after German reunification in 1991. The results showed that the educational system played a much greater role in channelling career paths for the East German cohort. The study also drew attention to adolescents' restricted career opportunities in East Germany. As a consequence, these young people had higher levels of career maturity, and were better prepared for making career decisions. The dynamic labour markets in modern societies by contrast have resulted in a far more difficult career decision-making context. Thinking about graduate occupations for example, Elias and Purcell (2004) add three additional graduate occupations (modern, new and niche) to traditional graduate occupations. The world of work is more complex, offers many opportunities (for some) and yet is also extremely challenging to youth.

In this more fluid world Generation Y individuals (also known as the dot-coms, bull market babies, twixters and millennials) have higher expectations of employment in terms or pay, working conditions and progression than previous generations (e.g.Oliver, 2006)[1]. To add to the more demanding nature of Generation Y's attitudes towards employment, according to Kerslake (2005) they can be loyal, subject to the achievement of personal goals. If these are not met they will simply move on. These individuals 'have by necessity embraced constant change and adaptability as a way of life' (Kerslake, 2005:45). In contrast with Kerslake however, the world is no longer this generation's oyster, at least not for many who continue to face high levels of unemployment, even those with higher level skills and degrees. As the earlier comments by Noreena Hertz (see page 62) suggest, Generation K's attitudes have changed again. No longer the 'yes we can' generation, they are racked by fears, by the precarious nature of the economy, by the fear of threats from terrorism and the fear of not succeeding in their chosen careers.

Generation Y was also described in the WTTC (2013) study of undergraduate perceptions of tourism employment, which was then backed up by a survey of more than 2,500 graduates across the UK, USA and China. One of the key

---

1   There is no universal agreement as to the precise begin and end points of Generation Y but according to Barron (2007), who has researched this issue in hospitality, it is those born between 1977 and 1994, i.e. who were/will be in their youth (16-24) between 1996 and 2018.

outcomes of this study was WTTC's (2013:13) insight that:

> the personality of someone who seems naturally attracted to the sector sees success defined by factors such as work-life balance, international opportunities, travel and good benefits... For those who are driven by more traditional approach to career and are attracted to messages promoting financial returns or achieving senior leadership positions, Travel and Tourism performs less well.

If this is true, then Generation Y may be more attuned to careers in tourism than the preceding generation.

There are sources that query the extent of changes in attitudes towards careers. Leading on from the fears of Generation K, job security, especially in tough economic conditions, is still important. In Kim *et al.*'s (2010) study of hospitality students, job security was the second most important out of a list of eight job attributes. Table 6.1 compares a study from 1987 with a more recent study published in 2012. Both studies sought to document and rank factors that tourism students'/recent graduates' considered important in employment.

Table 6.1: Factors playing a role in tourism students'/graduates' career decision-making

Rank	Blumenfeld, Kent, Shock, and Jourdan (1987)	Richardson and Butler (2012) *top 10 (out of 20)*
1	Type of work	An enjoyable job
2	Advancement opportunities	A pleasant working environment
3	Company reputation	Good promotion prospects
4	Salary	High earnings over length of career
5	Job security	A secure job (=5)
6	Hours of Work	Offers training opportunities (=5)
7	Benefits	A job that gives responsibility
8	Working conditions	Job mobility (ease of getting job elsewhere)
9	Nature of co-workers	Transferable skills
10	Nature of supervisors	Good starting salary

From the above comparison in Table 6.1, we can still see many similarities between the two groups despite the twenty-five year gap. Job security was placed in equal fifth position which contrasts with much of the career literature that emphasises increased job mobility. Earnings are regarded as important although starting salary was not regarded as that important by the 2012 group. Opportunities for career advancement are more important than earnings for both groups. The nature of the work features in first place for both groups. A difference that is discernible is the latter (2012) cohort's concern for working conditions, something that was less pronounced in the earlier cohort. Whether tourism and hospitality students are driven more by extrinsic or intrinsic rewards is unclear. Chuang and Dellmann-Jenkins (2010), who have researched this with a sample of students from the USA, suggest it is more the intrinsic rewards that lead people to seek hospitality employment, whereas in another US study (Kim *et al.*, 2010) it is extrinsic rewards that hold sway over career intentions and decisions. The fact is, it is simply very difficult to make robust generalisation across vast swathes of tourism and hospitality students. Trying to generalise to tourism and hospitality students in one country seems difficult enough, let alone doing so on a global scale.

Early work experiences

It may seem peculiar to focus on early work experiences as a separate item in a book on youth employment; after all, all of youth employment may be regarded as forming part of an individual's early work experience. However, even within the relatively short period of youth, individuals go through a career development process and here the earliest work experiences, such as those represented by work placements, and part-time work while still at school or in higher education, may have enormous repercussions for an individual's long term career. Sometimes these early work experiences set the trajectory upon which careers are then founded, even if young people are not aware of this at the time. According to the stepping stone hypothesis, early work experiences serve as a crucial first step into the world of work, and tourism, with its low entry barriers, can be very useful in this regard (Ryan, 1995).

Early work experiences may reach back into childhood. The term 'child labour' has pejorative connotations as pointed out by the ILO (undated), where it is defined as work that:

> deprives children of their childhood, their potential and their dignity, and that is harmful to physical and mental development.

The ILO also points out though that not all work undertaken by children is child labour. Helping parents, or assisting the family business is not necessarily child labour as defined above, as long as it is not harmful to the child's physical or mental development. Whether work can be classified as child labour or not will depend on the type of work, its duration and the context within which the work is performed as well as individual countries' objectives (ILO; as above).

For our purposes we will only focus on early work experiences insofar as they relate to youth, defined as 15-24 years of age. Thus, although it is quite possible, indeed probable, that the earliest work experiences for many young people employed in tourism and hospitality occurred while they were children, this remains outside the scope of this text.

Barron and Maxwell (1993), with reference to hospitality students in Scotland, claimed that the vast majority had no experience of working in the hospitality sector. The idea that the majority of students have no experience working in hospitality may still hold true, but there are today many students that have at least had some work experience. Moreau and Leathwood (2006) cite a number of studies that relate to the uptake of term-time work in the UK. Taking a chronological perspective, they highlight Ford *et al.* (1995) who surveyed second year students at four universities and reported that 30% of students had at some point held a part-time job during term-time. Leonard's (1995) study of Queens University Belfast suggested 46% of students were working during term-time and James *et al.* (2010:49 cited in Baron and Corbin, 2012) report that 61% of full-time first-year students were in paid work in 2009. Callender and Wilkinson (2003) provide further evidence that students are increasingly working while studying. Based on a survey of full time students in England and Wales, the proportion of students undertaking part-time work grew from 47% in 1998–1999 to 58% in 2002–2003, while the proportion of those working during the academic year, including vacation time, grew from 64 to 70%. To have a job while at university is now the norm, and not just in the UK. Data from Australia indicate that 52% of 20-24 year-olds in full time education are also employed (Australian Bureau of Statistics, 2008).

Averages mask differences however. Moreau and Leathwood (2006) review a number of studies that indicate term-time work is not evenly distributed across students irrespective of type of institution (e.g. pre- or post-1992 universities in the UK), social class or ethnicity. If you are male, White, middle-class and attending a prestigious university you are much less likely to be working part-time during your studies. Universities UK (2003) demonstrate that students from poorer backgrounds are more likely to engage in employment and to work longer hours while in higher education than students from more privileged backgrounds (Barke *et al.*, 2000). There is also evidence that students in post-1992 universities undertake more employment than those at pre-1992 institutions (Callender and Wilkinson, 2003). On the understanding that social class affects young people's choice of subject (or track) and that academic and scientific subjects are more highly regarded than vocational or utilitarian ones (Van de Werfhorst and Luijkx, 2010) there is an assumption that tourism and hospitality draw disproportionately on students from non-traditional backgrounds (non-traditional to HE). If this is the case, and the fact that tourism can perceived as a lesser subject (e.g. Walmsley, 2012a), term-time employment is likely to be elevated for tourism students.

People 1st's *State of the Nation Report*, 2013, presents data on employee characteristics in a range of tourism occupations. Students made up:

☐ 19% of kitchen and catering assistants

☐ 41% of waiting staff

☐ 31% of leisure and theme park attendants

☐ 27% of bar staff

These work experiences are important for numerous reasons, many of which mirror those of the work placement. They provide for many students their first taste of work, and if not their first then certainly one of the earliest work experiences. These early work experiences can be fundamental to individuals' long term career development in terms of forming attitudes to work and shaping career intentions. There are also many debates as to the impact of these work experiences on education outcomes, which in turn may impact career outcomes. Furthermore, the increased uptake of part-time employment while studying relates to HE funding requirements, student fees and labour market characteristics. Lastly, tourism and hospitality, but particularly hospitality along with retailing, are sectors of choice for many students in search of part-time work (Ford *et al.*, 1995; Curtis and Shani, 2002), given these sectors' workforce requirements (part-time work, unsocial hours, irregular hours). These issues will now be discussed in more detail.

The marketization of higher education, where higher education is not seen as a right or as a state benefit but as a product that is to be purchased like any other commodity, has led to increased financial pressure on students. This has led to increased student employment, something which employers are readily benefitting from in their desire for a flexible workforce (Moreau and Leathwood, 2006). Studies in tourism and hospitality have dealt in some detail with flexible labour arrangements to accommodate fluctuations in demand. A workforce that can work unsociable hours, such as at evenings and over weekends, also at short notice is provided by a growing number of students seeking work (James *et al.* 2010 cited in Baron and Corbin, 2012). The impact of these arrangements for the working student have been less explored. Moreau and Leathwood (2006) speak of 'juggling' work and study – a far cry from the image of students as a leisured class.

An ongoing debate surrounds the extent to which students should work, and if so how much work should be undertaken. Self (2005) has investigated the perceptions of hospitality students who did not upon graduation get their desired job. In hindsight many of these students wished they had obtained some work experience prior to graduation because this was important to employers who 'did not want to waste money on training' (Self, 2005:36). The danger with term-time work is that it can detract too much from one's studies but there is evidence that some work can 'focus the mind' and improve students' time management skills. In many respects the increased demands from employers, not just for good grades but for students who demonstrate a list of extra-curricular activities, is placing increasing amount of pressure on this generation of young people.

An important aspect of early work experiences in the tourism industry is the extent to which it fosters a desire to work in the sector or actually detracts from it; there is some evidence of the latter. Kusluvan and Kusluvan (2000), who looked at Turkey, found that students who had undertaken a formal work role as part of their education in the sector thereafter were less keen on seeking employment therein. Barron and Maxwell (1993) discovered a discrepancy between attitudes of those tourism students who were about to embark on employment in the sector with those that had undertaken some work experience in it, with the latter being less sanguine about tourism employment. Getz (1994) similarly reviewed the impact of work experiences in tourism on students' attitudes towards employment in the sector and concluded that attitudes were negatively impacted. These results contrast with conclusions of Ross (1992, 1997) and Murphy (1985), who argued that direct experience with the tourism industry leads to more favourable evaluations of careers in tourism. Again, countering this view is Chuang et al.'s (2007) study which cites a number of other studies that suggest many recent hospitality graduates leave the sector 3-5 years after joining it.

A common perception amongst tourism scholars and industry leaders is that tourism graduates should find employment in the sector, while numerous studies demonstrate that many tourism graduates neither enter the sector in the first place, nor stay in the sector subsequently (e.g. Hjalager and Andersen, 2000; Johns and McKechnie, 1995). Data from the UK's DLHE survey suggest (Higher Education Careers Services Unit, 2014) that of the 61.2% of 2013 graduates in Hospitality, Leisure, Tourism and Transport, six months after graduating the greatest proportion (24.1%) found work in 'Marketing, PR and sales professionals' only then followed by 'Retail, catering, waiting and bar staff' (18.7%).

For Chuang *et al.* (2007:29) 'preparing students for successful and satisfying careers in the hospitality industry is one of the important missions of most hospitality management programs' and in fact 82% of respondents to their study indicated they planned to pursue a hospitality career upon graduation. While it is clear that those undertaking tourism or hospitality programmes should be better prepared for work in the sector than non-tourism graduates, the premise seems to be that if employment is gained in other sectors something has gone wrong. If not mentioned explicitly then this is certainly implied in studies such as that by Chang and Tse (2012:12) where it is questioned 'why only limited number of students end up in the sector' although in this study 57% of graduates had found employment in tourism.

Hjalager and Andersen (2000:126) provide possibly a more realistic assessment of the sector's potential to retain tourism graduates arguing that:

> the tourist industry does not have its own distinct career system with clear internal career paths: staff come to tourism with quite varied backgrounds and obviously irrelevant professional educations and leave it for a range of other economic activities. The tourist industry thus shares its labour market with other trades, and the benefits are – potentially at least – mutual.

What is often neglected in comparing or ascertaining graduates' pre- and post-employment experiences in the sector is to disentangle attitudes towards the sector from attitudes towards employment. The shock (Hughes, 1958) or surprise (Louis, 1980) of starting a new work role itself should not be underestimated. Wanous *et al.* (1992) describe the organisational newcomer often as having over-inflated expectations, which often results in disappointment. Van Maanen and Schein (1979) and MacKenzie-Davey and Arnold (2000) likewise argue that entry into a new work setting has the potential to shock and as such we should not be too surprised that students or graduates who have little or no work experience in the sector face a degree of surprise. Negative early work experiences may then reflect in part unfamiliarity with work as well as de facto disappointment with sector specific elements.

An example from Barron and Maxwell (1993) serves to extend the analysis. Their pre-and post-placement data indicated that new students' perceptions of the effort-reward relationship were fair (18% believed it wasn't) whereby this figure changed dramatically for post-placement students who at 73% believed that effort outweighed rewards. This is clearly not an endorsement for the sector and yet students or graduates with little or no work experience may encounter similar effort-reward relationships across other industries where the surprise is as much about being in work in general as it is about being in tourism employment.

The role of work placements / internships

The embedding of work experience in formal educational programmes comes under different terms. Kusluvan *et al.* (2003) offer: industrial placement, industrial experience, cooperative education, student placements, supervised work experience and internship or sandwich courses. Ryan *et al.* (1996) write of the practicum as an umbrella term for field experience, cooperative education, sandwich programme, internship, clerkship and clinical practicum. Despite the diverse terminology, the fundamentals behind what is henceforth referred to as placements are very similar. The variation mainly comes down to duration and intensity of the work placement, and these may range from a few hours a week over a number of weeks to full time employment for a year.

A very common form of placement in HE is the so-called sandwich placement as it occurs either in the second or third year of a four year undergraduate programme. Sandwich placements are not a recent phenomenon, with guidelines from the then UK Department of Education and Science (1985) pointing out that they should be a form of supervised work experience and linked in some way to course content. Ryan *et al.* (1996) distinguish between two types of sandwich placement: the thick model is a year in duration, the thin model comprises shorter placements distributed throughout the course.

Perhaps the most common justification for the work placement is its role in providing a venue for the application of theory to practice, or the honing of practical skills, for fear of too much theory in the curriculum – see, for example, King's (1994) view on supplementing theoretical training with the attainment of necessary skills. Based on the previously described policy initiatives targeted at forging closer links between HE and industry, it should come as no surprise that placements are regarded favourably in policy circles. The UK Government's *Dearing Report* recommended that:

> ...all institutions should, over the medium term, identify opportunities to increase the extent to which programmes help students to become familiar with work. (Dearing, 1997: Annex A)

Nonetheless, a number of placement purposes have been described in tourism in addition to applying theory to practice, albeit in the broader vein of developing skills. Daresh (1990, cited in Ryan *et al.* 1996) provide a list of aims that include the testing of career intentions, the development of competencies and the recognition of areas where personal development is required. Busby *et al.* (1997) amalgamate aims with actions, such as accepting responsibility for the completion of tasks, becoming involved in the diagnosis and solution of problems, and the development of confidence and maturity. In an earlier paper, West and Jameson (1990) place much emphasis on the work placement's role in developing career intentions and building networks for career purposes. These authors state that for hospitality students the main objectives of the placement are to:

☐ Develop contacts with potential employers and to construct work experience profiles commensurate with the demands of future employers;

☐ Identify career paths within hospitality businesses and related organisations.

It is these kind of considerations that presumably led Sherrel (1987) to describe the work placement as the shop window of the industry, Ducat (1980) describes it as a career laboratory, and Collins (2002), with reference to the often encountered clash between work expectations and reality of the workplace, likens the placement experience to 'the sting of battle'. In Schaafsma's (1996:12) words, the work placement assists in 'sorting out what constitutes the real world'. Early reality checks either via placements or other work experiences may thereby increase satisfaction with first jobs after graduation, leading to lower labour turnover (Chuang *et al.*, 2007; Self, 2005).

The work placement is often viewed from the perspective of the student, although there are benefits also for employers and HE institutions and even beyond these groups (Busby, 2005). For the student, the benefits of having undertaken a work placement on employment prospects are well documented (e.g. Bowes and Harvey, 1999; Gault *et al.*, 2000; Purcell *et al.*, 1999; Callanan and Benzing, 2004; Walmsley *et al.*, 2006; Purcell and Pitcher, 1996). Harvey *et al.* (1997) were so convinced of the benefits of undertaking a work placement that they concluded their report on graduate employment by stating:

> If there was to be a single recommendation to come from the research, it would be to encourage all undergraduate programmes to offer students an option of a year-long work placement and employers to be less reluctant to provide placement opportunities.

Thus far the placement and its role have been regarded positively, as something that is to be encouraged within formal education. There remain however some concerns about the value of work placements to students' career prospects, which it would be negligent to dismiss out of hand, even if they go against the grain of accepted wisdom, or at least paint a more nuanced picture of the effects of placements on career outcomes. Indeed, there is some evidence that placement benefits accrue differentially depending on subject studied. Saniter and Siedler (2014), whose research involved students at German universities, found that the positive returns on placements (in terms of wages which are on average 6% higher than for those who do not undertake a placement) vary depending on whether the individual chose an area of study with a weak labour market orientation or not. Weak labour market orientation refers to areas of study that teach more general skills and qualify graduates for a wide range of different jobs, e.g. history, philosophy, languages as opposed to subjects like engineering or medicine with quite clear career trajectories. Tourism and hospitality as areas of study may lie somewhere between the more prescribed areas such as medicine, accounting or engineering but is stronger in labour market orientation than less vocational, generalist subjects such as history or philosophy.

Wilton (2012) conducted a longitudinal analysis of data from business students who had undertaken placements and completed their degrees in 1999. While the qualitative data from the study's participants in relation to the skills they had gained on their placements was positive, the quantitative data on labour market outcomes were inconsistent. Wilton found that the benefits of placements were less clear for graduates who opted for specialisms rather than more generic programmes of study (within the broader business management subject area). Wilton argues that intervening factors, such as gender and type of university attended, possibly blur the effect of the placement, which points to broader difficulties in assessing the impact of educational interventions. Interestingly, Wilton also discovered differences in perceived benefits (perceived by the students) depending on whether they were generic business management students or were pursuing a specialism such as tourism or marketing. Students on generic business courses commented on greater added value as a result of having undertaken the placement on skills development than students who had undertaken a specialism. No explanation as to why this was the case is provided but overall we might agree with Wilton's rather general conclusion that more research is needed before universal claims are made about the benefits of placements.

Bullock *et al.* (2009) in the aptly titled paper 'Work placement experience: should I stay or should I go?' explored the perspectives of students who had decided against undertaking a placement. This paper brings a new twist to the impact of placements by focussing not on career outcomes but on academic achievement (ignored here is the relationship between academic achievement and career outcomes). Bullock *et al.* remind the reader that evidence pertaining to a positive relationship between work placement and academic achievement remains weak. She and her co-authors acknowledge some studies that appear to demonstrate the relationship does exist. However, Bullock *et al.* also add that the relationship may be spurious, specifically that high achieving students are more likely to go on to do placements. Thus, as Wilton (2012) highlighted, despite students' satisfaction with placements, the link between placement and employment outcomes is difficult to establish due to the scope of intervening variables.

Bullock *et al.*'s study suggested students who did not go on a placement can be broadly separated into two groups: one well informed, the other less so, who 'lost out by default' (Bullock *et al.*, 2009:491). A number of reasons for students' lack of placement uptake are provided, including the increasing number of students who already have work experience. This is also noted elsewhere in this text and clearly, if the placement is to have its desired effects then it must provide students with novel learning experiences and opportunities for development. This is particularly important in an area such as tourism and hospitality where students often find part-time work in hotels and catering either before or during their studies (see also previous section). Morgan (2006), who investigated the attitude of accounting students towards placements, cites concerns around costs, quality, no formal assessment of the placement, not enough time to apply, uncertainty around career aspirations and high employer entry requirements as factors that detract from undertaking a placement. Aggett and Busby's (2011) study of tourism and hospitality students who had opted out of the placement cite similar reasons with the addition of fears around losing one's accommodation and/or work. Ultimately, Aggett and Busby (2011) also suggest that many students are unclear about the advantages of the placement.

It is furthermore perhaps startling, given the widespread endorsements work placements receive, that current trends suggest students are choosing not to undertake placements. In the UK, the most recent ATHE report on tourism higher education (Walmsley, 2012b) suggests that 24.1% of students enrolled on tourism courses in 2010/11 were enrolled on a sandwich placement whereas the figure for 2007/08 was 25.1%. This is not a dramatic difference and yet given the difficult labour market situation in developed economies following the global financial crisis one may have expected the number of students trying to delay labour market entry as well as enhance their employability to increase, a fact also queried by Aggett and Busby (2011). In fact, more generally Wolf (2011) argues that the postponement of entry into the labour market is only in part due to the economic pull of higher qualifications. In part young people are pushed into education by a lack of jobs.

SMEs and graduate entrepreneurship

The distribution of employment by size of firm in tourism is skewed towards both the very small and the very large organisation. On the one hand there are a few big players, on the other the vast majority of businesses in tourism are not only small but micro-enterprises, i.e. those with between 0 and 9 employees (the commonly used EU definition of a micro enterprise is one that employs fewer than 10 persons and whose annual turnover/and or annual balance sheet total does not exceed EUR 2 million, Eur-Lex, 2007). Precisely because of the preponderance of small and medium-sized enterprises (SMEs) in tourism, often referred to as their lifeblood (Wanhill, 2000), one might have expected tourism scholars to have fully engaged with them. That this is palpably not the case has been argued by Thomas *et al.* (2011). According to these authors there was a wave of research activity at the turn of the millennium on tourism SMEs, but since then research into tourism SMEs has languished with some notable exceptions (e.g. Ateljevic and Page, 2009, Thomas and Augustyn, 2007). By way of contrast, in the generic business literature, i.e. outside of tourism, scholarship that focusses on small businesses continues to flourish. One specific area that has witnessed enormous growth in scholarly, policy making and educational circles is that of graduate entrepreneurship, especially business start-up. Before we turn our attention to graduate entrepreneurship in tourism however, we first explore youth employment in tourism SMEs.

Graduate employment in SMEs

Graduate employment in tourism SMEs continues to attract only limited attention despite concerns about the opportunities for graduate employment with traditional, i.e. large, graduate recruiters. At the outset it should be noted that the employment generation potential of tourism SMEs, in particular in relation to regional economic development is widely recognised. Wanhill (2000:133), for example, claims:

> The tangible expression of the welfare consideration of public investment support for tourism SMEs in many countries and in the policies of the European Union is the generation of employment.

Perhaps what we are about to say in relation to tourism education and its lack of SME focus is even more surprising precisely for this reason.

Ronstadt (1987), in a discussion about the rise of entrepreneurship education, makes some interesting observations which relate to the overriding focus on large organisations in business education in the United States. It could be argued that within tourism education the same dominance exists. Ronstadt (1987:10) proposes that it was easier for academics, and more lucrative, to research larger organizations, which could lead to consulting contracts, board positions or funded professorial chairs. The result was:

> the evolution of a system of management education with an implicit value system that clearly favoured the large organization versus the small, the established entity versus the new, the ongoing business versus the emerging…

Clarke and Gibson-Sweet (1998) have likewise pointed to what they call a large business paradigm in business courses in the UK. Whether this is also the case in tourism is harder to identify, as less research exists here relating to curriculum content and firm size, but one may imagine that this large business paradigm also holds some sway in tourism education.

Concerns exist in relation to the promotion of the large firm paradigm because of a relative lack of large firm employment opportunities in the labour market more generally, but also specifically in tourism. Authors such as King (2003) and Holden *et al.* (2007) argue that increased graduate employment in SMEs is inevitable precisely because more students are graduating from higher education than there are positions being created in large, traditional graduate employers. Data from ATHE and CHME reports referred to earlier also indicate that a considerable proportion of tourism and hospitality graduates' first employment in the UK occurs in SMEs. The employment of tourism graduates in SMEs is, according to these DLHE figures, not small scale.

The relatively high proportion of tourism graduates that go on to work in SMEs can be explained by the structure of the sector. Where there are many SMEs it is unsurprising to find much graduate employment in SMEs. However, this still leaves the issue as to whether graduates go on to work in SMEs by default or by design. One would hope that tourism graduates who find employment in SMEs do so not solely because of a lack of opportunities elsewhere.

Matching the demand for SME employment on the part of graduates with the supply of SME employment on the part of employers has featured in a number of papers, albeit usually without a specific tourism sector focus. Holden and Jameson have explored graduate employment in hospitality SMEs (1996, 1996 and 2009) but these publications aside, the use of SMEs as an analytical category in studies of the tourism graduate labour market remains limited.

To summarise very briefly the nature of graduate demand for SME employment, weak uptake of employment in SMEs by graduates is explained either by an ignorance barrier or a preference/attitude barrier (also referred to as a market barrier by Belfield, 1999). The former refers to graduates simply not being aware of the extent of graduate employment opportunities. The latter explanation suggests that graduates are aware of SME employment opportunities but tend to prefer large firms for a range of additional benefits associated with these, such as higher pay, enhanced career prospects, prestige and the like (e.g. Hesketh, 2000; Brindley and Ritchie, 2000; Belfield, 1999). When looking for employment, applicants are looking not only for positions, but also for organisations after all (Schwab *et al.*, 1987), and one would assume that large, well-known employers are at an advantage here.

Despite the convincing nature of the preference barrier explanation, there is likely to be some truth in the existence of an ignorance barrier concerning SME employment opportunities. Numerous studies have suggested that career advice tends to focus disproportionately on large firms (Bowen *et al.*, 2004; Booth, 2004; Pollard *et al.*, 2004; Otter, 2005). Westhead and Matlay (2005) suggest that graduates have few models of success relating to SME employment, which again can be linked to a possible large firm bias in tourism education as well as adding to the ignorance barrier. That tourism and hospitality education does tend to favour particular sub-sectors was demonstrated by Doherty *et al.* (2001), who claim that in hospitality higher education many industry contexts are being neglected in favour of the upmarket hotel sector. It is furthermore plausible to assume that there is a positive correlation between size of organisation and attempts at hiring graduates in so-called 'milk round' type recruitment exercises. Certainly, there is a positive correlation between size of firm and the proportion of the workforce who are degree holders (Harris and Reid, 2005). In all likelihood the transition from education to SME employment is shaped by both ignorance and market factors.

Once employed, the experience of working in a tourism SME seems variable. This confirms the literature around SME employment more generally, where employee relations have been described as both better and worse than in large organisations. Early research in this area (Ingham, 1970; Talacchi, 1960) argues that small organizations are more satisfying from a human point of view. Going back even further, Durkheim (1933) proposed that small scale industry, with less division of labour, promoted more harmonious relations between worker and employer. This was then picked up by Goss (1991) in his description of a 'Green' approach to business. Martin and Chapman (2006) investigated the experience of marketing graduates in SMEs and came to the conclusion that for many of their respondents there were a number of positive facets that they had not initially considered, such as a great deal of autonomy and the assumption of responsibility fairly early on in the employment relationship. Martin and

Chapman therefore write of a socialisation towards large firms in HE where students and graduates-to-be are not deliberately, but almost by default, led to consider transition into large firms as the 'normal' route into graduate employment.

Further research by Jones *et al.* (2001) explored placement experiences in SMEs and found that participants had appreciated the flexibility they were given, which increased participants' desire to work in an SME. These findings were confirmed by Walmsley *et al.* (2006) who focussed specifically on tourism and hospitality students in their study of SME placement experiences. Initially driven by the desire to understand how SME placements might impact career intentions, specifically with regard to SME employment, the study provided insights into the employment experience in tourism SMEs. It confirmed that levels of responsibility, flexibility and autonomy were judged highly by students, although there was also an absence of formal training in these firms. For some participants the employment experience had been very satisfactory, for others less so. It is difficult to therefore generalise across all tourism SMEs, as disappointment was at times down to what may be termed the classic attributes of tourism employment, long hours, low pay, low skilled, which are not firm size related, at other times it was down to an overbearing owner/manager in what may be described as a simply structured (also: entrepreneurial) organizational configuration (Mintzberg, 1979). Sometimes, rather than being autocratic, the owner/manager was amenable and caring and this attitude then pervaded the organisation in a way that would be difficult to be achieved in a large organisation.

It would be extremely short-sighted to ignore SMEs as graduate destinations (given the structure of the sector, they are by default a major source of non-graduate youth employment). Unless the number of positions in large firms increases at the same rate of growth as numbers graduating from university, it may seem clear that graduates will have to seek other sources of work. Particularly in tourism which is dominated by SMEs, to assume all graduates will, should or indeed can find employment in large firms is to misunderstand the nature of tourism labour markets. More research is needed to assist in understanding a range of issues in the tourism-SME relationship, for example, the transition into SME employment, working conditions once employed and how SMEs can benefit from a graduate's skills and knowledge are all areas that merit further attention.

Graduate entrepreneurship

Just as employment in SMEs can be turned to as an alternative source of youth employment, particularly graduate employment, a different employment avenue opens itself up in the form of entrepreneurship, i.e. self-employment. In tourism as we have seen (Chapter 2) much economic activity occurs in the informal economy and much of this relates to informal entrepreneurship. Tourism, with its low entry/start-up barriers is frequently a sector of choice for entrepreneurs in the informal economy and so a discussion around the role of entrepreneurship and youth employment, here self-employment, is very pertinent.

However, often regarded as solely relating to venture creation (e.g. Vesper, 1983), entrepreneurship can take place in an existing firm, whether newly created or long established. There exist two perspective of entrepreneurship and by implication graduate entrepreneurship, a narrow definition that focuses solely on venture creation and a broad definition that focuses on entrepreneurial behaviour per se, irrespective of context (Bridge *et al.*, 2003). Chapter 5 (page 129 ff.) covered the contribution of youth to the achievement of organisational objectives, including the 'new blood' argument which referred to harnessing the creativity and drive of youth, one might say their entrepreneurial zeal. The following therefore focuses predominantly on the venture creation perspective.

Policy makers have their eyes on enterprise in its broad definition as it is widely regarded as a key driver of economic growth and job creation. Kuratko (2005) writes of entrepreneurial firms, and the two key contributions they can make to market economies. The first is that they play a crucial part of the renewal process. They are needed for productivity growth and promoting technological change. Second, they provide the means by which many individuals can enter the economic mainstream. Kuratko mentions women, minorities and immigrants to which we could add young people. Drawing on Kuratko's recognition of the job creation potential of entrepreneurial firms for economically side-lined groups, as well as the view that tourism as a sector is well placed to provide these groups with work, we can summarise that the entrepreneurial tourism firm holds immense potential for youth employment.

The origins of entrepreneurship are often traced back to the Industrial Revolution. Schumpeter who defined entrepreneurship as 'the carrying out of new combinations (of means of production)' (Schumpeter, 1934:74) and his notion of creative destruction are often held up as initiating or in fact re-awakening a spirit of enterprise that began with the Industrial Revolution, and yet as Casson and Casson demonstrate, the study of entrepreneurship can be pushed back to the medieval period by focussing on the individual entrepreneur rather than on the firm. A further interesting feature identified by Casson and Casson (2014:1237) given a re-awakened spirit, or culture of entrepreneurship is that in the medieval period 'no-one considered themselves too important to be engaged in trade. Kings, bishops and abbots all regarded the profits of trade as an indispensable source of income'. They contrast this with the notion that the 'political and social elite cannot be seen to soil their hands with trade' which appears to be a late Victorian invention. Notwithstanding such temporary blips in the history of enterprise, its recent history, that relating to the latter half of the twentieth century and the beginning of the twenty first, displays a greater degree of contention between commentators and political elites as to where the source of enterprise lies.

In today's climate the view that small businesses are an anachronism of a bygone age, a remnant of the cottage-type industries described by Weber (2002/1905), seems almost risible. But that is frequently how small firms were in fact perceived by many with the rise of the corporation after the Second World War (Burrows and Curran, 1989, Curran, 1990). As Casson and Casson (2014:1224) point out: 'Modern Capitalism was identified with corporatism and bureaucracy rather than individualism and enterprise'. Small firms were frequently regarded as inward-looking and stuck in their ways (and arguably, many in tourism still are), unable to compete with the large enterprises. The small business sector was quite simply perceived to be in decline.

That this view changed in the 1970s is evidenced by, amongst other things, the publication of the 1971 *Bolton Report* in the UK which sought to emphasise the importance of small firms to the economy (this report was also subsequently heavily criticised for its sanguine depiction of employee relations in small firms). Meanwhile in the United States in 1979, David Birch presented his report, *The Job Generation Process,* in which it was argued that the majority of new jobs in the US were being created by small companies. As the title of Bannock's (1981) book, *The Economics of Small Firms: Return From the Wilderness,* suggests, small firms were indeed 'returning from the wilderness'.

This renewed recognition of the importance of SMEs was closely linked to an interest in enterprise and the growth of an enterprise culture, which may itself be regarded as part of the neo-liberal Washington Agenda that spread throughout Western and Southern countries in the 1980s (Helleiner, 2003). Audretsch (2009:104) explains that entrepreneurship extends beyond the realms of industry and is in fact a societal phenomenon:

> Just as it has been important to understand how to manage entrepreneurial firms, it has now become at least as important to understand

how to achieve an entrepreneurial society. While this emphasis on small entrepreneurial firms as engines of dynamic efficiency may seem startling after decades of looking at the corporate giants as engines of growth and development, it may not be so new.

Audretsch (2009) confirms small firms' new-found role in driving forward economic progress, but goes beyond this in this notion of an entrepreneurial society. The novelty here is that being entrepreneurial is not the preserve of the small firm; in its reach entrepreneurship is pervasive, and it becomes embedded in a society's culture. At least this is what has been promoted by policy makers in the hope of stimulating economic growth, though Hundley and Hansen (2012) also note that culture can be a dependent variable, explaining that people in countries with below average economic performance may be less enterprising.

This drive to create an entrepreneurial culture and society fed through to education. Entrepreneurial individuals can provide a stimulus to growth, which again creates employment for others. Nonetheless, there was one sticking point that needed to be overcome – the question of whether entrepreneurship can in fact be taught. A key position here that would undermine much entrepreneurship education is the view that entrepreneurship is a character trait that one either has or does not have; the issue of whether entrepreneurs are born or made. This has been discussed extensively in the literature, to a degree even in tourism (Gurel *et al.*, 2010) and while a resolution to what entrepreneurship is may never, definitively, be provided, there exists now an abundance of literature that suggests entrepreneurship can be taught. Drucker (1985) is often referred to in this regard, where he is vociferous in his defence of the notion that entrepreneurship is neither mysterious nor magical. Based on reviews of studies on entrepreneurship education (Gorman *et al.*, 1997; Pittaway and Cope, 2007) the verdict that entrepreneurship can be taught is compelling. Policy makers certainly believe in investing in entrepreneurship education. The European Commission (2013) has for example very high hopes for entrepreneurship education which it explains thus:

> Entrepreneurial education and training = growth and business creation. (European Commission, 2013)

To suggest that the rise in entrepreneurship education in the last two decades has been dramatic is anything but an overstatement. This growth has been global and is now expanding beyond universities into secondary and primary schools (Fayolle, 2013). The United States which is still the 'market leader' in entrepreneurship education (Lourenço and Jones, 2006) is a case in point. Fiet

(2001) claims that in 1971 there were only 16 universities teaching entrepreneurship in the United States, whereas in 2000 it was over 800. Solomon (2007) claims that entrepreneurship and small business education is now offered at more than 1,200 post-secondary institutions in the United States. In the United Kingdom the National Council for Graduate Entrepreneurship (NCGE) was created in 2004 with the aim of enhancing the number and sustainability of graduate start-ups. (It has since been renamed the National Council for Entrepreneurship in Education.) An NCGE report (2006) suggests that 7% of students in English HE institutions are now engaged in enterprise activities.

There also appears to be considerable demand for business start-up among young people. Taken at face value numerous studies suggest an interest in entrepreneurship amongst young people. Fiet (2001) cites a US Gallup Poll where no less than 70% of high school students expressed the desire to start their own business 'some time in the future'. Eurobarometer (2002 cited in Greene and Saridakis, 2007) suggests 56% of young people have a preference for starting their own business. Nabi *et al.* (2010) take stock of a series of entrepreneurial intentions surveys at universities in the UK region of Yorkshire and Humber between 2002/03 and 2007/08 (total sample size > 28,000). Although there was a decrease in those answering either 'definitely' or 'probably' to the question as to whether they would start a business between 2002/03 and 2007/08, a third of students still placed themselves within this group. In Barron *et al.*'s (2007) study of largely Scottish undergraduate hospitality students, there was a clear desire to start their own businesses among half of the sample (which was albeit quite small), which the authors relate to characteristics of Generation Y. An exception here to the strong levels of interest in business start-up is Jenkins' (2001) study where only two students in a combined sample of students of a British and Dutch university expected to own a business five years after graduating (the figure increased to four for ten years after graduating).

Globally, i.e. including developing countries, levels of entrepreneurial intent are likely to be far higher. Data from the Global Entrepreneurship Monitor (GEM) the largest ongoing study of entrepreneurial dynamics in the world, indicate that the lowest level of entrepreneurial intentions is found in European and North American economies, while the highest corresponds to African economies. This appears to conflict with Hundley and Hansen's (2012) view that high levels of economic performance foster entrepreneurial behaviour and vice versa.

If these entrepreneurial preference and intent surveys are anything to go by, one might ask why entrepreneurship education is needed. Entrepreneurship education to stimulate entrepreneurial intent is less useful if levels of entrepreneurial intent are already very high. Despite these high levels of intent and positive attitudes towards entrepreneurship, actual rates of youth venture creation are relatively low. The problem seems to lie with the follow through on intent. Based on a number of studies, Greene and Saridakis (2007) claim that in the UK graduate start-up rates are approximately 4%. Nabi *et al.* (2010:549) in a review of research into the relationship between entrepreneurial intent and actual business start-up rates similarly raise this issue emphasising 'particular research focus on those who express intent (i.e. a commitment to pursue the entrepreneurship career path), but who do not fulfil this intent, or at least not in the first three or four years post degree'.

The plethora of papers in entrepreneurship education that seek to understand how graduates can be encouraged to start businesses is indicative of an understanding of entrepreneurship as involving new venture creation. The substantial amount of literature in the area of entrepreneurial intent should not detract from the fact that venture creation represents a narrow understanding of what enterprise or entrepreneurship is. In addition to venture creation, enterprising behaviour within organisations, corporate entrepreneurship (Bridge *et al.*, 2003), reflects a broader definition of what constitutes enterprise with implications also for what should be taught within the remit of enterprise education. Shepherd and Douglas' (1997, cited in Solomon, 2007:169) definition of entrepreneurship, although at first glance indicating a focus on business start-up may arguably be understood more broadly:

> The essence of entrepreneurship is the ability to envision and chart a course for a new business venture by combining information from the functional disciplines and from the external environment in the context of the extraordinary uncertainty and ambiguity which faces a new business venture. It manifests itself in creative strategies, innovative tactics, uncanny perception of trends and market mood changes, courageous leadership when the way forward is not obvious and so on. What we teach in our entrepreneurship classes should serve to instil and enhance these abilities.

Here, entrepreneurship involves new business ventures, which can relate to an entirely new business, or a new venture within a business (e.g. entering a new market, developing a new product, introducing a new process etc.). Vesper (1984) extends this further, providing three activities characteristic of corporate entrepreneurship:

☐ The creation of a new business unit by an established firm;

☐ The development and implementation of entrepreneurial strategic thrusts;

☐ The emergence of new ideas from various levels within an organisation.

There are many factors that influence firm-level entrepreneurship as identified by an analysis of 45 papers in this area (Zahra *et al.*, 1999). According to these authors, firm-level entrepreneurship is characterised by the nature of the activities themselves (e.g. corporate venturing, innovation and proactivity), the source of entrepreneurship (internal or external to the organisation), and the focus of entrepreneurship (formal or informal). Furthermore, Zahra *et al.* (1999) identified various labels being used for firm-level entrepreneurship from corporate entrepreneurship, intrapreneurship, entrepreneurial posture, strategic posture and entrepreneurial orientation.

Returning to the theme of entrepreneurship education, we can now say that on the one hand it is about assisting and encouraging individuals to create their own businesses, but we can also say that developing entrepreneurial behaviour more broadly understood is likewise an important element of entrepreneurship education, or education more generally for that matter. There is still much that is being taken for granted and that does not provide an answer to Ronstadt's (1987) needing to know the what and how of entrepreneurship education. This is strongly evident in Fayolle's (2013:693) reflection on the state of entrepreneurship education where he claims:

> There is commitment, intellectual and emotional investment and passion among the educators, instructors and all the people engaged in the entrepreneurship education. Yet, we need to stand back and reflect upon our practices and what we talk about when we talk about entrepreneurship education. What are we really doing when we teach or train people in entrepreneurship, in terms of the nature and the impact of our interventions? What do we know about the appropriateness, relevance, coherence, social usefulness and efficiency of our initiatives and practices in entrepreneurship education?

That this reflection is necessary is demonstrated in a number of studies that propose entrepreneurship education has no impact on entrepreneurial intentions or indeed can even decrease them. Souitaris *et al.* (2007) found no significant relationship between entrepreneurship education programme learning and intentions, for example. Studies by Oosterbeek *et al.* (2010) and Von Graevenitz *et al.* (2010) suggest that entrepreneurship education has led to a reduction in entrepreneurial intentions. If true, this would add to the dilemma of youth unemployment rather than detracting from it. There are few studies in tourism that focus on entrepreneurial intentions, though they do exist. Using Ajzen's Theory of Planned Behaviour and Shapero and Sokol's notion of the Entrepreneurial Event, Walmsley and Thomas (2009) discuss how tourism education, including placements in SMEs, can increase the intention to start a business. Gurel *et al.* (2010) conducted a survey of tourism students in Turkey and the UK where they explored factors influencing entrepreneurial intentions, including education. Gurel *et al.* also argue that education does not play a role in fostering entrepreneurial intentions, neither for the Turkish nor for the UK group. They explain this using a quotation from Krueger and Carsrud (1993:327 cited in Gurel *et al.*, 2010):

> teaching people about the realities of entrepreneurship may increase their entrepreneurial self-efficacy, but simultaneously decrease the perceived desirability of starting a business.

Entrepreneurship education could be a double-edged sword in the desire to foster entrepreneurial intent (Souitaris *et al.*, 2007).

Within-firm entrepreneurship, or corporate entrepreneurship, in tourism lacks much by way of empirical research also. With respect to youth employment and self-employment in regard to tourism and entrepreneurship, there is little more than anecdotal evidence of either young people starting tourism firms or bringing entrepreneurial skills to existing firms. This does not mean this is not happening. In fact, the theoretical case for both playing a large part in the sector is very strong. As has been discussed, entry barriers to tourism can be low in terms of technical skill requirements, and capital requirements can be relatively low also. This invites entrepreneurship, especially where other employment opportunities are scarce, i.e. there is a push into entrepreneurship rather than a draw (pull) into it (Nabi *et al.*, 2013). The rise in tourism education globally should ensure that more young people today are equipped and ready to contribute to the companies that hire them. A barrier here could in fact be business owners themselves, or managers, who are unable to appreciate and therefore use the skills and knowledge that a young person may bring with them to the job as outlined by Froy (2013).

References

Aggett, M. & Busby, G. (2011) Opting out of internship: Perceptions of hospitality, tourism and events management undergraduates at a British University. *Journal of Hospitality, Leisure, Sport and Tourism Education,* **10** (1), 106-113.

Akande, T. (2014). Youth unemployment in Nigeria. A situation analysis. *Africa in Focus.* Brookings. Available: http://www.brookings.edu/blogs/ africa-in-focus/posts/2014/09/23-youth-unemployment-nigeria-akande

Arthur, M., Hall, D. and Lawrence, B. (Eds) (1989) *Handbook of Career Theory*. Cambridge: Cambridge University Press.

Arthur, M. & Rousseau, D. M. (1996) *The Boundaryless Career: A New Employment Principle for a New Organizational Era*, Oxford: Oxford University Press.

Ateljevic, J. & Page, S. (2009) *Tourism Entrepreneurship*, Oxford: Butterworth-Heinemann.

Audretsch, D. (2009) The Entrepreneurial Society. *In:* Audretsch, D., Dagnino, G. B., Faraci, R. & Hoskisson, R. (eds.) *New Frontiers in Entrepreneurship: Recognizing, Seizing, and Executing Opportunities*. New York: Springer.

Australian Bureau of Statistics. (2008) Education and work, Australia. Available: http://www.abs.gov.au/AUSSTATS/abs@.nsf/Lookup/6227.0Main+Features1May%202008.

Bandura, A. (1986) *Social Foundations of Thought and Action. A Social Cognitive Theory*, New Jersey: Englewood Cliffs.

Bannock, G. (1981) *The Economics of Small Firms: Return From the Wilderness*, Oxford: Basil Blackwell.

Barke, M., Braidford, P., Houston, M., Hunt, A., Lincoln, I., Morphet, C., Stone, I. & Walker, A. (2000). *Students in the labour market. Nature, extent and implications of term-time employment among University of Northumbria undergraduates*. London: Department for Education and Employment.

Baron, P. & Corbin, L. (2012) Student engagement: Rhetoric and reality. *Higher Education Research and Development*, **31 (**6), 759-772.

Barron, P. & Maxwell, G. (1993) Hospitality management students' image of the hospitality industry. *International Journal of Contemporary Hospitality Management*, **5 (**5), 5-8.

Barron, P., Maxwell, G., Broadbridge, A. & Ogden, S. (2007) Careers in hospitality management: Generation Y's experiences and perceptions. *Journal of Hospitality & Tourism Management*, **14 (**2), 119-128.

Bauman, Z. (2000) *Liquid Modernity*, Cambridge: Polity Press.

Belfield, C. R. (1999) The behaviour of graduates in the SME labour market: Evidence and perceptions. *Small Business Economics*, **12** 249-259.

Bendit, R. & Miranda, A. (2015) Transitions to adulthood in contexts of economic crisis and post-recession. The case of Argentina. *Journal of Youth Studies*, **18 (**2), 183-196.

Blumenfeld, W. S., Kent, W. E., Shock, P. J. & Jourdan, L. F. (1987) Job attributes preferences of a group of potential hospitality industry managers: What makes a job good or bad. *Hospitality Education and Research*, **10 (**2), 79-93.

Booth, J. (2004). *Get Ahead. Supplying high level skills to smaller companies.* Loughborough: East Midlands Universities Careers Task Force.

Bowen, E., Lloyd, S. & Thomas, S. (2004) *Changing Cultural Attitudes Towards Graduates in SMEs to Stimulate Regional Innovation.* School of Technology, University of Glamorgan, Wales. Available: www.tti-ltd.com/tti2004/presentations/12d_lloyd.doc.

Bowes, L. & Harvey, L. (1999). *The impact of sandwich education on the activities of graduates six months post-graduation.* Birmingham: Center for Research into Quality.

Bridge, S., O'Neill, K. & Cromie, S. (2003) *Understanding Enterprise, Entrepreneurship and Small Business,* Basingstoke: Palgrave Macmillan.

Brindley, C. & Ritchie, B. (2000) Undergraduates and small and medium-sized enterprises: opportunities for a symbiotic partnership? *Education and Training,* **42 (**9), 509-517.

Brown, D. (2002) Introduction to theories of career development and choice. origins, evolution, and current efforts. *In:* Brown, D. & Associates (eds.) *Career Choice and Development.* 4 ed. San Francisco: Jossey-Bass.

Brown, P. & Scase, R. (1994) *Higher Education & Corporate Realities. Class, Culture and the Decline of Graduate Careers,* London: UCL Press.

Bynner, J. (2001) British Youth Transitions in Comparative Perspective. *Journal of Youth Studies.* **4**(1), 5-23.

Bullock, K., Gould, V., Hejmadi, M. & Lock, G. (2009) Work placement experience: should I stay or should I go? *Higher Education Research & Development,* **28 (**5), 481-494.

Burrows, R. & Curran, J. (1989) Sociological research on service sector small businesses: some conceptual considerations. *Work, Employment and Society,* **3 (**4), 527-539.

Busby, G. (2005) Work experience and industrial links. *In:* Airey, D. & Tribe, J. (eds.) *An International Handbook of Tourism Education.* Oxford: Elsevier.

Busby, G., Brunt, P. & Baber, S. (1997) Tourism sandwich placements: an appraisal. *Tourism Management,* **28 (**2), 105-110.

Callanan, G. & Benzing, C. (2004) Assessing the role of internships in the career-oriented employment of graduating college students. *Education and Training,* **46 (**2), 82-89.

Callender, C. & Wilkinson, D. (2003). *2002/03 student income and expenditure survey: students' income, expenditure and debt in 2002/03 and changes since 1998/99.* London: Department for Education.

Casson, M. & Casson, C. (2014) The history of entrepreneurship: Medieval origins of a modern phenomenon. *Business History,* **56 (**8), 1223-1242.

Chang, S. & Tse, E. C.-Y. (2012) Understanding the initial career decisions of hospitality graduates in Hong Kong: Quantitative and qualitative evidence. *Journal of Hospitality & Tourism Research,* published online 09.10.2012.

Chuang, N.-K. & Dellmann-Jenkins, M. (2010) Career decision-making and intention: a study of hospitality undergraduate students. *Journal of Hospitality & Tourism Research,* **34** (4), 512-530.

Chuang, N.-K., Goh, B., Stout, B. & Dellmann-Jenkins, M. (2007) Hospitality undergraduate students' career choices and factors influencing commitment to the profession. *Journal of Hospitality & Tourism Education,* **19** (4), 28-37.

Clarke, J. & Gibson-Sweet, M. (1998) Enterprising futures: training and education for small businesses. *Education and Training,* **40** (3), 102-108.

Collin, A. (1998) New challenges in the study of career. *Personnel Review,* **27** (5), 412-425.

Collins, A. B. (2002) Gateway to the real world, industrial training: dilemmas and problems. *Tourism Management,* **23** (1), 93-96.

Curran, J. (1990) Rethinking economic structure: exploring the role of the small firm and self-employment in the British economy. *Work, Employment and Society,* **4** (5), 125-146.

Curtis, S. & Shani, N. (2002) The effect of taking paid employment during term-time on students' academic studies. *Journal of Further and Higher Education,* **26** (2), 129-138.

Dearing, R. (1997). *Report of the National Committee of Inquiry into Higher Education. Higher Education in the Learning Society.* Norwich: HMSO.

Department of Education and Science (1985). *An assessment of the costs and benefits of sandwich education.* London: Committee on Research into Sandwich Education, DES.

Doherty, L., Guerrier, Y., Jameson, S., Lashley, C. & Lockwood, A. (2001). *Getting ahead: graduate careers in hospitality management.* Council for Hospitality Management Education.

Drucker, P. (1985) *Innovation and Entrepreneurship. Practice and Principles,* London: Elsevier.

Ducat, D. (1980) Cooperative education, career exploration, and occupational concepts for community college students. *Journal of Vocational Behavior,* **17** 195-203.

Durkheim, E. (1933) *The Division of Labour in Society*: Glencoe, Ill.

Elias, P. & Purcell, K. (2004). Researching Graduate Careers Seven Years On. Research paper No. 6. SOC (HE): A classification of occupations for studying the graduate labour market. Warwick: Warwick Institute for Employment Research.

Eur-Lex. (2007) *Definition of micro, small and medium-sized enterprises*. Available: http://eur-lex.europa.eu/legal-content/EN/TXT/?uri=URISERV:n26026 [Accessed 23.02.15].

European Commission. (2013) *Entrepreneurship as a main driver for economic growth*. Available: http://ec.europa.eu/enterprise/newsroom/cf/itemdetail. cfm?item_id=6368&lang=en [Accessed 30.06.15].

Fayolle, A. (2013) Personal views on the future of entrepreneurship education. *Entrepreneurship and Regional Development*, **25** (7/8), 692-701.

Fiet, J. O. (2001) The pedagogical side of teaching entrepreneurship. *Journal of Business Venturing*, **16** (2), 10-117.

Ford, J., Bosworth, D. & Wilson, R. (1995) Part-time work and full-time higher education. *Studies in Higher Education*, **20** (2), 187-202.

Froy, F. (2013) Global policy developments towards industrial policy and skills: Skills for competitiveness and growth. *Oxford Review of Economic Policy*, **29** (2), 344-360.

Gati, I., Krausz, M. & Osipow, S. (1996) A taxonomy of difficulties in career decision making. *Journal of Counseling Psychology*, **43** (4), 510-526.

Gault, J., Redington, J. & Schlager, T. (2000) Undergraduate business internships and career success: are they related? *Journal of Marketing Education*, **22** (1), 45-53.

Getz, D. (1994) Students' work experiences, perceptions and attitudes towards careers in hospitality and tourism: a longitudinal case study in Spey Valley, Scotland. *International Journal of Hospitality Management*, **13** (1), 25-37.

Giddens, A. (1991) *Modernity and Self-identity: Self and Society in the Late Modern Age*, Cambridge: Polity Press.

Ginsberg, E., Ginsberg, S., Axelrad, S. And Herma, J. (1951) *Occupational Choice. An approach to a general theory*. New York: Columbia University Press.

Gorman, G., Hanlon, D. & King, W. (1997) Some research perspectives on entrepreneurship education, enterprise education and education for small business management: a ten-year literature review. *International Small Business Journal*, **15** (3), 56-77.

Goss, D. (1991) *Small Business and Society*, London: Routledge.

Gottfredson, L. S. (1981) Circumscription and compromise: A developmental theory of occupational aspirations. *Journal of Counseling Psychology Monograph*, **28** (6), 545-578.

Gottfredson, L. S. (2002) Gottfredson's Theory of Circumscription, Compromise, and Self-Creation. *In:* Brown, D. (ed.) *Career Choice and Development.* 4 ed. San Francisco: Jossey-Bass.

Greene, F. & Saridakis, G. (2007). *Understanding the Factors Influencing Graduate Entrepreneurship.* Birmingham: National Council for Graduate Entrepreneurship.

Guichard, J., Pouyaud, J., De Calan, C. & Dumora, B. (2012) Identity construction and career development interventions with emerging adults. *Journal of Vocational Behavior,* **81** 52-58.

Gurel, E., Altinay, L. & Daniele, R. (2010) Tourism students' entrepreneurial intentions. *Annals of Tourism Research,* **37** (3), 646-669.

Hall, D. T. (1996) Protean careers of the 21st century'. *Academy of Management Executive,* **10** (4), 8-16.

Harris, R. & Reid, R. (2005) Graduate employment and training in SMEs in Northern Ireland. An overview using the 2000 Labour Force Survey. *Industry & Higher Education,* **17** (4), 55-63.

Harvey, L., Moon, S. & Geall, V. (1997). *Graduates' Work: Organisational Change and Students' Attributes.* Birmingham: Centre for Research into Quality.

Heggli, G., Haukanes, H. & Marit, T. (2013) Fearing the future? Young people envisioning their working lives in the Czech Republic, Norway and Tunisia. *Journal of Leisure Studies,* **16** (7), 916-931.

Helleiner, E. (2003) Economic liberalism and its critics: the past as prologue? *Review of International Political Economy* **10** (4), 685-696.

Herr, E. L. (1990) Issues in career research. *In:* Young, R. A. & Borgen, W. A. (eds.) *Methodological Approaches to the Study of Career.* New York: Praeger.

Hesketh, A. J. (2000) Recruiting an elite?: Employers' perceptions of graduate education and training. *Journal of Education and Work,* **13** (3), 245-271.

Higher Education Careers Services Unit (2014). *What do Graduates Do?* Higher Education Career Services Unit.

Hjalager, A.-M. & Andersen, S. (2000) Tourism employment: contingent work or professional career? *Employee Relations,* **23** (2), 114-129.

Hodkinson, P. (1998) The origins of a theory of career decision-making: A case study of hermeneutical research. *British Educational Research Journal,* **24** (5).

Hodkinson, P. (2008). Understanding career decision-making and progression: Careership revisited. John Killeen Memorial Lecture, Woburn House, London: Leeds University. Available: http://www.crac.org.uk/CMS/files/upload/fifth_johnkilleenlecturenotes.pdf

Holden, R. & Jameson, S. (1999) Employing graduates in hospitality small to medium-sized enterprises: Context and issues. *In:* Lee-Ross, D. (ed.) *HRM in Tourism and Hospitality.* London: Cassell.

Holden, R., Jameson, S. & Walmsley, A. (2007) New graduate employment in SMEs: Still in the dark? *Journal of Small Business and Enterprise Development,* **14 (**2), 211-227.

Hughes, E. C. (1958) *Men and their Work,* Glencoe, Illinois: Free Press.

Hundley, G. & Hansen, D. (2012) Economic performance and the enterprise culture. *Journal of Enterprising Culture,* **20 (**3), 245-264.

ILO (undated) What is child labour. Available: http://www.ilo.org/ipec/facts/lang--en [Accessed 27.04.14].

Ingham, G. (1970) *Size of Industrial Organization and Worker Behaviour,* Cambridge: Cambridge University Press.

Jameson, S. (1996) Small firms and the hospitality graduate labour market. *International Journal of Contemporary Hospitality Management,* **8 (**5), 37-38.

Jameson, S., Holden, R. & Walmsley, A. (2009) Tourism graduates in Yorkshire: An emerging role for SMEs? *In:* Thomas, R. (ed.) *Managing Regional Tourism: A Case Study of Yorkshire, England.* Otley: Great Northern Books.

Jenkins, A. K. (2001) Making a career of it? Hospitality students' future perspectives: an Anglo-Dutch study. *International Journal of Contemporary Hospitality Management,* **13 (**1), 13-20.

Johns, N. & Mckechnie, M. (1995) Career demands and learning perceptions of hotel and catering graduates ± ten years on. *International Journal of Contemporary Hospitality Management,* **7 (**5), 9-12.

Jones, A. J., Woods, A., Coles, A.-M. & Rein, M. (2001) Graduates as strategic change agents in small firms: a case study of graduate placements and lifelong learning. *Strategic Change,* **10 (**1), 59-69.

Kerslake, P. (2005) Words From the Ys. Leading the demanding dot-coms. *New Zealand Management,* **52 (**4), 44-48.

Kim, B., McCleary, K. & Kaufman, T. (2010) The new generation in the industry: Hospitality/tourism students' career preferences, sources of influence and career choice factors. *Journal of Hospitality and Tourism Education,* **22 (**3), 5-11.

King, B. (1994) Co-operative education for hospitality and tourism students: An Australian case study. *Australian Journal of Hospitality Management,* **1 (**2), 17-24.

King, Z. (2003) New or traditional careers? A study of UK graduates' preferences. *Human Resource Management Journal,* **13 (**1), 5-26.

Krieshok, T., Black, M. & Mckay, R. (2009) Career decision making: The limits of rationality and the abundance of non-conscious processes. *Journal of Vocational Behavioru,* **75 (**3), 275-290.

Kuratko, D. (2005) The emergence of entrepreneurship education: Development, trends, and challenges. *Entrepreneurship Theory and Practice,* **29 (**5), 577-598.

Kusluvan, S. & Kusluvan, Z. (2000) Perceptions and attitudes of undergraduate tourism students towards working in the tourism industry in Turkey. *Tourism Management,* **21 (**3), 251-269.

Kusluvan, S., Kusluvan, Z. & Eren, D. (2003) Undergraduate tourism students' satisfaction with student work experience and its impact on their future career intentions: a case study. *In:* Kusluvan, S. (ed.) *Managing Employee Attitudes and Behaviors in the Tourism and Hospitality Industry.* New York: Nova Science Publishers.

Lent, R. W., Brown, D. & Hackett, G. (1994) Toward a unifying social cognitive theory of career and academic interest, choice, and performance. *Journal of Vocational Behavior,* **45**, 79-122.

Leonard, M. (1995) Labouring to learn: students' debt and term time employment in Belfast. *Higher Education Quarterly,* **49 (**3), 229-247.

Leung, S. A. (2008) The big five career theories. *In:* Athanasou, J. A. & Van Esbroeck, R. (eds.) *International Handbook of Career Guidance.* Springer

Lewin, K. (1951) *Field Theory in Social Science,* New York: Harper & Row.

Littleton, S., Arthur, M. and Rousseau, D. (2000) The Future of Boundaryless Careers. In: *The Future of Career,* edited by Collin, A. and Young, R. (pp101-114) Cambridge: Cambridge University Press.

Louis, M. R. (1980) Surprise and sense making: What newcomers experience in entering unfamiliar organizational settings. *Administrative Science Quarterly,* **25 (**2), 226-252.

Lourenço, F. & Jones, O. (2006) Developing entrepreneurship education: Comparing traditional and alternative approaches. *International Journal of Entrepreneurship Education,* **4**, 111-140.

Mackenzie Davey, K. & Arnold, J. (2000) A multi-method study of accounts of personal change by graduates starting work: Self-ratings, categories and women's discourses. *Journal of Occupational and Organizational Psychology,* **73 (**4), 461-486.

Marler, J., Barringer, M. & Milkovich, G. (2002) Boundaryless and traditional contingent employees: worlds apart. *Journal of organizational behavior,* **23 (**4), 425-453.

Martin, P. & Chapman, D. (2006) An exploration of factors that contribute to the reluctance of SME owner-managers to employ first destination marketing graduates. *Marketing Intelligence and Planning,* **24 (**2), 158-173.

Mintzberg, H. (1979) *The Structuring of Organizations,* Englewood Cliffs, NJ:

Prentice Hall.

Moreau, M.-P. & Leathwood, C. (2006) Balancing paid work and studies: working (-class) students in higher education. *Studies in Higher Education,* **31 (**1), 23-42.

Morgan, H. (2006). Why students avoid sandwich placements. *Education in a Changing Environment.* University of Salford.

Murphy, P. E. (1985) *Tourism: A Community Approach,* New York: Methuen.

Nabi, G., Holden, R. & Walmsley, A. (2010) Entrepreneurial intentions among students: towards a re-focused research agenda. *Journal of Small Business and Enterprise Development,* **17 (**4), 537-551.

Nabi, G., Walmsley, A. & Holden, R. (2013) Pushed or pulled? Exploring the factors underpinning graduate start-ups and non-start-ups. *Journal of Education and Work,* **10 (**1), 1-26.

National Council for Graduate Entrepreneurship (2006). *Enterprise and Entrepreneurship in English Higher Education* (National Summary Report). NCGE.

Oliver, D. (2006) An expectation of continued success: the work attitudes of Generation Y. *Labour and Industry,* **17 (**1), 61-84.

ONS (2012). Graduates in the Labour Market, 2012. Available: http://www.ons.gov.uk/ons/dcp171776_259049.pdf

Oosterbeek, H., Van Praag, M. & Ijsselstein, A. (2010) The impact of entrepreneurship education on entrepreneurship skills and motivation. *European Economic Review,* **54 (**3), 442-454.

Otter, S. (2005). *Graduate Placement Evaluation Study.* Otter Consulting Limited.

Parsons, F. (1909) *Choosing a Vocation,* Boston: Houghton Mifflin.

Pittaway, L. & Cope, J. (2007) Entrepreneurship education. a systematic review of the evidence. *International Small Business Journal,* **25 (**5), 479-510.

Pollard, E., Williams, M. & Hill, D. (2004). *Graduate Employment in the East Midlands.* Brighton: Institute for Employment Studies.

Purcell, K. & Pitcher, J. (1996). *Great Expectations: the new diversity of graduate skills and aspirations.* Coventry: Institute for Employment, University of Warwick.

Purcell, K., Pitcher, J. & Simm, C. (1999). *Working Out - Graduates' Early Experiences of the Labour market.* London: DfEE.

Richardson, S. & Butler, G. (2012) Attitudes of Malaysian tourism and hospitality students' towards a career in the industry. *Asia Pacific Journal of Tourism Research,* **17 (**3), 262-276.

Riley, M. & Ladkin, A. (1994) Career theory and tourism: The development of a basic analytical framework. *Progress in Tourism Recreation and Hospitality Management,* **6** 225-237.

Ronstadt, R. (1987) The educated entrepreneurs: A new era of entrepreneurial education is beginning. *American Journal of Small Business,* **11** (4), 37-53.

Ross, G. F. (1992) Tourism management as a career path: vocational perceptions of Australian school leavers. *Tourism Management,* **13** (2), 242-247.

Ross, G. F. (1997) Career stress responses among hospitality employees. *Annals of Tourism Research,* **24** (1), 41-51.

Ryan, C. (1995) Tourism courses: A new concern for new times? *Tourism Management,* **16** (2), 97-100.

Ryan, G., Toohey, S. & Hughes, C. (1996) The purpose, value and structure of the practicum in higher education: a literature review. *Higher Education,* **31** 355-377.

Saniter, N. & Siedler, T. (2014). Door opener or waste of time? The effects of student internships on labor market outcomes. Bonn: IZA Discussion Paper 8141.

Savickas, M. (2002) Career construction. A developmental theory of vocational behaviour. *In:* Brown, D. (ed.) *Career Choice and Development.* 4th ed. San Francisco: Jossey Bass.

Schaafsma, H. (1996) Back to the real world: work placements revisited. *Education + Training,* **38** (1), 5-13.

Schmitt-Roedermund, E. & Silbereisen, R. (1998) Career maturity determinants: individual development, social context, and historical time. *Career Development Quarterly,* **47** (1), 16-31.

Schumpeter, J. (1934) *The Theory of Economic Development,* New York: Oxford University Press / Galaxy 1961.

Schwab, D., Rynes, S. & Aldag, R. (1987) Theories and research on job search and choice. *In:* Rowland, M. & Ferris, G. R. (eds.) *Research in Personnel and Human Resources Management*

Self, J. (2005) 20-20 Hindsight: A qualitative analysis of hospitality graduates. *Journal of Hospitality & Tourism Education,* **17** (1), 33-37.

Sennett, R. (1998) *The Corrosion of Character. The personal consequences of work in the new capitalism.,* London: W.W. Norton & Company.

Sharma, Y. (2014). Rising unemployment – Are there too many graduates? University World News. Available: http://www.universityworldnews.com/article.php?story=20140213153927383

Sherrel, S. (1987). Give us a chance. *Caterer and Hotelkeeper.*

Solomon, G. (2007) An examination of entrepreneurship education in the United States. *Journal of Small Business and Enterprise Development,* **14**(2), 168-182.

Souitaris, V., Zerbinati, S. & Al-Laham, A. (2007) Do entrepreneurship programmes raise entrepreneurial intention of science and engineering students? The effect of learning, inspiration and resources. *Journal of Business Venturing,* **22** (4), 566-591.

Sullivan, S. and Arthur, M. (2006) The evolution of the boundaryless career concept: Examining physical and psychological mobility. *Journal of Vocational Behavior.* **69**(1), 19-29.

Super, D. (1953) A theory of vocational development. *American Psychologist,* **8** 185-190.

Talacchi, S. (1960) Organization Size, individual attitudes and behavior: An empirical study. *Administrative Science Quarterly,* **5** (3), 398-420.

Thomas, R. & Augustyn, M. (2007) *Tourism in the New Europe: Perspectives on SME Policies and Practices,* Oxford: Pergamon.

Thomas, R., Shaw, G. & Page, S. (2011) Understanding small firms in tourism: A perspective on research trends and challenges. *Tourism Management,* **32** 963-976.

Universities UK (2003). Attitudes to debt: school leavers and further education students' attitudes to debt and their impact on participation in higher education. London: Universities UK. Available: http://www.universitiesuk. ac.uk/highereducation/Documents/2003/DebtSummary.pdf

Van De Werfhorst, H. & Luijkx, R. (2010) Educational field of study and social mobility: Disaggregating social origin and education. *Sociology,* **44** (4), 695-715.

Van Maanen, J. & Schein, E. H. (1979) Towards a theory of organizational socialization. *Research in Organizational Behavior,* **1** 209-264.

Vesper, K. (1984) The three faces of corporate entrepreneurship: A pilot study. *In:* Hornaday, J., Tarpley, F., Timmons, J. & Vesper, K., (eds.) *Frontiers of Entrepreneurship Research, Proceedings of the Conference, 1984* Wellesley. Babson College Center For Entrepreneurial Studies, 294-320.

Von Graevenitz, G., Harhoff, D. & Weber, R. (2010) The effects of entrepreneurship education. *Journal of Economic Behavior & Organization* **76** (1), 90-112.

Walmsley, A. (2012a) Pathways into tourism higher education. *Journal of Hospitality, Leisure, Sport and Tourism Education,* **11** 131-139.

Walmsley, A. (2012b). Tourism Intelligence Monitor. ATHE Report on Tourism Higher Education in the UK, 2012.

Walmsley, A. & Thomas, R. (2009) Understanding and influencing entrepreneurial intentions of tourism students. *In:* Ateljevic, J. & Page, S. (eds.) *Tourism and Entrepreneurship. International Perspectives.* Oxford: Elsevier.

Walmsley, A., Thomas, R. & Jameson, S. (2006) Surprise and sense making: undergraduate placement experiences in SMEs. *Education + Training,* **48** (5), 360-372.

Walmsley, A., Thomas, R. & Jameson, S. (2012) Internships in SMEs and career intentions. *Journal of Education and Work,* **25** (2), 185-204.

Wanhill, S. (2000) Small and medium tourism enterprises. *Annals of Tourism Research,* **27** (1), 132-147.

Wanous, J. P., Poland, T. D., Premack, S. L. & Davis, K. S. (1992) The effects of met expectations on newcomer attitudes and behaviors: A review and meta-analysis. *Journal of Applied Psychology,* **77** (3), 288-297.

Weber, M. (2002) *The Protestant Ethic and the 'Spirit' of Capitalism and other writings,* New York: Penguin.

West, A. J. & Jameson, S. (1990) Supervised work experience in graduate employment. *International Journal of Contemporary Hospitality Management,* **2** (2), 29-32.

Westhead, P. & Matlay, H. (2005) Graduate employment in SMEs: a longitudinal perspective. *Journal of Small Business and Enterprise Development,* **12** (3), 353-365.

Whyte, W. (1956) *The Organization Man.* New York: Simon and Shuster.

Wilensky, H. L. (1960) Work, careers and social integration. *International Social Science Journal,* **12** (4), 553-338.

Wilkinson, N. (2008) *An Introduction to Behavioral Economics,* Basingstoke: Palgrave Macmillan.

Wilton, N. (2012) The impact of work placements on skills development and career outcomes for business and management graduates. *Studies in Higher Education,* **37** (5), 603-620.

Wolf, A. (2011) *Review of Vocational Education. The Wolf Report.* Department for Education and Department for Business, Innovation and Skills.

WTTC (2013). *A Career in Travel & Tourism.* London: World Travel and Tourism Council.

Zahra, S., Jennings, D. & Kuratko, D. (1999) The antecdents and consequence of firm-level entrepreneurship: The state of the field. *Entrepreneurship Theory and Practice,* **24** (2), 45-66.

7 Conclusion

This aim of this book was to establish a baseline of information on youth employment in tourism and hospitality, as well as to review the nature and determinants of youth employment in the sector. In doing so it has covered a broad body of literature and, on occasion, been quite critical in the process, notably in relation to educational policy but also in relation to working conditions. Notwithstanding the critique, the text seeks to offer a conciliatory tone and acknowledges that many young people go on to find extremely satisfying careers in the sector. As examples throughout have demonstrated, being a responsible employer and being successful are not mutually exclusive – far from it. Ultimately, ensuring young people are offered meaningful work, which tourism is well placed to do, is in everyone's interest, from key stakeholders such as young people and the business community, to policy makers, and educational institutions, as well as to wider society who all suffer the effects of high rates of youth unemployment.

The absence of any substantive text in this area to date is surprising for a number of reasons, not least because of the widespread acknowledgement of the sector's reliance on frequently marginalised groups including young people. Moreover, given the continued concerns about youth unemployment in both developed and developing economies, as well as tourism's ability to provide avenues into employment, the surprise is even more justifiable. There is some evidence of a growing concern with issues relating to youth employment in the sector and this text is indicative of this increased awareness. This final chapter draws together key themes that have arisen within the text, summarising what we know but also reviewing ongoing dilemmas surrounding youth employment in tourism of which plenty exist.

At the outset it can be concluded that data on youth employment are still found wanting. In fact the same could be said for data on tourism employment more generally. What Wanhill (1992:78) stipulated over twenty years ago in relation to the availability of tourism statistics: 'compared to other human activity tourism is not well served in terms of published statistics' certainly still holds true for tourism employment. Ladkin (2011) shares this view, claiming that one explanation for the relatively scarce research in the area of tourism labour is a lack of reliable employment data. Official statistics in advanced economies suggest youth employment in tourism, defined as employment by those aged 15-24, hovers at around 20 percent but can vary quite considerably from one country to the next. Non-governmental statistics frequently offer a higher proportion of youth employment in tourism, often between 30-35% (and sometimes even higher than this). Effectively, the figure will vary depending on which definition or proxy for tourism is used as well as the prevalence of informal employment in tourism (the assumption here is that youth are disproportionately affected by informal employment). What data exist suggest youth employment is particularly elevated in certain sub-sectors of hospitality (e.g. bars) but lower in others (e.g. campsites and short-stay accommodation). When speaking of a rate of youth employment in tourism these distinctions and 'data difficulties' should be borne in mind.

Global levels of youth unemployment remain stubbornly high. Being unemployed can have deep-seated and long term negative implications for the individual and for society. Doyle (2003:336) writes: 'The sad fact is that our earliest, often least-considered decisions can determine the rest of our lives, and each generation has to learn this anew'. While undoubtedly true, this presumes a degree of personal agency but in many instances young individuals have very limited agency as there are few alternatives to choose from. Levels of youth employment in tourism are determined by a host of factors, not least wider economic circumstances. An example was provided where, based on recent economic data, an inverse relationship was established between general levels of unemployment and levels of youth employment in tourism. A possible explanation was offered that suggested with rising levels of unemployment, those who might traditionally not have sought employment in tourism (i.e. non-youth) then turn to tourism as a quasi refuge sector (a similar argument in relation to economic change in Hungary has previously been made by Szivas and Riley, 1999).

Upon a challenging economic backdrop tourism and hospitality can offer a vital source of work for youth. The kind of employment presented by the sector varies greatly, from permanent, full-time positions offering rapid career development to short-term, precarious forms of employment with limited career prospects. Even this latter type of employment can prove beneficial for some youth however who are struggling to obtain any form of work and, by implication, work experience. Whether used as a stepping stone into other forms of employment subsequently, or as a source of sustained employment in the sector, tourism will continue to play a role in many youth's career development.

This sanguine view should not detract from a variety of dilemmas relating to youth employment in tourism. Poor working conditions and limited career opportunities are two main areas of concern. It is all too easy to extoll the virtues of tourism employment whereby in reality many youth are trapped in 'dead end' jobs with limited career prospects. Today, many youth are caught in a vicious cycle of periods of unemployment and precarious short-term employment. Employers are in a powerful position where demand for jobs is so great that low pay and poor working conditions are simply tolerated because there are few alternatives. A move towards a more responsible tourism sector is of course to be welcomed and yet the employment perspective seems to be regularly side-lined. Labour standards as stipulated by the ILO along with its Decent Work agenda are moves in the right direction but ongoing reports of employment malpractices demonstrate there is still some way to go to ensure workers' rights are not simply overlooked. It is worth noting that examples of enlightened human resource management practices can be found in many large tourism firms, but equally, there are many large employers who are shirking their responsibilities towards their employees. Poor working conditions are not restricted to small and medium-sized tourism organisations and moreover, while generalisations about youth employment in the sector need to be made, there is a danger that we overlook the specific. This would impoverish understanding of what is arguably a fascinating precisely because complex, at times seemingly contradictory, phenomenon.

A case in point is youth employment in tourism in developing countries. It was noted that not only are official data on youth employment lacking, but the majority of academic studies of employment in the sector relate to advanced economies. This can be explained on the basis of data access issues but it does not remove the need to acknowledge that what holds true for advanced economies may not necessarily hold true elsewhere. The review has provided some evidence that tourism in developing countries is frequently regarded more favourably than other alternatives, particularly where the other alternative relates to physically demanding, low-paid agricultural work. In many developing countries tourism provides an important route out of poverty, offers relatively decent working conditions and work that is on par with other available alternatives in terms of esteem.

Rarely are academics provided with unfettered access to an organisation's employees. Where relatively open access has been provided (e.g. Font *et al.*,

2012) it is very clear that for some tourism organisations corporate social performance is weak as what is promised in policies is not implemented in practice. This was also demonstrated here in relation to levels of sexual harassment in the sector, which continue to be high, and disproportionately affect youth, despite policies aimed at curbing it. Trade unions continue to provide a vital source of information on corporate malpractices in the area of employment but also to assist in social dialogue. It is unfortunate therefore that many leading tourism and hospitality employers refuse to recognise them. The liberalisation of communication channels with the rise of ICT, i.e. the ease with which the individual can share information with a potentially global audience, may work in favour of bringing into the public sphere poor employment practices in the sector but there are also personal risks attached to this of course.

Business models premised entirely on seeing employees as a cost, where exploitation is possible given labour market circumstances that provide a willing source of labour even where working conditions are poor cannot ultimately be healthy for society as a whole. Blair (1998) has provided a conceptual basis for understanding employment as an output of a firm, rather than as a cost. It remains to be seen whether growing pressure on businesses to look at more than the bottom line may result in a reappraisal of the place of business in society. However, if moral reasons are insufficient to sway employers towards more responsible employment practices, which as we have seen disproportionately affect youth, then recourse to the business case may be made. This is more difficult for employment issues admittedly than for many environmental ones whereby in the latter case the link between responsible behaviour and the bottom line is often more direct, primarily in the form of cost savings. Nonetheless, where empirically the argument has yet to be won, at a theoretical level the coupling between responsible HRM and business success is strong. Increased productivity, customer satisfaction and staff retention are, for example, all issues that a more enlightened human resource management approach may offer. Furthermore, where businesses themselves claim there is a 'war for talent' this text points to studies that indicate the existence of a relationship between a firm's corporate social performance and its attractiveness as an employer.

Baum's (2007) review of tourism employment suggests that in many respects we are still waiting for change, for the theory of what counts as progressive and/or enlightened human resource management practices to extend into practice and indeed it would be difficult not to reach this conclusion on the basis of current evidence. We should not ignore however that examples of good practice clearly exist and that tourism employment is very attractive to many young people. While progressive employment practices in tourism may simply be regarded as exceptions to the rule this misses an important point: their value lies in the demonstration that an alternative approach to employment in tourism is possible. The WTTC (2013:7) is frank in its appraisal of the suitability of tourism employment: 'the personality of someone who seems naturally attracted to the sector sees success defined by factors such as work-life balance, international opportunities, travel and good benefits…For those who are driven by more traditional approach to career and are attracted to messages promoting financial returns or achieving senior leadership positions, Travel and Tourism performs less well'. Although it is often things like a lack of work-life balance that turn individuals away from sector employment, to pretend that it does not offer satisfying careers to many would be to take a very parochial view. Perhaps tourism is in fact more attuned to this generation of youth's attitudes towards employment and careers, i.e. a move away from long-term employment with one organisation, gradually working one's way up the corporate ladder. Instead, tourism may offer more rapid progression based on movement within but also between companies and/or employment aligned with lifestyle considerations. Employment practices are increasingly acknowledged as an important consideration in responsible tourism and it is to be seen to what extent a review of employment practices in the future will echo Baum's (2007) conclusion.

As we have seen, the review of youth employment in tourism is fraught with numerous apparent contradictions. In prime place here is the concern of employers who complain about skills shortages, while at the same time youth unemployment is elevated, vocational education has expanded and employment in the sector itself is characterised as low-skilled. One frequently encounters assurances that staff are an organisation's most important asset while simultaneously observing poor levels of pay and working conditions. The text has pointed to a number of factors that might explain these paradoxes. The notion of tourism being low-skilled can be queried, quite convincingly in fact if one considers demands on the employee relating to emotional and aesthetic labour. What may at first glance and to the uninitiated appear to be a simple job, can if understood more fully demonstrate the numerous demands placed on the tourism worker. Certainly, for those businesses aiming to exceed customer expectations, the notion that their staff are low (or even un-) skilled is hard to comprehend. While an individual may be able to perform required tasks, this does not mean they will be performed well. Categorising jobs according to skills levels does not take into account variation in task performance and as such many jobs in tourism may be categorised as low- or even unskilled where in fact to consistently exceed customer expectations is extremely demanding.

Furthermore, what may be regarded as a skills shortage might only be a skills shortage at a certain wage level. Standard economic theory suggests the supply of labour increases as wages increase. If paying a minimum wage (or possibly less if one considers the extent of informal employment in the sector) then one should not expect highly-skilled applicants (although labour market conditions may leave youth with few options but to take on low-skilled employment). Here again the devil is in the detail where within tourism, and particularly hospitality, there are shortages for certain occupations, e.g. chefs. Another consideration in relation to skills shortages concerns the expectation that employees should be able to hit the ground running when they enter employment and require little or no further training. Context specificity of work environments which may prevent a complete preparation for work aside (Keep, 2012), this expectation is not universally shared. In some countries there is an anticipation that employers contribute to the education of youth; frequently this takes the form of apprenticeships. Rather than just stating what kind of employee they desire, businesses can contribute to the preparation for work. The UK government's recently-announced Trailblazers apprenticeship scheme which seeks an ambitious 3 million 'starts' during the period of the current parliament is evidence that this approach is now being taken seriously (in other countries such an approach is not new of course). Ultimately, if businesses are the primary beneficiaries of a trained and educated workforce then their contribution to the preparation for employment seems a reasonable request to make. In fact, this has been recognised by business leaders themselves. In a foreword to a report of employers' perspective into tackling youth unemployment we find an open admission: 'if we want young people who are ready for the workplace we need to be willing to help build their employability skills' (UKCES, 2011). Ensuring youth are prepared for the workplace is a shared responsibility.

Tackling both supply and demand side barriers to youth employment in the sector is necessary if tourism is to fulfil its potential as a source of meaningful employment. Numerous studies have suggested tourism's image does detract from sector employment, and alas early work experiences do often seem to detract from sector employment. Returning to the corporate social performance issue, improving working conditions can provide a business benefit in terms of the firm being able to draw on a larger talent pool. There is growing evidence that a company's reputation, to include how staff are treated, can have a positive impact on recruitment. The premise here is that tourism employers understand this but in reality recruitment practices in the sector continue to be informal and poorly designed (to an extent poor recruitment practices are also to blame for the poor perception of tourism employment). The text has argued, based on a review of job postings, that there is frequently little explicit demand for formal education by tourism firms seeking employees, even in what one might consider higher skilled jobs. There is furthermore some evidence that for many tourism employers looks are more important than skills or education when hiring staff (e.g. Nickson *et al.*, 2005). A further point to note is the under-employment of skilled staff in the sector. The concept of a low skills equilibrium was discussed whereby it was noted that employers are not always best placed to make use of the skills of their recruits. This results in a missed opportunity for the business and for the skilled employee.

This review has been critical of much current education policy, reflecting admittedly a UK-centric perspective, but one that sees parallels in many nations that are putting forward the well-trodden arguments about the need for an educated workforce to remain competitive in a globalised knowledge economy. This text does not argue against education of course, and indeed education is the best protection against un- and underemployment. The concern lies with an overly utilitarian approach to education which tends to focus and therefore measure only short-term, employment-related outcomes. If these are not met does this mean that education has failed, or that it was 'useless' in the literal meaning of the term? Others have written about this far more cogently (Wolf, 2002, Maskell and Robinson, 2001) and yet the point is worth raising again given the persistence of the education-for-employment discourse, frequently promoted even by those in education. In an arguably vocational subject such as tourism the danger of wholly neglecting aspects of education where the link to work is not immediately apparent is very real.

The structure of the sector suggests that substantial levels of youth employment in tourism SMEs is inevitable, despite what some suggest would be a bias towards large firms in tourism education. Just as it is expedient to ignore the diverse facets of tourism employment, generalisations have been made about tourism SME employment that call at least for closer scrutiny. This text has discussed employee relations in this regard where a review of non-tourism specific literature paints a mixed picture, certainly not a simplistic 'big is good, small is bad' perspective. Although large firms may provide for clearer career progression routes and more formal employment practices, SMEs are not necessarily worse places to work from an employee relations perspective and with regard to early levels of autonomy and responsibility may offer more than large organisations. Alas, there is limited literature on employment in tourism SMEs. We would therefore echo Thomas *et al.*'s (2011:972) concerns: 'How can public policy initiatives to enhance quality, to create jobs, to regenerate destinations do so without understanding the dynamics of smaller enterprises that are endemic in tourism?'

A further area that is likely to see a growth in interest is entrepreneurship and youth employment in tourism. Graduate entrepreneurship has received considerable attention outside of tourism and some, albeit limited attention in the tourism literature. Youth entrepreneurship is certainly not just about graduate entrepreneurship. Although figures are not available because undertaken on an informal basis, much youth employment in tourism in developing economies relates to entrepreneurial activities. This is certainly an area where policy makers might usefully channel resources, financial support as well as capacity building.

Realistically, the blight of high levels of youth unemployment is unlikely to be resolved in the near future, requiring as it would a wholesale restructuring of the economic base. Nonetheless, tourism and hospitality can and should be regarded as a sector that can directly provide some welcome alleviation from it. While tourism employment might not appeal to all, and employment practices in some tourism firms are evidently poor, it should not be ignored that for many youth the sector provides meaningful and satisfying employment. This text set out to explore the underlying complexities of youth employment in tourism and as was demonstrated it is characterised by numerous, at first sight at least, paradoxes. There is ample scope then for further research in this area that extends beyond the traditional avenues of large employers in developed economies if policy is not to run blind on this issue.

References

Baum, T. (2007) 'Human resources in tourism: Still waiting for change'. *Tourism Management,* **28** 1383-1399.

Blair, M. (1998) For whom should corporations be run?: An economic rationale for stakeholder management. *Long Range Planning,* **31** (2), 195-200.

Doyle, C. (2003) *Work and Organizational Psychology. An introduction with attitude.,* Hove: Psychology Press.

Font, X., Walmsley, A., Coggoti, S., Mccombes, L. & Häusler, N. (2012) 'Corporate social responsibility: the disclosure-performance gap'. *Tourism Management,* **33** (**6**), 1544-1533.

Keep, E. (2012). Youth Transitions, the Labour Market and Entry into Employment: Some Reflections and Questions. *SKOPE Publications.* Cardiff: SKOPE.

Ladkin, A. (2011) 'Exploring Tourism Labour'. *Annals of Tourism Research,* **38** (3), 1135-1155.

Maskell, D. & Robinson, I. (2001) *The New Idea of a University,* London: Haven Books.

Nickson, D., Warhurst, C. & Dutton, E. (2005) 'The Importance of Attitude and Appearance in the Service Encounter in Retail and Hospitality'. *Managing Service Quality,* **15** (2), 195-208.

Szivas, E. & Riley, M. (1999) 'Tourism employment during economic transition'. *Annals of Tourism Research,* **26** (4), 747-771.

Thomas, R., Shaw, G. & Page, S. (2011) 'Understanding small firms in tourism: A perspective on research trends and challenges'. *Tourism Management,* **32** 963-976.

UKCES (2011). The Youth Inquiry. Employers' perspectives on tackling youth unemployment. UK Commission for Employment and Skills.

Wanhill, S. (1992) 'Methodologies for tourism and hospitality'. *Tourism Management,* **13** (2), 78.

Wolf, A. (2002) *Does Education Matter? Myths about Education and Economic Growth,* London: Penguin.

WTTC (2013). A Career in Travel & Tourism. London: World Travel and Tourism Council.

 **Index**

New titles from
Goodfellow Publishers

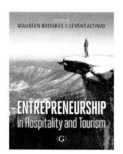

Entrepreneurship in Hospitality and Tourism
Maureen Brookes and Levent Altinay

Packed with case studies, designed to develop understanding of the different types of entrepreneurship within hospitality and tourism from an applied and theoretical perspective.

Hardback: 978-1-910158-27-2 £75, Euro 96, US$ 120

Paperback: 978-1-910158-28-9 £29.99, Euro 36, US$ 48

Ebook: 978-1-910158-29-6 £36, Euro 36, US$ 48

How to Buy and Manage your own Hotel
Miles Quest and Peter Nannestad

A clear toolkit and action plan for those looking to make the leap to buying their own hotel, from getting the initial finances in place, to successful marketing techniques and staffing issues.

Hardback: 978-1-910158-21-0 £75, Euro 98, US$ 120

Paperback: 978-1-910158-22-7 £29.99, Euro 36, US$ 48

Ebook: 978-1-910158-23-4 £36, Euro 36, US$ 48

Winter Sport Tourism
Simon Hudson and Louise Hudson

A fresh look at this rapidly growing multi-million dollar industry, covering issues such as the consumers, marketing, economics and environmental impacts.

Hardback: 978-1-910158-39-5 £75, Euro 98, US$ 120

Paperback: 978-1-910158-40-1 £29.99, Euro 36, US$ 48

Ebook: 978-1-910158-41-8 £36, Euro 36, US$ 48

Thanatourism: case studies in travel to the dark side
Tony Johnston and Pascal Mandelartz

Uses international case studies to provide a new philosophical perspectives and a wealth of empirical material on the contemporary and historical consumption of death, designed to stretch and challenge current discourse.

Hardback: 978-1-910158-33-3 £75, Euro 96, US$ 120

Paperback: 978-1-910158-34-0 £29.99, Euro 36, US$ 48

Ebook: 978-1-910158-35-7 £36, Euro 36, US$ 48